CRICKET
in the
shadows

For Bev and Sharon

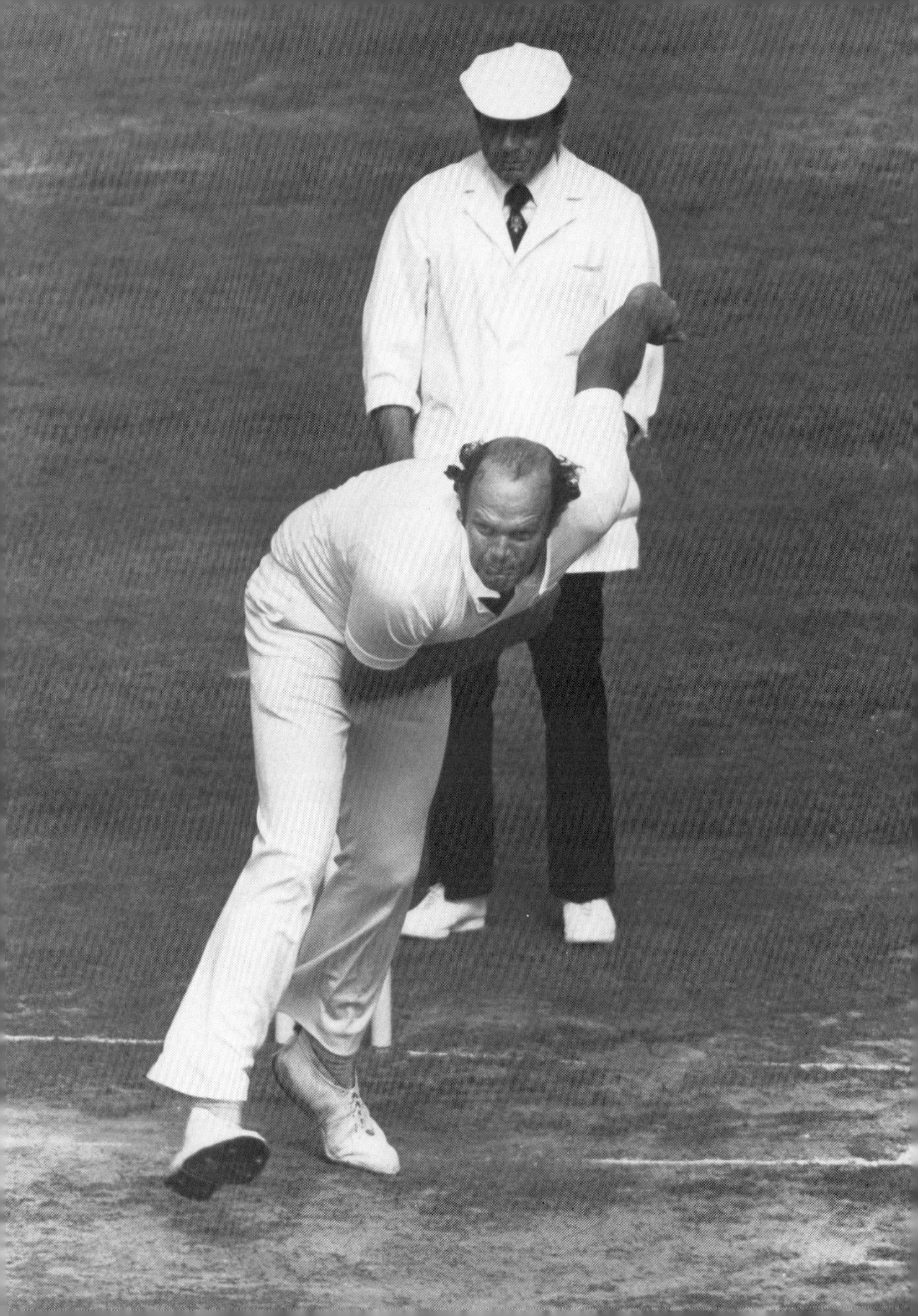

CRICKET in the shadows

VINTCENT VAN DER BIJL
with
JOHN BISHOP

Foreword by
Mike Brearley

Postscript by
Barry Richards

Shuter & Shooter
PIETERMARITZBURG

Shuter & Shooter (Pty) Ltd
Gray's Inn, 230 Church Street
Pietermaritzburg, South Africa 3201

Copyright © Shuter & Shooter (Pty) Ltd 1984

All rights reserved. No part of this publication may be
reproduced or transmitted, in any form or by any means,
without permission of the publishers

First edition 1984

ISBN 0 86985 797 5

Set in 12 on 14pt Bembo
Printed by The Natal Witness (Pty) Ltd, Pietermaritzburg
7014L

Foreword

Southend is notorious for its pier and its whelks. It also boasts a cricket ground, called Chalkwell Park, with a duck-pond behind the pavilion, into which Wayne Daniel, when batting, would regularly attempt to launch any spin bowler operating from that end (and would occasionally succeed).

The pavilion had seen better days than in 1980, when Vintcent van der Bijl paid it what was presumably his only visit. It consisted of two small dressing rooms with splintery floors opening from a narrow corridor that led to a staircase. There was little chance of splinter-injury in ours, as within a few minutes nine-tenths of the floor-space was taken over by Vince's bag and its overspill.

In the second innings of the match, Keith Fletcher, the Essex captain, was given out lbw to Daniel. The ball would, I thought, have missed the stumps by six inches or more, and Fletcher thought so too. So, in the privacy of his dressing room he did the time-honoured thing — he threw his bat. The bat happened to hit the fire extinguisher, which happened to be fixed near his peg, and the fire-extinguisher happened to go off. John Lever considerately tossed it into the passage, where most of its foamy contents erupted into our room. We reckoned that Vince would not have noticed if the whole lot had landed in his bag.

This extraordinary untidiness off the field was matched by a remarkable accuracy on it. In this same match, Vince's figures were 51,3 overs, 25 maidens, eight wickets for 65 runs. He was a prodigious bowler. If conditions helped, he bowled sides out cheaply; if they didn't, he would close up one end *and* pick up a few wickets. At the time of writing, in August 1984, Joel Garner seems to be at his peak; and the one bowler from any epoch who undoubtedly challenges the Big Bird is Vintcent van der Bijl. My assessment is that though Vince may not have been quite as hostile as the great West Indian, he moved the ball more and had, perhaps, slightly more range.

He was, of course, a captain's dream, but not only on the field (though if he slept in your house, the dream could turn into a nightmare, as this naked ox of a man was liable to sleepwalk his way into one's marital bed, and sleep deeply till late morning). Middlesex were a robust team in those days, bristling with strong characters, with rivalries, and with a biting and usually enjoyable humour that could, however, turn acid when things went wrong. Self-criticism was a rare commodity. In this atmosphere Vince stood out like a beacon, and his influence was extremely helpful. I remember a John Player match against Kent. On a damp pitch, we allowed them to score 177 — too many by thirty or forty runs. Between innings, before any criticisms could start, Vince immediately announced 'Jeez, I'm sorry, Mike; it's all my fault, bowling those two half volleys'. Without a trace of false modesty, he would invariably notice others' strengths and his own shortcomings.

But much self-deprecation never affected his own game adversely. Never? Well, perhaps once. In the Gillette Cup semi-final that he humbly refers to in the book — a tense battle with Sussex before a partisan crowd at Hove — he actually bowled eight wides in his nine overs. And they weren't ordinary wides; most of them would have hit second slip if not third! He didn't lose his length, however.

Even the most reliable performer may suffer from nerves. And perhaps it was a sign of the tendency to be preoccupied with one's own anxiety, and not enter into that of others, that I did not realize how anxious Vintcent was at the start of his only season in English cricket.

I suppose I too was nervous about our meeting. I had, in fact, briefly met his sisters in Cape Town sixteen years before, and shaken hands with the fresh-faced sixteen-year-old himself. But there had, in the weeks before his arrival in April 1980, been a few questions from the media about how I'd get on with a South African, as if all members of that tribe would be anathema to me. I suppose I did wonder at first just how this improbable giant with his almost effeminate run and his infectious bellow of a laugh would feel about my attitude to South Africa and the effect of such attitudes on his career.

For during my time in South Africa as a member of MCC's last tour there in 1964–65, I had become cynical about the prospects of changing apartheid in sport by 'bridge-building'. By 1970, I was prepared to argue publicly that a tour by South Africa in England would be an insult to coloured people living in this country, and that any slight improvement in the situation in South Africa was more likely to come from a policy of isolation than in any other way.

I soon discovered that Vince and I shared a wide area of agreement. We did differ on the current situation. He stressed the moves towards integration in sport made during the 1970s, and believed that further progress would be hindered by South Africa's continued exclusion from the international cricket arena. I, on the other hand, was more struck by the fact that, despite the brave efforts of many cricketers and others to make sport multi-racial, not one of the laws that sustain apartheid had been abolished. The changes had been made against the background of entrenched injustice and inequality, and were still permitted only on the whim of government officials. Moreover, I felt, and still feel, that we in England have a responsibility to respect the sensibilities of the Blacks and Asians who make up a significant part of our society. Symbolic it may be—but the ban on international cricket stresses the fact that we are aiming at a totally different type of solution to the problems of racial and cultural diversity.

Enough of that. As Vince says, his own arrival on the international scene was perfectly ill-timed. For that reason, amongst others, he is the ideal man to give an account of South African cricket and his own career during the years of isolation.

Dear Vince,
Baie dankie to you, too, for your stimulating and generous friendship, not to mention your tremendous cricketing talent which has given so much pleasure. *And* you were an excellent ambassador for your country.

MIKE BREARLEY

"I don't care WHOSE they are . . . . . as long as he's on our side . . . . . ."

Contents

1	The watershed	1
2	The Road to Newlands	11
3	The changing face of cricket	31
4	Procter and Richards in the Seventies	51
5	The early tours: An international flavour	74
6	The Middlesex Venture	93
7	Mike Brearley — The pick of captains	113
8	After Middlesex	124
9	The men in the middle	134
10	The first rebels	147
11	The West Indians	165
12	The end of the road	186
13	The Characters	200
14	At the crossroads again	215
	Vintcent Adriaan Pieter van der Bijl	221
	Postscript and gallery	224

Acknowledgements

The publishers and authors wish to record their gratitude to: Mike Brearley and Barry Richards for kindly writing, respectively, the Foreword and Postscript to this book; Peter Robinson and Richard Steyn for reading and commenting on early drafts; Patrick Eagar and Bill Smith for the photographs taken during the Middlesex season; and Sharon Bishop for providing numerous photographs, and for her presence of mind to record the Vince's only Currie Cup hat-trick.

Thanks are also due to:
The Natal Witness, Sunday Tribune, Daily News, Natal Mercury, Sunday Times, Rand Daily Mail, Die Burger, Cape Argus, Beeld, Eastern Province Herald and the *Kentish Gazette* for other photographs in this book. To Jock Leyden and Mike Watkins, a special word of thanks for their cartoons.

Vince's particular thanks go to Derek Smith and Wiggins Teape for encouraging his continued involvement in the game.

CHAPTER ONE

The watershed

Newlands on a grey Saturday morning in April 1971 provided the backdrop for the most extraordinary protest in the history of cricket. The spectators at this three-day match between the Rest of South Africa and Currie Cup champions Transvaal, played as part of the Republic Sports Festival, had hardly settled into their positions when the players left the field.

Mike Procter, opening the bowling for the Rest of South Africa, delivered just one ball which Barry Richards, guesting for Transvaal, pushed to the off-side, scampered through for a single and then joined the other players on their quiet but purposeful walk to the pavilion. The expectant buzz of the crowd had given away to a bemused hush as the umpires, like two sentinels guarding the traditions of the game, stood alone out in the middle.

The inactivity on the field contrasted sharply with the feverish bustle off it as administrators and cricket journalists tried to find out what had happened to their game of cricket. Minutes later the players handed a statement to the Press and returned to the field. The first political stand by cricketers was over.

The background to the Newlands walk-off, and the reasons for it, are familiar to most South African cricket followers. The Springbok team to travel to Australia that year was to be announced during this Festival match, and the South African Cricket Association, as it was known then, had asked the Nationalist Government to allow the two best Black players to be included in the tour party.

In the light of the many changes that have taken place in South Africa over the last 14 years, such a request now appears insignificant, but at the time it had enormous implications politically.

The Government turned down the request, further damaging the flagging South African cause on both the sporting and political fronts. The Australian tour, already hanging by the thinnest of threads, seemed doomed.

Peter and Graeme Pollock lead the Newlands walk-off, 3 April 1971.

On the eve of the Festival game Graeme Pollock (who was captaining the Rest of South Africa XI in the absence of Ali Bacher), his brother Peter, Mike Procter, Denis Lindsay and Barry Richards, who joined the group later, had decided over dinner that the players should show their support for the SACA. Initially, they agreed that the Rest of South Africa XI should simply boycott the match. As it was being staged as part of the Republic's 10th anniversary celebrations, it was a perfect platform for a political statement.

The respected Charles Fortune, later to become secretary of the SACA, but down in Cape Town to commentate on the game, was staying in the same hotel and the players decided to consult him. He advised the group against their proposed action, believing that many sympathisers and cricket followers would be alienated by a refusal to play. He did suggest, however, that if there was a genuine wish to make a stand, then a walk-off might be more appropriate. When the teams met the next morning the remaining players were found to be in favour and the timing of the walk-off, and the wording of the statement, were settled.

It was decided that only the umpires and team managers would have prior knowledge of the walk-off, and that to achieve greater impact the Rest of South Africa XI would field first.

Careful thought was given to the wording of the statement. It read: *'We cricketers feel that the time has come for an expression of our views. We fully support the South African Cricket Association's application to include Non-Whites on the tour to Australia if good enough and, furthermore, subscribe to merit being the only criterion on the cricket field.'*

Left-wing commentators later described the protest as window-dressing and simply a last-ditch effort by South African cricketers to save the Australian tour. To an extent this was true. But it was also an unequivocal and independent plea for equality in sport and selection totally on merit. It was not the first stage of a well-conceived plan to alter the state of South African cricket, but was the spontaneous reaction of a frustrated group of young cricketers who had already seen two international tours cancelled for political reasons.

It was the first time the players had made a public stand against racial and political influence. On tours to England in the sixties, South African teams had been subjected to small but vocal demonstrations at grounds and airports. But the players never involved themselves and the future of South African cricket was left solely in the hands of the administrators. They, in turn, believed that the International Cricket Conference's sense of fair play would ensure South Africa's speedy return.

The statement made by the players at Newlands, in fact, indicated only qualified support for the SACA. The cricketers did not want to see the token selection of Blacks, but simply wanted to see selection on merit alone.

Fred Goldstein, the Transvaal opening batsman, made this clear at the players' meeting, saying: 'If this is just an attempt to save the Springbok tour to Australia, I'm not interested. But, if it is a genuine effort to promote equality on the sporting field, then count me in all the way.'

The response to the walk-off was remarkable. A friend of mine, Clive McDonald, happened to be playing in a charity golf day with the Prime Minister, B. J. Vorster, at Beachwood in Durban. The Prime Minister was just settling down to play an approach shot when an overweight aide came puffing up to tell him of the Newlands walk-off. Mr Vorster, nestling his six iron behind the ball, scarcely looked up. 'Don't worry me with that now. Let me finish my game of golf and then I'll worry about the blerrie cricketers.'

Mr Vorster was to have presented festival medals to the players on the Monday of the Newlands game, but he failed to fulfil his commitment while an invitation to the teams to attend a braai at the house of Mr Frank Waring, the Minister of Sport, was abruptly withdrawn.

Mr Waring dismissed the walk-off as 'merely a gesture for local and particularly popular overseas consumption'.

Mrs Helen Suzman, for years the lone liberal voice in Parliament, remarked cryptically: 'Good for them. It's nice to see they are coming along so well.' She then added that the more active the cricketers were in showing their opposition to the Government's racial policy, the better the chance for South Africa to maintain its tenuous place in international sport.

While the reaction from the politicians was predictable, the response from the cricket administrators was not. There was annoyance that the cricketers had stepped into their domain and a witch-hunt was begun to find out who had been behind the protest.

Talented all-rounder Don MacKay-Coghill, leading Transvaal in the absence of Springbok captain Ali Bacher, was a strong contender for the Australian tour, but was told by a national selector that he would never be picked for South Africa — a forecast which proved horribly accurate.

Efforts were made to find out who had been the ringleaders in the South African side. The selectors clearly felt Peter Pollock was to blame and Graeme Pollock was called before them and asked about his brother's involvement. Graeme told them it had been a team decision.

On the day after the walk-off, with the Springbok team for the Australian tour due to be announced after the game, a concerned Arthur Coy approached Peter Pollock and told him that he might be made a scapegoat for the players' actions. The inference was clearly that the selectors were considering leaving Pollock out of the tour party, but the message quickly went back to the selectors that they would have problems with the other players if Peter was omitted. Springbok captain Ali Bacher and his vice-captain Eddie Barlow, who had both missed the Newlands match, immediately pledged their support for the players' stand.

The public and media reaction to the walk-off was intense and varied: cynicism from the left, aggression from the right and bewilderment in the centre. The man in the street, told often enough that politics and sport did not mix, could not understand how cricketers could now make a stand on racial issues. The players themselves saw the walk-off as a last ditch attempt to salvage the wreckage of South African sport which was foundering helplessly in political waters. It was a plea from the players (who happened to be cricketers) to rid sport of political and racial influences.

The repercussions of the walk-off were not immediately felt, but I believe it heralded a change in attitude amongst the players nationwide. In Pietermaritzburg, two years later, a multi-racial cricket club was formed. Aurora, with the support of local cricket officials and the City Council, flew a defiant banner in the face of the country's laws and police intimidation. Their courage and persistence helped significantly in the advance of mixed cricket in South Africa.

As little Aurora began calling the Government's bluff, so pressure for change grew. While administrators and players were making demands internally, the effects of Peter Hain's persistent campaign overseas were being felt by all sportsmen.

Mike Procter later remarked that Hain had done more than any other person to further the cause of multi-racial sport in South Africa. This drew an angry reaction from many South Africans, but Procter was merely voicing the feelings of many of the country's cricketers who felt that isolation was now inevitable anyway.

Yet, in spite of the events of 1971, and the changes that have taken place since, South Africa is no nearer its goal of returning to genuine international cricket. We are, in fact, still in the embryonic stages of our development. It has taken 14 years for the appointment of a sports ambassador to London, ironically one of the 1971 Springboks, Eddie Barlow. And while the country's leading cricketers stood together for the first time in 1971, it took more than a decade before a South African Players' Association was formed.

Politically, too, the left hand still does not know what the right hand is doing. We have Cabinet Minister Dr Piet Koornhof admitting the mistakes of the past and acknowledging that his former colleague, Prime Minister Mr B. J. Vorster, was wrong in his handling of the D'Oliveira affair which led to the cancellation of the 1968 England tour. Then, only days later, the Government refused Mr Krish MacKerdhuj, president of the South African Cricket Board, a passport to enable him to travel to the International Cricket Conference in London to present his Board's case.

The protest at Newlands on 3 April 1971 obscured another event of significance which took place in the minute's play before the cricketers left the field.

Facing that first ball, and taking a single off it, Richards earned himself R2 to become the first player to be paid on an individual basis in South Africa. Commercial sponsorship of cricket had arrived.

It had, in fact, been pre-arranged that Richards would simply pat Procter's first delivery back down the wicket before the players left the field. But Richards angled it away for a single and, when Procter chided him, replied: 'Well, that's R2 in the bank, anyway.'

Richards, just back from his record-breaking season in Australia and suffering from jet lag, ground out an uncharacteristic 140 in a couple of minutes under six hours. Crossing between overs when Richards had reached the 50-mark, Graeme Pollock suggested that he should adopt a more aggressive approach, to which Richards retorted:

'A quick 50 doesn't buy me a lot of breakfasts.'

In the years ahead cricket's new 'mercenary' would be constantly defending his right to earn a living by exploiting his batting skills — a professional approach which has become acceptable today.

England all-rounder Basil D'Oliveira, an innocent pawn in the game of international politics.

The fact that South Africa's political isolation was to coincide with the advent of sponsorship and one-day cricket proved an unexpected boon for South African cricket administrators. It enabled them to keep South African cricket vibrant and healthy in spite of the lack of international competition.

With money playing an increasing role, cricket in South Africa was revolutionised over the next decade.

The one-day game, first introduced to South Africa in 1970, immediately became popular. Advertisers were quick to exploit this new product and, with the passing years, the game became more gimmicky until a new phenomenon, night cricket, was started in the eighties.

Coloured gear, live commentaries and blaring advertising at matches, numbered players, the increased involvement of the media and uninitiated spectators, along with all the other Kerry Packer trimmings and refinements, transformed the quiet, traditional game of 1971 into a noisy, colourful, entertaining roadshow.

In contrast, South Africa's premier competition, the three-day Currie Cup, began to look dowdy and pedestrian. With rumblings coming from the sponsors, who naturally wanted a slice of the cake, the administrators took the extraordinary step of introducing a sudden-death final to the Currie Cup league competition. Whether that is enough to satisfy the sponsors is doubtful, and there are now hints that the Currie Cup format will be drastically altered, perhaps even reduced to a one innings, two-day event.

Another result of our political isolation was that the emphasis switched from international to provincial cricket. Currie Cup matches began to be played with the ferocity of test matches and, with more money available, provinces went shopping for overseas professionals.

The first minute of the match at Newlands in April 1971 can therefore be seen as a watershed for South African cricket in more than one respect. Evident in that fleeting piece of cricket were the influences of politics and money, operating together for the first time.

Fortunately or unfortunately, my career coincided almost exactly with a period which can be considered the most crucial, and certainly the most distressing, in South African cricket history.

The Newlands match saw my inclusion in the team to tour Australia, but my joy at becoming a Springbok was tempered by the uproar over our walk-off, and by the fact that we knew the tour would never take place. On the last afternoon of the game, in fact, our 12th man, Peter Swart, came on with the drinks and brought with him the news that South Australia had announced a boycott of the tour. We knew before the tour party was announced that it would be no more than a phantom Springbok side.

It was to be 11 long years before another Springbok side was chosen and again I was included. This time the nagging feeling that the 'tests' against Graham Gooch's Englishmen were not genuine spoilt what should have been a very special moment for me.

With overseas tours out of the question, I took the same path as many other South Africans and found some international experience with a season on the English county circuit.

In a way, then, my career mirrored the frustrations, the joys, the conflicts and the dramatic changes of this period — an era in South African cricket moulded by political and financial forces.

The culmination of this momentous decade came when the forces of politics and money clambered into bed together to end South Africa's isolation. The product of this bizarre union was a West Indian tour which shook the cricket-playing world. While the rebel tours provided South African cricket with a timely and welcome boost internally, they left the Springboks further than ever from international acceptance.

10 *Cricket in the Shadows*

The Western Province Craven Week trials at Newlands in 1966. The days of the old-fashioned toe-poked place-kick.

CHAPTER TWO

The Road to Newlands

My path to Newlands, and selection for the ghost Springbok cricket team, had followed a relatively direct, easy and uncomplicated course. As a youngster in Cape Town I had enjoyed all the advantages of a White South African schoolboy, living in comfortable surroundings and spending most of my leisure hours playing sport.

At Bishops, I dabbled in athletics and rugby, and my limited success in these winter sports was the result of my height and strength rather than any outstanding talents.

I managed to make the Western Province Schools rugby side — at lock forward, naturally — and my selection can be attributed to two factors: my ability to hoof goals and my lineout work which enabled me to gain possession without jumping too high. For the rest, I tackled very seldom, was slow about the field and was usually last into the loose scrum.

Craven Week at Loftus Versfeld did provide me with one memorable moment. As I was lining up an attempted penalty on my own 10-metre line, a voice boomed down from the stands, 'If you kick that over, I'll buy you a farm in Adderley Street.' I happened to have a friend in the grandstand who identified the Cape Town pessimist, and a couple of days later I wrote to him, reminding him of the offer. I'm still waiting for his reply!

My ability, as a junior, to putt the shot and hurl the discus gained me selection for the Western Province and, later, the Natal athletic teams.

But these moments on the rugby and athletic fields were just brief flirtations, and cricket was my genuine love.

My pedigree, if not my early prowess with the ball, suggested that I would one day play first-class cricket. My grandfather Vintcent had represented the 1892 Western Province side which won the Currie Cup at the first attempt. His brother Voltelin was chosen for the 1894 South African side to tour England, but business commitments forced him to withdraw, and then problems with varicose veins further curtailed his career.

My father Pieter played in the 1938–39 home series against England before the Second World War, and serious wounds in the Italian campaign ended his active sporting life. He was, however, the only one of the three Van der Bijls selected to play for South Africa who actually saw action in a genuine test match.

Pieter van der Bijl, hands too far apart on the handle for the purist, batting with Eric Rowan in the 'Timeless Test' against England in 1938–39 in Durban. With his captain, Alan Melville, he produced opening stands worth 131 and 191.

My father was a man of many talents; a Rhodes Scholar, who won Blues for boxing and cricket at Oxford, a wartime commanding officer of the Duke of Edinburgh's Own Rifles (the Dukes), headmaster of Bishops Preparatory School, a top cricket administrator and a Springbok selector. He set standards, morally and in cricket, that I always respected and tried to emulate.

As a soldier and a batsman, stoicism was his watchword. In Abyssinia, his troops came under a heavy bombardment, though the shells were dropping short. Lt-Col van der Bijl, unperturbed, shouted to his men, 'Never mind the long-hops, chaps, it's the full tosses that count.'

He failed by only three runs to become the first South African batsman to score a century in each innings of a test match, taking a patient 125 and 97 off the England attack in the famous Timeless Test in Durban. Cricket journalist Dick Stent was watching and he later wrote: 'Van der Bijl, scoring at a rate of 17 runs an hour, continued to bat as if saying to himself, "They may get my wicket but it will be over my dead body" as fast bowler Ken Farnes (an old Oxford friend) continued to pound his legside assault, frequently hitting Van der Bijl and bruising him through the padding of towels he had wrapped round his body . . . He withstood this bombardment with only an occasional grunt and a slowly-uttered gibe to the bowler: "Cut it out now, Ken. That's enough!"'

But he could occasionally play the part of the cavalier, once clubbing 28 off the last over of the day to steer Western Province to a Currie Cup victory against Eastern Province at Newlands. And not only on the field! When I first went to the Durban Country Club in 1968, an old waiter came up and told me he had served my father with a gin and tonic during the Timeless Test. He added that later that night Van der Bijl had been banned from the Country Club for using the car park to launch rockets at the approaching enemy. Part of his army training, I gather, but certainly it was a side of him I would dearly love to have known.

My father had a powerful influence on my cricket career. As a headmaster, he refused to advise me on style and the technical details of the game, believing that the cricket master should coach that area of the game. But for years we spoke about approach and attitude on the field, and the lessons he gave me, though some of them were forgotten for a period towards the end of my playing days, were crucial in my development as a cricketer.

There was one trait I inherited from my father which I would rather have done without. It has, to say the least, caused me acute embarrassment. After lengthy cocktail parties he had a habit of sleep-walking and then, according to my mother, using the broom cupboard as a toilet. It was only after I was married in 1973 that I discovered I was following in his footsteps.

Warm congratulations from my father on my selection for the 1971–72 Springbok tour to Australia. Both of us knew when this photograph was taken that the tour would not take place.

Graeme Pollock was once on the receiving end. We were sharing a room at the Holiday Inn in Cape Town during the South African XI — Derrick Robins game at Newlands in 1975 and, on the morning of the final day, I awoke first, flung open the curtains and then turned to shake Pollock from his slumbers.

He looked at me rather strangely for a moment and then said, 'Vince, won't you just feel that pair of pants over there,' pointing to his smart grey longs neatly folded over the back of a chair. 'Hell, Graeme,' I replied, 'they're all wet.'

Pollock sat bolt upright in bed. 'I don't believe it!' he said. 'I saw you peeing all over my pants in the middle of the night. I thought it had to be a dream so I just went back to sleep.'

More recently, I travelled down from Johannesburg to Pietermaritzburg to address a function at a local hotel. I was spending the night with co-author John Bishop and his wife Sharon, and when I arrived back from the function at about midnight they were already asleep.

At about 2 a.m. my hosts awoke to find me standing stark naked at the end of their bed. 'What do you want, Vince?' John asked. 'Shut up, and move over,' I replied, and jumped into bed with them. Not prepared to antagonise a naked giant in the middle of the night, they reluctantly made space and the three of us fell into an uneasy sleep. At one stage during the night I smoothed the blankets over John — believing I was sleeping next to my wife Bev — snuggled down, and started snoring contentedly in spite of the muffled laughter from my bed-mates. The end came shortly before dawn when I threw my arm around John and tried to give him a hug. His loud bellow finally shook me from my sleep and, with a conciliatory, 'Sorry, folks, just one of my turns,' I stumbled back to my own bed, reflecting that our friendship might have been tried even more severely had I decided to get into the other side of the bed.

I showed little sign of having picked up any of my father's cricketing ability while I was at school. I generally made the various teams as a number four batsman and it was only when I reached Under 15 level that I bowled seriously for the first time. Our attack was one short for the match against Rondebosch and the coach, considering my height rather than my ability to bowl straight, suggested I have a spell. I happened to get three for 0 in the first innings and three for 10 in the second, so I started to regard myself as a bowler, even if others, including my father, did not.

I went on to captain the Western Province Schools Nuffield cricket side but, as a batsman who could bowl a bit, I did nothing to suggest that I had any real future in cricket. My father was resigned to the fact that I had little aptitude for the game and would be no more than an average club cricketer. The change only came when I moved to Natal University in Pietermaritzburg on the completion of my schooling. I planned to go into teaching and my father advised me to move away from Cape Town to broaden my outlook. Four happy years as a student certainly did that, but the impetus given my cricket career was even more important.

For some time I was considered something of an oddball on campus. I breezed into my first net practice — in March 1967 — immaculately attired in white longs, cricket shirt and boots, as was the custom at Bishops. That caused a fair amount of amusement among the other players, who were dressed in an assortment of T-shirts or rugby jerseys, shorts and tackies. I made less of an impact with my cricket and played second team for the first term. My fortunes changed at the end of the year when I gained late selection to an injury-hit Natal University side to play in the annual South African Universities Week in Cape Town.

Colin Fletcher, brother of Zimbabwe captain Duncan, and I made the 1 600 km trip to Cape Town by car, and I assiduously studied the MCC coaching manual during the long trip. I had been chosen as additional medium-pacer, but the formal coaching I had received at school — from English professional Tom Reddick — had been aimed at improving my batting rather than my bowling.

We arrived in Cape Town a week before the SAU Week started and, armed with my manual and an old ball, I spent three hours every day bowling to Fletcher in the concrete nets. On the last day I took a new ball and discovered that I had developed the ability to bowl an outswinger.

On the eve of the tournament I received a letter from my father:

'Dear Vintcent,

Play is called tomorrow and I hope that it will be an enjoyable week.

Billy Griffiths (secretary of the MCC) taught me last week (even at my age!) that it is better to be charitable than bloody-minded; that it is better to be tolerant than intolerant (I knew this, but I had to be reminded of it). Bear this in mind. Not that I think you err in this respect!

Whether you make runs or take wickets, or do neither, always think of the other *fellow. Sometimes he might need to be quietly reprimanded but, of course, balance is the answer. This is what makes a good leader, and you have it.*

It is so easy to win, and so easy to make excuses when things go astray.

Mum and I will never be disappointed when you are not successful in the matter of making runs or taking wickets. We like you to do well only for your sake.

May you enjoy yourself.

Your loving Dad.'

I enjoyed only reasonable success during the Week, but on the final day, playing against a strong University of Cape Town team at the Vineyards, my best spell of five for 20 coincided with the presence at the ground of the SA Universities selectors, and that night I was in their team.

I returned to University in Pietermaritzburg for my second year in 1968 to find that Springbok all-rounder Trevor Goddard had been appointed Sports Director on campus, and he played with us in the first league side. Goddard had an extraordinary influence on my career and he, more than any other, helped me develop as a bowler.

He was a most interesting mix. Off the field a deeply sensitive man, on it he was a totally uncompromising opponent. Playing in the same side as the veteran Springbok, I saw first hand how an expert could manipulate the umpire. Watching Goddard, quiet and undemonstrative, was seeing a master at work. He would run up to bowl, left-arm over, strike the batsman on the pads wide down the leg-side and then stand on line with the stumps, hands on his hips, and peer down the wicket. As he walked back to his mark, he would remark, 'Going down leg, wasn't it?' and the umpire would have to agree. A couple of deliveries later he might hit the pads well outside off-stump and again he would go through his routine. 'Missing off, wasn't it?' he would enquire and the umpire would nod his head gravely. And then would come the sting. Goddard would hit the pads in a more favourable position, not straight in front, but a marginal decision when the batsman would usually get the benefit of the doubt. Up he would go in a most vociferous appeal and, inevitably, he would find the umpire agreeing with him again.

Goddard spent hours with me in the nets, constantly encouraging and advising me, even coaching me during matches for the University and later Natal. He taught me the very basics of fast bowling and to this day I find myself repeating his words when I am trying to help a youngster. There are three aspects to be grasped by fast bowlers — the run-up, the delivery from side-on and the follow-through, he would tell me. And if anything was wrong with my bowling, he would always return to basics in order to get to the root of the problem. It is difficult to impress on young bowlers that swing, speed and seam are not as important as line and length. Additional nip off the wicket can be generated by simply having the correct action, not by bowling faster.

Springbok all-rounder Trevor Goddard. His tips were not confined to the coaching manual, but all were valuable.

Goddard also taught me several other important tricks of the fast bowler's trade, such as how to pick the seam.

But it was Berry Versfeld, in fact, who showed me how lip-ice can be used for more than just protection against the wind and sun.

Unfortunately, he failed to issue a safety warning. Playing in my very first match for Natal — against Eastern Province at St George's Park — we were preparing to go back onto the field after lunch on the second day when Versfeld turned and asked if I had the juice. 'What juice, what are you talking about?' I asked. 'The juice, man, the lip-ice,' he replied. I was puzzled. 'What do you want lip-ice for, haven't you seen all the clouds?'. 'No, you idiot,' he said, surprised at my ignorance, 'it's to put on the ball to make it shine.'

I dutifully ran off and fetched the lip-ice which I kept in my pocket. The ball became very old very quickly because Graeme Pollock was batting. For the first time I used lip-ice on a cricket field, rubbing it on one side of the tattered ball. Suddenly, after 70 overs, the ball starting swinging prodigiously and I was highly delighted with my new ploy. The umpire at my end, Carl Coetzee, must have realised something odd was happening, and the end came when, in my total naïveté, I took the lip-ice from my pocket and started rubbing it on the ball while I was standing next to him. 'What on earth are you doing?' an astonished Coetzee asked. 'I'm just putting some lip-ice on the ball,' I replied innocently.

Versfeld had failed to inform me that my action was illegal and I found myself reported to the South African Cricket Association for irregular tactics — on my Currie Cup debut!

I had been drafted into the Natal team for the second match of the season. Perhaps because I had stopped growing physically, I had begun to find my co-ordination and rhythm, picking up wickets in the early league games.

With Goddard at my shoulder, I began appreciating the intricacies of the game and that it was possible to work a batsman out. Trevor did it so easily and well in one game against Old Collegians when Neville McDonald, their number 11 batsman, was holding us up. McDonald, friendly and likeable, was a typical tail-ender but, as he enjoyed telling anyone who would listen, he could look back on a maiden first-class century scored against Griquas while batting at number 10. He had a very awkward, cramped stance and you could see both cheeks of his backside when you ran in to bowl to him. Anyway, Goddard turned to me and said, 'I think I'll just open him up a bit.' He pitched his first delivery in line with the leg-stump, and bowled the next three wider and wider down the leg-side. Gradually McDonald opened his stance, attempting to counter this new line of attack, and then with his fifth ball Goddard bowled him middle stump through the gate. It was the first time I had seen a thinking bowler in operation and I was fascinated.

I had some success against the clubs that mattered in the early days of the 1968–69 season, taking 10 wickets in a match against Barry Richards' DHSOB, another 10 against Berea Rovers, with Mike Procter and Lee Irvine in their side, and bowling well to Durban Collegians and Natal captain Versfeld. I heard later that it was only at the insistence of Versfeld and Richards that I came into the team for the game against Eastern Province. The selectors had first wanted to blood me in the Natal B team.

When I telephoned my father on Sunday evening to tell him that I had been selected for Natal, he was pleased, but not particularly enthusiastic. However, at 5 a.m. the next morning, he called back in great excitement. He had just seen the morning newspaper and realised that I had been picked for the Natal Currie Cup side and not the B team — as a specialist bowler!

My first taste of Currie Cup cricket was a terrifying one. We made a dismal 166, and I contributed only seven, but I will never forget my brief stay at the wicket. I had gone in to face Springbok fast bowler Peter Pollock. My first two deliveries were bouncers, but I managed to stand up straight and play them down defensively from shoulder height. As Pollock was walking back to his mark, I looked into the cordon of slips where I saw my University clubmates, Arthur Short and Dassie Biggs, who played their provincial cricket for EP, laughing at me. I smiled nervously at them but, unfortunately, Pollock chose that moment to turn round. He saw me grinning, presumed I was amused at his inability to get the ball up, and proceeded to bowl me three more bouncers which flew viciously over my head.

I had received five bouncers in my first over of Currie Cup cricket and, after scrambling my seven runs, returned to the dressing-room, at least expecting some words of comfort. No mention was made of Pollock's fiery assault. The lesson was obvious. I had to learn that Currie Cup cricket was hard and uncompromising, and advantage had to be taken of an opponent's weakness.

We were in the field for two hours that evening and I opened the bowling, foolishly in new boots. I did not perform particularly well, bowling five overs for 17, but when I took my boots off at the close I found the sock on my right foot drenched in blood. I had taken all the skin off my toes and yet, in the excitement, had not felt any pain. Years later the slightest twinge would have sent me scurrying off to the change-room for treatment!

On the second day I found fate on my side. At one stage I had bowled 25 overs, conceding 52 runs without a wicket but I ended the innings with four for 65 in 29 overs (was it the lip-ice?). My first Currie Cup victim was one any bowler would have treasured — Graeme Pollock. The Springbok left-hander was becalmed on 91 and, looking for a couple of quick boundaries off the new boy to take him to his century, swung at a delivery on the leg-stump, missed and the ball clipped his pads on the way into his stumps.

Pollock was only 25 years old at the time, and I had already collected scrapbooks around him. But I was surprised to see how vulnerable he was on the leg-side. When I first bowled to him, he was on 80 and Versfeld, setting an on-side field, told me to bowl on or outside the leg-stump. My first four overs to him were, in fact, all maidens. He did not then have the ability, which he developed so devastatingly later in his career, to hit the ball with power and freedom to all quarters of the field.

My performance cemented my place in the side and, apart from withdrawing from two Currie Cup games because of university examinations in the years that followed, I played in Natal's next 101 Currie Cup matches over the following 14 years before moving to Johannesburg.

Peter Pollock was another to have a profound influence on my career, and it started on my Currie Cup debut. He had shown me what Currie Cup cricket involved, providing me with a fiery baptism when I batted in the first innings, and then using a piece of gamesmanship to talk me into a taking a wild, and unsuccessful swipe at spinner Neville Mallett in the second. In the years which followed, however, his efforts were confined to helping me with my bowling.

In my second Currie Cup outing — also against Eastern Province — in Pietermaritzburg I walked into the hotel dining-room after the first day's play to find Peter Pollock having dinner alone. He asked me to join him and that was the start of an extraordinary tutor/pupil relationship which was to have a considerable impact on my career. I had taken four for 51 in EP's first innings of 228 and over dinner we discussed the day's play. He spoke about my attitude on the field, said he thought I should be more aggressive and gave me some advice about my bowling action. My respect for him was immense. He was 27, in his prime as an established world-class fast bowler, and yet had gone out of his way to help an opponent, a rookie medium-pacer, in the middle of a crucial game.

Sweet revenge in a friendly rivalry. Bowling Peter Pollock at Kingsmead while bespectacled brother Graeme looks on. Graeme sent a flutter through the hearts of South African cricketing followers when he suddenly donned glasses. Later he was to discard them but he never stopped scoring runs.

In the years ahead, while he was still playing and later when he had retired, I constantly turned to him for advice.

Probably the most remarkable feature of my first three games for Natal was playing under four different captains. Versfeld ducked into a

Peter Pollock bouncer in the second innings of the EP game and was carried off. The blow sidelined him for over a month and left him with a speech impediment which lasted even longer. Trevor Goddard took over as skipper but, in the very next match, the second-round fixture against Eastern Province in Pietermaritzburg, he broke a thumb while making 145. We moved on to the Wanderers to play Transvaal in our traditional Christmas contest and Grayson Heath, the new captain, developed a virus and Dennis Gamsy took over.

We came second to Transvaal in the Currie Cup that summer and I ended with 20 wickets from five matches at 21,60 apiece, finishing second to Don MacKay-Coghill on the national averages. But my arrival on the scene coincided with a radical change in Natal's fortunes. Under the leadership of Jackie McGlew, Natal had won the Currie Cup for the previous seven years, but it was to be another five before Barry Richards would again bring the Currie Cup back to Kingsmead.

For Natal the season 1968–69 was largely one of failure, but for me the experience I had gained in playing alongside several world-class players was invaluable. At full strength, the Natal attack included Mike Procter, Pat Trimborn, Trevor Goddard and Norman Crookes, all Springboks. I was the new boy, the bowler the opposition would look to score off while keeping out the rest of the attack. I did not realise it at the time, but the others were setting up wickets for me to take.

Had I, as an inexperienced 20-year-old, been required to fill the role of a strike bowler, I believe I would have been unsuccessful. Two of my successors in Natal, Evan Hodkinson and young Mike Clare have, I believe, battled to establish themselves for this very reason.

I had indeed been fortunate. An ideal cricketing background, excellent coaching when it was most needed, the right breaks at club level and then inclusion in a powerful Natal attack, had all facilitated my climb to first-class cricket.

My luck was not over. Tiger Lance, the Springbok all-rounder, was a late withdrawal from the Wilf Isaacs tour party to visit Britain in July and August of 1969, and I was invited to replace him.

The tour, the only overseas one I ever went on, was another considerable and timely boost to my career, providing me with the opportunity of bowling on a variety of wickets.

The cricket was, however, overshadowed by anti-apartheid demonstrations. South African cricketers had been met by protestors before. Jackie McGlew's 1960 Springboks, arriving at Heathrow, were welcomed by banner-waving demonstrators galvanised into action by the recent Sharpeville shootings. But, for most of us, it was the first time politics had disturbed the calm waters of our lives.

Over the next few years political influences — both internally and from overseas — swept through South African sport and were to remain unwelcome companions for the rest of my playing days.

But this was July 1969, a year since Mr B. J. Vorster's dreadful bungling of the D'Oliveira affair, and small groups of protesters were able to show for the first time how effectively they could disrupt cricket matches.

The Isaacs tour was, of course, a private one, but for South African sport the implications were enormous. Both the anti-apartheid demonstrators and the cricket authorities learnt from the experiences. The demos went on to better and bigger things against Dawie de Villiers' Springbok rugby players just months later, turning that tour into a military operation. The ease with which they invaded grounds during the Isaacs games, and their success in ruining the Springbok rugby tour, dismayed officials at Lord's and were major factors in the last minute cancellation of the 1970 Springbok cricket tour to England.

We opened the tour at Basildon against Essex where we had our first taste of demonstrators. Five of them came on to the pitch and sat in a tight knot just short of a length. Keith Boyce, the Essex and West Indian all-rounder who was capable of bowling at great pace, was at the end of his run and came charging in to bowl, determined to put a quick end to the protest. Brian Taylor, captaining Essex and keeping wicket, had to run up to the stumps to restrain him and it took a couple of minutes to cool him down.

Before our next match, against Oxford University at the Parks ground, vandals dug a 40 metre trench across the table, damaging 17 pitches. We were still able to play though and Graeme Pollock, in scintillating form, cracked 231 not out to dominate the game.

I had an unpleasant brush with a demonstrator at this match. At the end of the first day's play, a young, unkempt man, came up to me and called me a 'racist pig' and spat in my face. Fortunately, there was someone with me and he restrained me from what might easily have been the first, and only physically violent act of my life. We were a bunch of young cricketers — most of the tour party were in their early twenties — and, at that stage, we thought politics were beyond our sphere of activity and influence.

With the tour nearly over, I took the first hat-trick of my career against the Derrick Robins XI at Eastbourne, bowling Colin Ingleby-MacKenzie and Don Bennett, who was to sign me for Middlesex more than 10 years later, and then trapping former SA Schools player Giles Ridley in front.

Pelham Henwood and I returned home as the two most successful bowlers. The opportunity of playing in strange conditions, and mixing with established and talented players, had been a wonderful experience, giving me confidence in my ability and cricketing future.

The Springbok team to tour England was to be announced at the end of the new South African season, and the fact that several critics, including former Springbok fast bowler Neil Adcock, were tipping me as a candidate, was another important boost for my morale. It had only been nine months since my Currie Cup debut at Port Elizabeth and, while I did not take the critics entirely seriously, I did believe a productive Currie Cup season would give me an outside chance of selection.

Right through the 1969–70 summer, I vied with Transvaal paceman Gary Watson for the one remaining place in the tour party. We had almost identical seasons, taking 18 wickets apiece, and I topped the averages with 14,5 with Watson second on 15,5.

Natal's game against the touring Australians that season was obviously crucial for me. If I was to stake a claim for the England tour, I had to prove my worth against international opposition. I did not, however, bowl with any great penetration and, for most of the drawn match, filled the role of a stock bowler, taking four for 93 in 30 overs as the Australians made 385.

Watson, a cricketer of boundless energy and excellent physique, was by far the faster bowler. Obviously the South African selectors were looking for speedsters, particularly as Peter Pollock would be in his 30th year by the end of the tour, and Watson was chosen ahead of me.

While not as naïve as I had been in my first season, I was still shaken by a couple of incidents during the Australian tour. Don MacKay-Coghill told me of one in the Transvaal game against the tourists. He had dismissed Bill Lawry, Keith Stackpole and Dougie Walters, who played and missed at his first two deliveries and then gave an easy catch off the third, and was excited about his form. But some of the wind was taken out of his sails when he reached the dressing-room and heard the background to Walters' dismissal. The Australians were apparently playing poker and Walters, the next man in, had just drawn two cards when a wicket fell. He glanced at his hand and saw his first-ever Royal Flush. He asked the others in the school, Brian Taber and Ian Chappell, to leave the hand untouched, adding that he did not plan to be away long. Striding to the middle, he contrived his own dismissal and then hurried back to the dressing-room — to find the other players shuffling the cards. Everything is not always as it seems out in the middle!

In the Australian game against Natal, Bill Lawry, who was having an unhappy tour leading the outclassed Australians — they were whitewashed 4–0 — and occasionally reacting petulantly when decisions went against him, was out in controversial circumstances. When he had 11, he aimed to drive me through the covers, but the ball cut back to take the inside edge. I started to appeal and then stopped, believing the ball had pitched short of the keeper's gloves. Gamsy and the slips went on with the appeal and the umpire gave Lawry out. The Australian captain, who had followed the ball as it went through to Gamsy, said a few choice words and then dragged himself forlornly back to the pavilion, looking round a couple of times as the crowd shouted 'walk, walk'. Natal captain Trevor Goddard ran up to Gamsy and asked him if he had caught it. 'Think so,' replied Gamsy. Goddard turned to the slips, but they would not commit themselves for several moments until eventually one, who had been following Lawry's slow progress to the pavilion, suddenly admitted he thought it had bounced. Goddard swung round to recall Lawry, but the Australian had disappeared from view.

I was shaken by the incident, but I believe that by this stage of the tour many South African cricketers had become tired of Lawry's behaviour and had little sympathy for him.

I enjoyed my batting in this match, making 22 and, with Dave Dyer (55 not out), added 61 in 77 minutes for the last wicket as Natal made 259. I had gone to the wicket to face the second new ball which was being shared by the admirable Graham McKenzie and Alan Connolly. I had been in awe of McKenzie since watching him bowl the Australians to a magnificent victory over the Springboks — their only win of the series—on a flat Newlands wicket three years previously. Pat Trimborn had been bowled by McKenzie's second delivery with the new ball and we crossed at the players' gate. I stopped, hoping for some words of encouragement and advice. 'That guy is quick!' said a wide-eyed Trimborn and scurried off to the dressing-room, clearly relieved to be out of the firing-line. It did very little for my confidence, but I survived for some time before being bowled by the unorthodox spinner John Gleeson.

Natal had a strong Currie Cup side, led by Trevor Goddard in his last season of first-class cricket, but our middle-order, now without the services of two Springboks, Mike Procter and Lee Irvine, who had moved to Cape Town and Johannesburg respectively, was young and inexperienced. Natal finished third on the log as Transvaal and Western Province tied at the top.

I had missed the opening game of the season against Western Province because of university examinations, but played in the remainder and, though disappointed at missing selection for the England tour, I was happy with my form. I like to think I made it possible for the province of my birth to share the Cup. In the game against Transvaal at the Wanderers, Natal, chasing a victory target of 267, were in a hopeless position at 88 for eight when I joined Trimborn with 20 overs remaining. For 13 overs we held out and then Trimborn departed, caught by Ray White off MacKay-Coghill. Colin Burnhill was the last man in and together we saw out play and denied Transvaal a victory which would have put the Currie Cup on ice.

In the last moments of the match, I had to contend with the bowling of Springbok all-rounder Tiger Lance. He did everything to unsettle me, bowling skilfully and intelligently, and then cursing me when I played and missed. The last ball of the match was a Watson bouncer on off-stump and, as I let it fly harmlessly by, Lance ran across to me from leg-gully, shook my hand and congratulated me warmly for my efforts. It was a most generous and sporting gesture from an established and highly competitive Springbok, and it made a deep impression on me.

The tour to England was cancelled at the last minute when Harold Wilson's Government, fearful of the public disruption it would cause, put enormous pressure on Lord's. In South Africa, at the time, there was widespread anger with the part the British Government and Peter

Hain's anti-apartheid movement had played. But, of course, South Africans were reaping what they had sowed. Two years earlier the South African Government had cancelled the England tour because of D'Oliveira's inclusion, openly mixing politics and sport for the first time.

The 1970–71 season nevertheless started with hopes high that the tour to Australia during the following summer would go ahead. Pat Trimborn took over the captaincy of a very young Natal side which had lost Goddard, Richards, Procter, Irvine, Ackerman and Versfeld in two seasons. The gaps were frighteningly wide, but the team performed commendably and, had Natal won the last match of the season against Transvaal, instead of losing by 36 runs, we would have shared the Currie Cup with eventual winners Transvaal and Western Province.

It was a vital period of rebuilding for Natal cricket, and there were several richly gifted youngsters who should have emerged to form the core of the side for the next decade. Two all-rounders, Dave Orchard and Dougie Morgan, were particularly exciting prospects, but neither fulfilled his undoubted potential. The 22-year-old Orchard did reveal glimpses of his ability in the 1970–71 season, and Clive Rice was perhaps a shade fortunate to gain the all-rounder's berth for the Australian tour ahead of him, though, in the end, it was purely academic. Had the ultimate goal of a Springbok cap been attainable in the years which followed, Orchard might have produced the results to do justice to his talents.

In a young, untried side, Trimborn did not have the necessary backing and support of senior players. He had to marshal his inexperienced troops in fairly dictatorial style and this weighed heavily on him. His delightful sense of humour almost disappeared as his approach changed, and I believe that he would have been a far more successful captain had he been able to retain his perspective. But, by having to lead alone, he became isolated, and he occasionally emerged from matches bitter and critical. Later he clashed with Natal administrators and was replaced as captain for the 1972–73 season.

As far as I was concerned, however, Trimborn could not have treated me more fairly. He and I developed an effective opening attack, a happy partnership which continued until his retirement at the end of the 1975–76 season. He was an excellent bowler, able to move the ball prodigiously both ways, and both Barry Richards and Mike Procter, with their overseas experience, considered him and Tom Cartwright as the two best bowlers they had seen on seaming wickets.

Trimborn and I were challenging for the Springbok side as medium–fast seamers — and were both, eventually, included in the party for Australia — but this did not cloud his treatment of me, and he bent over backwards to give me every opportunity to prove myself. He was 30 at the time, an experienced Springbok and still bowling as well as ever, yet he always offered me every advantage when we shared the new ball, often going into the wind himself to allow me to bowl with it.

At the time it used constantly to amaze me that I took more wickets than he did in the Currie Cup as I felt he was the better bowler. It was probably the height difference which was the telling factor as batsmen played him largely horizontally, worrying about his deviation off the wicket, while my height, and the bounce it produced, tested the batsmen vertically as well.

I missed the first game of the season again because of examinations — the last Natal game I was to miss for the next 13 years — and ended with 26 wickets at an average of 19,5 while Trimborn took 23. I felt we had both done enough to gain selection for the Australian trip. But, as the final Springbok 'trial' — the Rest of South Africa v Transvaal at Newlands early in April 1971 — drew nearer, it became increasingly clear that the tour would not take place.

Standing in the shadow of the Newlands pavilion after the match — a game remembered for the historic walk-off by the players — I heard my name included in the Springbok tour party. I was standing next to Arthur Short, and he was the first to shake my hand, though he must have been acutely disappointed at his own omission. He and I had digs in a large communal house in Pietermaritzburg at the time, and a year earlier we had been involved in a farewell party on the eve of his departure with the 1970 Springboks for England when news of the cancellation of the tour was broadcast.

I felt relief at having made the side, but we knew then it would be no more than another ghost team, and that clouded the moment. Two days later I received a letter from my father, advising me not to harbour any hopes of the tour taking place. He added, 'Nothing, I repeat nothing, can take away the achievement of being chosen to play for your country.'

And so we entered the most unsettled period in South African

The Springbok team to travel to Australia is read out at Newlands in 1971 and Arthur Short, raising a brave smile, is the first to congratulate me. Short, selected for the aborted Springbok tour to England a year previously, was originally overlooked for the Australian visit but later replaced Eddie Barlow who withdrew. In the end, however, it was all academic.

cricket history, a time of intense frustration for the players, heightened by inept and contradictory Government policies, and the well-intentioned but ineffectual attempts by administrators to break the deadlock.

I had floated to the top at a most unpropitious moment.

CHAPTER THREE

The changing face of cricket

When I made my first-class debut in 1968, the game in South Africa was still conducted along traditional lines. Eight three-day games were played during the season and there were no incidental competitions or pre-season friendlies to clutter up the programme. The game was for amateurs with no financial incentives — the latter hardly being necessary with a Springbok cap in the offing.

When I retired in 1983 the game had changed markedly. Politics had ushered genuine test cricket from the stage, one-day games had become the biggest crowd-pullers, and sponsorship was influencing the game at every level.

The Currie Cup, the premier competition in South Africa, was losing its unequal struggle with one-day cricket and, as a result, the sponsors sought changes to the well-tried format. To appease the sponsors, South African Breweries, and provide a climax to the Currie Cup season, the administrators had taken the unusual step of introducing a four-day final between the two sides heading the league competition.

Cash incentives were offered in all provincial games, and most of the Currie Cup sides fielded several local and two overseas professionals.

The first of these changes came in 1970 when an unofficial Gillette Cup, one-day competition was introduced. It was master-minded by Eric Rowan, but without the full blessing of the SACA, and the teams appeared under the captains' names.

As with the Packer World Series years later, the Press and the traditionalists were sceptical, yet by the end of the competition there was no doubt that one-day cricket had enormous appeal and was here to stay.

In the semi-final of the first Gillette Cup, between Wesley's XI (Natal) and Bacher's XI (Transvaal) an extraordinary incident took place which I have never seen repeated. I had taken four early wickets in the Transvaal innings and, with nine wickets down, still had two of my allotted 12 overs to bowl. There was a R100 bonus award for any bowler taking five wickets and this was obviously to be shared amongst the team. Springbok wicket-keeper Dennis Gamsy, and the cordon of slip fielders, decided that they could not stand by idly and let this sum of money slip through their fingers. The result was that when Dave Orchard, bowling at the other end, found the edge of tailender Gary Watson's bat, the catch was intentionally grassed. I went on to trap Watson leg-before in the next over and we all went home nearly R9 richer.

The final was between Barlow's XI (Western Province) and Natal and, with the prize money of R45 a player, I had high hopes of being able to buy my first transistor radio.

It seemed my ambitions would be realised when we dismissed Western Province for 132 and reached 90 for four. But we then collapsed and, at 125 for nine, I found myself batting with Charlie Sullivan. We scrambled a further four runs and then Sullivan, aiming to hit the winning boundary, flayed wildly at Peter Swart and dragged the ball into his stumps.

As Charles Fortune told his radio listeners, 'there goes Charlie Sullivan, brandishing his willow as though to beat out a veld fire, but all he has succeeded in doing is beating out the hopes and aspirations of his team.' He might have added that the purchase of my transistor radio was delayed by several months.

After this first tentative step into the new world of one-day cricket, the changes came on rapidly and the game gained in popularity.

The one-day game still has its many detractors, particularly amongst the purists who regard it as hit-and-giggle cricket. They mourn the passing of the time-honoured contest when the batting side's aim was to score runs while the bowlers would try and bowl them out.

The changing face of cricket 33

The emphasis in the one-day game is on containment rather than taking wickets. In the one-day game a bowler capable of delivering his 11 overs for 20 is preferred to the one who might pick up three for 60 in his spell. The attacking leg-spinner, like Denys Hobson, who has taken years to develop his art, is replaced by the mediocre, boring medium-pacer.

To combat negative bowling and defensive field-placings, batsmen have resorted to the unorthodox; the classic batting skills are

The Numbers Game. Number three (Alvin Kallicharran) on the sweep watched by number four (Graeme Pollock) and number 10 (Richie Ryall).

adulterated in the desperate search for runs. The game rewards the batsman who can step away to leg and bludgeon the ball to the off, or angle the ball wide of the wicket-keeper. The beautifully executed cover drive often proves a waste as deep cover cuts it down to a single run.

The popularity of one-day cricket, and the money it generates, has resulted in a congested season. At present, we still have the right balance with the Nissan Shield limited-over competition and the Benson and Hedges Night Series to complement the three-day Castle Currie Cup competition. But the situation overseas is bewildering and even the most ardent follower, able to rattle off the scores and results of five-day test matches, will battle to remember the outcome of the numerous one-day internationals being played.

There is, of course, a positive side to one-day cricket. Apart from filling cricket's coffers, and boosting the game, it has improved cricketing skills in several areas.

It has taught many batsmen, who tend to be stodgy in their approach, to play a greater variety of attacking strokes. Glenn Turner, the former New Zealand captain and one of the most prolific batsmen in the English County Championship, ascribes much of his development to the influences of the one-day game. In this country players such as Robbie Armitage and Brian Whitfield should also benefit from having to tap their more adventurous resources.

I found in England in 1980 that the one-day game sharpened my control over line and length. One of the best overs I bowled all season was to Yorkshire and England wicketkeeper-batsman David Bairstow, an effective hitter of the ball. He was just short of his 50, and Yorkshire were looking for more than six an over, but I bowled six yorkers on the leg-stump and he was only able to add a further two to the score.

A further result has been the marked improvement in the running between wickets while fielding has also become more lively with the throwing faster and more accurate.

The introduction of the one-day game was particularly important for South Africa. It came at a time when we had been banished from world cricket, and its excitement and ability to draw large crowds kept the enthusiasm of the players and spectators high in those dark days.

The competition also takes the Currie Cup sides into the outlying areas in the early rounds, providing the likes of Free State, Griquas and

Springboks in colour. Mike Procter the centre of attraction in the first twilight international against the 1983–84 West Indians.

Border with an opportunity to play against the leading teams in the country.

This does, however, produce many one-sided matches. When Natal were down in East London one year for a first-round match against Border, skipper Barry Richards, conducting a pre-match team talk which was dragging on, said: 'Now let's deal with the Border attack.'

'That's not an attack, that's a defence,' remarked Pelham Henwood, bringing the team talk to a swift conclusion.

Henwood, an excellent left-arm spinner, was one of those unfortunate South African cricketers who peaked in the seventies when Springboks were an extinct breed. A serious motor accident in 1968, when he was 22, left him with a badly damaged leg and seemed certain to end his blossoming cricket career. But he fought back with great courage and, shrewdly handled by skipper Barry Richards, he became the country's leading spinner, turning out for South Africa against a succession of Derrick Robins touring sides.

He also had a sharp and dry wit. Playing against Rhodesia in intense heat, he was in the middle of a protracted spell when Richards, worried about his spinner's damaged knee which was held together by a pin, asked him if he was fit to continue. 'I'm fine,' replied Henwood, 'just a little bit of metal fatigue!'

He enjoyed particular success in the Gillette Cup competition, disproving the contemporary view that the spinner had no place in a one-day game, and his bowling analysis of seven for 21 against Border in the 1972–73 season has still to be bettered.

There is a heavy emphasis on one-day cricket in England where their greater exposure to the game has given them a more sophisticated approach. This is particularly true of selection where, even at national level, we are still choosing players on their prowess as three-day performers. In England, the composition of the sides varies enormously and some players, considered one-day specialists, rarely see action in the test or county game.

Batsmen have adapted particularly well to one-day cricket. When the 40-over John Player Sunday League was first introduced in England, teams scoring 120 were considered to be reasonably well placed. In fact, Somerset bowler B. A. Langford bowled eight consecutive maidens in 1969! Today, in spite of more scientific field-placing and better fielding, totals of 240 do not ensure victory.

The reasons for the popularity of one-day cricket are obvious. Spectators are treated to an instant match, a full day of aggressive cricket with a result guaranteed at the end. An added attraction is that the underdog has a far greater chance of upsetting the stronger opponent than in the three-day outing. With time for recovery limited, the one-day match can easily be turned by a great catch, a missed opportunity or an inspired piece of bowling or batting.

In the semi-final of the Datsun Shield (formerly Gillette Cup) competition in 1980, Procter and I had Transvaal struggling when Graeme Pollock came to the wicket. We knew that an early dismissal of the incomparable left-hander could settle the match. He was on four when Procter found an outside edge, but Natal wicket-keeper Tich Smith dropped the catch. 'I've just dropped the Datsun Shield,' was Smith's reaction, and Pollock went on to make 135 not out in a Transvaal total of 278.

He took 22 off my last over — that ultimately proved the difference between the two sides as we made 252 — twice hitting me for six over long-on. The second of these shots was perhaps the finest ever played off me. I pitched the ball in the blockhole, and any normal batsman would have had to hit it along the ground. But Pollock moved forward, turning it into a low full toss, and somehow contrived to club it high over the long-on fence.

In the style of soccer players, Alan Kourie gets to grips with Ray Jennings after the Springbok wicket-keeper's remarkable running catch to dismiss Dennis Amiss off the penultimate ball of the limited-overs clash against the 1982 SAB English at the Wanderers.

The fallibility of umpires, too, can prove a major factor in the abbreviated game. In the 1977 final between Eastern Province and Natal an umpiring error might so easily have cost us the Shield. Eastern Province, led by Chris Wilkins, still had the services of Pollock who was obviously a key figure.

Eastern Province had started disastrously, crawling to 46 for two off 20 overs, when Pollock came to the wicket. Natal left-arm seamer Aubrey Lilley, later to die tragically in a light aeroplane crash, almost immediately bowled the Springbok left-hander a poor delivery down the leg-side. Pollock flicked at it but succeeded only in getting an edge which Smith moved across to take. A catch down the leg-side is often the most difficult decision for the umpire to make, but in this case it looked a straightforward one. Umpire Syd Moore, however, gave Pollock not out and for a few moments there was turmoil out in the middle.

Crossing over at the end of the over, Procter remarked to Pollock that he thought he had been lucky.

'Lucky,' exclaimed Pollock, 'that wasn't luck, that was the worst decision I've ever seen in my life.'

There was a roar of laughter and the tension out in the middle evaporated. Fortunately, the error was not a costly one. Pollock had reached only eight when Lilley had him caught by Mike Madsen at point and we went on to a comfortable win.

The appeal of limited-over cricket has brought a new element to grounds; the spectator who enjoys the crowd participation and razzmatazz of the one-day contest, but cares little for the refinements of the game. But, accompanying this noise and excitement has been a general deterioration in the behaviour of spectators and, to a degree, the players.

Cricket fever hit a peak in Durban in 1982 when we played, and beat, Transvaal in the second-leg Datsun Shield semi-final and then in the midweek play-off days later. In mid-morning of the Wednesday clash, I had to nip off on an errand and found the city like a morgue. Hundreds of grandmothers must have been buried that day and Kingsmead had a capacity crowd of 16 000.

But what I also remember about those two matches was the disgraceful, drunken conduct of sections of the crowd. There was a tragic sequel when South Africa met the SAB England side in a one-day

Crowd participation at Kingsmead as Natal beat Transvaal by eight runs in the Datsun Shield semi-final in January 1982.

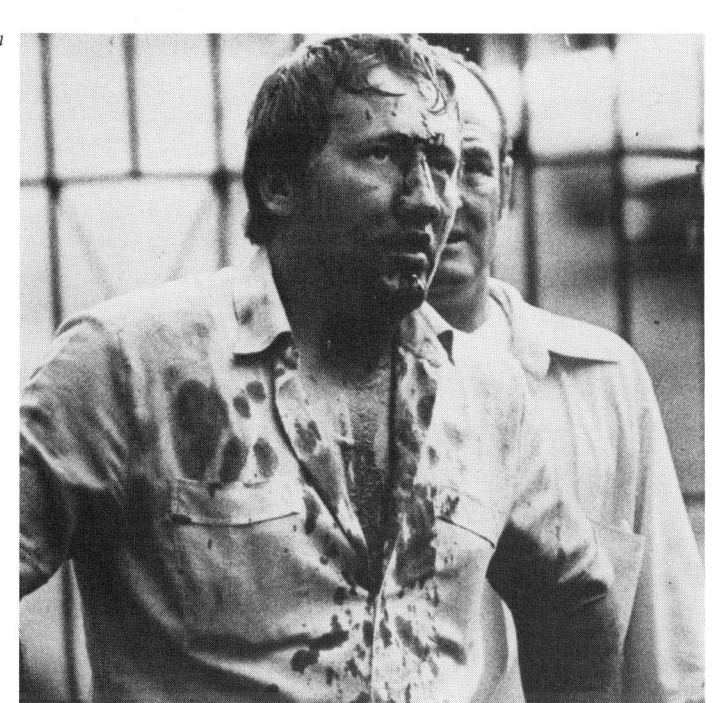

The ugly side of cricket crowds. A brawl during a Western Province–Transvaal clash in 1980 had this bloody result.

international two months later. When the match finished, and the Kingsmead crowd finally cleared late on that Wednesday afternoon, a small knot of people stood round a prone figure on the bank at the Umgeni end. A spectator had received a blow on the head during those final minutes and, while the Springboks were sweeping to victory, urged on by a deliriously happy crowd, this young man had died.

A total ban on alcohol on the banks has since been enforced at Kingsmead and it is quite noticeable how this has cut down the size of the crowds. For years a number of my Natal friends, genuine cricket lovers, used to pack a couple of beers with their lunch and enjoy the day on the banks at Kingsmead. The new and unruly cricket element has ensured the removal of this luxury and my friends now stay away and enjoy their cricket from the comfort of their lounges.

One of the most indelible memories of my stint in England in 1980 was the attitude of the one-day crowds. I found the crowd's reaction

The humour of the English crowds. The banners of rivals Surrey and Middlesex in the 1980 Gillette Cup final at Lord's.

and participation in the Gillette Cup final between Middlesex and Surrey at Lord's quite fascinating. Throughout the long day the spectators involved themselves with the players, but never in a malicious way. Whenever a player on either side did anything out of the ordinary, his particular group of supporters would burst into song. My ditty ran:

> *What's it like to have no hair,*
> *Are you young or are you old,*
> *Are you hot or are you cold,*
> *What's it like to be bald?*

More significant was the reaction of the Surrey supporters to their sound, seven wicket defeat by Middlesex that day. After the presentation, the Surrey supporters stayed on, a huge, banner-waving throng gathered beneath the players' balcony, and they sang to their team for nearly two hours.

The important issue, as far as the Surrey followers were concerned, was that their team had reached the final. The priority and honour was getting to Lord's even if Surrey were finally defeated.

South African crowds, in contrast, are largely interested in watching their sides succeed. Many of cricket's new followers care little for the game itself but are concerned only with winning. Provincialism is the real key to their involvement and they lack the humour and generosity of their English counterparts.

In my last year with Natal I was chatting to a young but avid Natal supporter. 'I hate Graeme Pollock,' he told me vehemently. Taken aback, I asked why and his disturbing reply was, 'He always scores runs against Natal.'

The unpredictability of one-day cricket has also added immensely to the flavour of one-day cricket. And no game I played in illustrates this more vividly than the 1981 Datsun Shield semi-final between Natal and Transvaal at the Wanderers. Transvaal held the whiphand for most of the day, and appeared to be cruising to a comfortable victory at 221 for six, needing only five to tie and take the Shield because they had lost fewer wickets. But, inexplicably, the pressure started getting to them in those closing moments, and they lost Alan Kourie and Henry Fotheringham to runs outs.

Procter, bowling fast and straight, tied the batsmen down in the final over and Gordon McMillan, batting with Dougie Neilson, was run out at the bowler's end as the batsmen tried to take two off the penultimate delivery of the game. Four were needed off the last ball if Transvaal were to win.

As we gathered in the middle of the wicket, awaiting the new batsman, Neville Daniels turned to me and said: 'Hell, I'm pleased Proccie is bowling the last ball. He's no fool.'

In the Transvaal change-room, Graeme Pollock was resigned to defeat. 'Well, chaps, we really flogged that one,' he said and started packing away his gear. And Procter, at the end of his long run, turned to me at deep mid-off and said that for the first time in the match he thought Natal would win.

But the cricketing gods had one more trick to play. The Wanderers had become decidedly murky and Procter decided, quite rightly, to bowl Neilson a yorker.

Unfortunately for him — and Natal — he pitched fractionally short and Neilson managed to heave the ball through mid-wicket where Kenny Cooper, picking up the flight late in the gloom, never had any hope of stopping it.

Later Procter was to be told repeatedly that he should have bowled a bouncer, and when we arrived at the Jan Smuts Airport to catch our flight home the next day, a fuming Natal supporter walked up to him and said, 'Why didn't you just give the game to Transvaal on a plate!'

However, there was praise, too, from several Transvaal critics who admired his sporting attitude in pitching the ball up to the bat instead of bowling short. But they had all misread the situation. Procter is one of the fairest cricketers I have met, but there is no doubt he would have bowled a bouncer had he thought it would have secured the match for Natal. We agreed that in the poor light neither third man nor fine leg would be able to follow the flight of the ball had Neilson edged it.

Transvaal had won a memorable match in tantalising fashion and, as we picked our way through the buoyant crowd on the way to the change-room, Daniels patted me on the back and, with a broad smile, said, 'Good judge, aren't I?'

There was an extraordinary atmosphere in the Natal dressing-room immediately after the game, and I have never seen a team take defeat better. There were no recriminations — possibly because Procter was captain! — but rather an air of excitement at having taken part in a remarkable contest.

Early the next day Procter's 11-year-old son, Greg, telephoned him from Durban and berated him for bowling a yorker. 'Dad, I've looked in the book of rules and you should have bowled underarm. They could never have hit you for four.' It was an alternative Procter would not even have contemplated, and yet he was to remember his son's advice three weeks later when, in similar circumstances, Australian captain Greg Chappell instructed his brother Trevor to bowl underarm to prevent New Zealand from winning the final one-day international.

If we thought we had been generous in defeat, our reaction pales when compared to a similar incident in my father's day. He was captaining Western Province in the match against Eastern Province in 1932 and his side had been set to score 120 to win in 43 minutes, or about 13 (eight ball) overs. Batting at number four, my father came to the wicket with the score on 51. He, and an opening bat by name of H. P. Jordaan, hurried the score along but 27 runs were still required off the last over. An off-spinner, J. Buchanan, bowled, Jordaan took a single off the first ball and then my father hit 28 runs off the next six (4, 4, 6, 6, 4, 4) to win the match.

To quote the respected Cape Town cricket writer A. C. Parker's report: 'The small number of spectators, who were privileged to witness this extraordinary feat, will never forget that final over at the end of which the Eastern Province team, surely the most sporting side of cricketers ever to visit Newlands, made a rush for the Province captain, hoisted him high on their shoulders and carried him off to the pavilion.'

The report went on: 'The crowd gave Van der Bijl and Jordaan a great reception and the Eastern Province players seemed just as pleased as everyone else. They lost the match, but in doing so they showed that it is still possible to put the game before the result. It is to their credit that they wasted not a minute in the field and they made no attempt at negative tactics.'

A few years ago I bumped into Mr Buchanan in Welkom and asked him what was going through his mind in that last over. He said that after the second six was hit off him — and seven runs were needed off the remaining three deliveries — his captain asked him to bowl a little 'flatter' and to pitch the ball on the leg-stump to make run-scoring more difficult.

'I couldn't do that,' Mr Buchanan told me. 'It seemed unsporting

THE CHANGING TIMES:
1970: Departure for Rhodesia. Short-back-and-sides, and in their team colours, the Natal line-up is Dereck Dowling (manager), Barry Richards, Norman Crookes, Dave Dyer, Pat Trimborn, Berry Versfeld, Dave Orchard, Gerald Katz, Arthur Short, Dennis Gamsy, Trevor Goddard and Vince van der Bijl.

1977: Returning after beating Rhodesia to win the Currie Cup — and complete the first-ever 'double'. Casually dressed and less than sober Alan Barrow, Bruce Groves, Tich Smith, Pelham Henwood, Jimmy Russell (12th man), Mike Procter, Vince van der Bijl, Aubrey Lilley, manager Julian Thornton (obscured) and Darryl Bestall.

and wrong, so I decided to keep trying to tantalise your father into hitting a catch into the outfield.'

We took our defeat at the Wanderers well, yet no one in the Natal side would have thought of hoisting Dougie Neilson on his shoulder and carrying him off.

Times, of course, have changed, and winning has become of paramount importance in an age when chivalry on the sportsfield is often seen as a sign of weakness. Nevertheless, there is a tendency to highlight the negative side of modern players and play down acts of sportsmanship.

Springbok spinner Jackie du Preez was one of the most sporting characters I have encountered. It must be a trait common to leg-spinners as Western Province's Denys Hobson is another with an admirable approach to the game.

Du Preez's scrupulously fair approach almost certainly cost Rhodesia victory in an excellent Gillette Cup semi-final contest in Salisbury in 1975. Rhodesia, batting first, had compiled a seemingly unassailable 275 as Stew Robertson hit a splendid century with strong support from Brian Davison (65) and Duncan Fletcher (35 not out).

We lost three quick wickets, including that of Barry Richards, and the Rhodesian spectators — not renowned for their impartiality — thinking their place in the final was assured, chanted, 'We're all going to Joburg'.

But Darryl Bestall and Henry Fotheringham began fashioning a splendid partnership which eventually turned the match. The decisive moment came when Bestall was on 25 and he lofted his drive off Fletcher to Du Preez at deep mid-on. Du Preez dived forward and appeared to bring off an excellent catch. The umpire immediately gave Bestall out and he was starting back to the pavilion when Du Preez, clambering to his feet, shouted 'no catch'. Bestall went on to make 60 and Fotheringham 90 and a solid contribution from Gerald Katz helped us to a narrow two-wicket win with five deliveries remaining.

At the presentations that evening, sponsors Gillette made a special award to Du Preez, perhaps their most important ever. They rewarded his honesty with a cheque. A further sign of the changing times — money being presented to players for sportsmanship.

In the same season we played Rhodesia in the Currie Cup on the pleasant Oval in Pietermaritzburg. Natal won comfortably enough, but the most memorable incident in the match was the dismissal of Du Preez. He had 18 in the second innings when he shuffled in front and was beaten by a delivery from English professional Bob Woolmer. The appeal had only just started when Du Preez turned towards the pavilion and, by the time the umpire's finger went up, he had already started to leave the wicket.

It was the only time I have seen a batsman walking for a leg-before decision, not that Du Preez found it surprising. 'I was so plumb, I couldn't just stand there, could I?' was his reply when I asked him about it.

Such displays of honesty are, however, regrettably rare. Sportsmanship, once synonymous with cricket, is rapidly disappearing from the game world-wide. In this new age of sponsorship and professionalism, cricket is being exploited, and has picked up a variety of nasty habits with umpires being intimidated, rules bent and decisions questioned.

As top-level cricket has changed, so new supports have been introduced. Today there are four, like legs of a table, and the removal of any one will leave the game tottering.

The first two legs are as old as the game — the players and the administrators. But, in this professional age, their motives and ideals have altered. The player, once a pure amateur, is paid today and he has his own union. The administrator has changed from the unpaid, part-time worker into a businessman who, apart from having to keep the game healthy, must ensure that the grounds are full and the bank manager is happy.

The two relatively new legs are the sponsor, who pours vast sums of money into the modern game, and the media, the promoters of the game.

These four elements are closely linked and, particularly in isolated South Africa, have played decisive roles in keeping the game in good health. But, while serving the game, they have also taken what they want from it and often their interests are in conflict.

Money, of course, is shaping cricket's future and there is a genuine concern among the purists that it will ultimately ruin the game as we know it.

At the start of my career, cricket matters — decisions regarding the introduction of new competitions, the modification of existing formats, or the changes to playing conditions—were handled by administrators intent only in serving the game. As South Africa still had regular international tours, and there were no professionals to be paid, provincial unions were financially viable and did not have to consider sponsors when making decisions.

By the time I left, sponsors were playing an increasing role in forcing changes on the game and, on occasions, dictating to the administrators and players. The result is that decisions are now being made which are not always in the best interests of cricket.

One obviously cannot blame the sponsor who has entered into a business transaction and wants a return on the money he is spending. Exposure is what he demands, even if it takes coloured gear, live commentaries and advertising jingles to get his message across.

Cricket is now being described as a medium of mass entertainment. The implications of this view are far reaching. The game itself is overshadowed by the need to generate excitement and interest which will attract the public and, in turn, television and newspaper coverage.

Television, of course, has become the crucial factor in the modern game. The sponsors naturally want coverage, but administrators often do not as their gate suffers. Yet the administrators need sponsorship if the game, now an expensive business, is to survive.

This clash of interests has taken place in Natal. The Jan Smuts Stadium in Pietermaritzburg, once the headquarters of a professional football club, pioneered night cricket in Natal and, to a degree, in South Africa. All Natal's home matches in the Benson and Hedges Night Series over the last two seasons have been played at this excellent venue where crowds have been good. The floodlighting, however, is no more than adequate, and the local City Council will not spend money improving the lights unless it has some guarantee that provincial night cricket will continue to be played there.

While the Natal Cricket Association wants night cricket to stay at the Stadium, the sponsors are insisting that it be moved to Durban—they are helping to pay for the installation of floodlights at Kingsmead—where bigger crowds are anticipated and matches will be televised.

The impact of limited-over, knock-out cricket, and particularly the very popular Night Series, has left South African Breweries, the sponsors of the three-day Currie Cup, more than a little peeved. For years SAB has poured vast sums into the country's premier competition, but it has not been able to match the exposure given the two limited-over competitions, backed by Datsun and Benson and Hedges, which climax with a final at the Wanderers.

The South African Cricket Union, concerned at losing a major sponsor, agreed to alter the time-honoured format of the Currie Cup in an effort to give SAB more mileage. The Currie Cup, played on a league system all season, now ends with a sudden-death final between the two top sides. Quite clearly, this is unsatisfactory as a team can outplay all opposition for the entire season, head the log by 30 points, and then have the worst of the conditions, or suffer a brief loss of form, and so lose the final.

The concern among the country's cricketers and administrators is that the popularity of one-day cricket will lead to the demise of the traditional three-day competition. Both in England and here, the County Championship and the Currie Cup have always been regarded as the premier competitions. The one-day trophies are sought after, but the team winning the three-day competition is recognised as the best in the country.

There are murmurings that the Currie Cup format is to be changed again with two one-innings matches played over two days. But, if this is the case, cricket will be the loser as many of the old skills, attacking spin bowling and classic batsmanship, will be lost.

Television has played a vital role in promoting cricket, and the widespread coverage given the recent West Indian tours raised interest in the game to a level last reached when the Australians made their tour here in 1969–70. But umpires will be less enthusiastic about its presence as controversial decisions are highlighted and replayed. The players, too, have to be aware of the cameras and need to be far more disciplined.

At the time of the Information Scandal, a picture of Eschel Rhoodie, waving two fingers rudely at the photographer while playing tennis, was published in a Sunday newspaper. An aide explained that Mr Rhoodie was simply telling his opponent that there were two serves to come. A few days later I was involved in a game against Western Province at Newlands and a section of the crowd was jeering me and hurling some very personal abuse at me. As I neared the end of my run, I quickly gave a two-fingered sign but just as the television cameras panned in on me. Pat Tebbutt, who was commentating, quickly said, 'That's not a rude sign, he's just telling the batsman there are two more balls to come in the over.'

Television has personalised players, bringing them closer to the public, but it has also shattered many preconceived ideas which cricketers have about themselves. I always thought I floated up to the wicket with a certain amount of agility and athletic prowess, but I now know that my trundling approach resembles a chicken trying to run with its wings strapped to its side.

Sportsmen have had to learn how to deal with television interviews and Martin Locke, for one, has earned a certain amount of notoriety among cricketers for his controversial, unexpected questions. Professional cricketer Clive Rice was one to be caught on the hop. Returning to South Africa from a stint with Kerry Packer's World Series, Rice had demanded that he should be paid to play for Transvaal in the closing matches of the season.

Locke asked for an interview with Rice to review the Packer Series, and told him he would steer clear of any tricky questions. But, in the middle of the interview, he suddenly pounced on the unprepared Rice and made him look somewhat foolish with several pointed questions on his financial demands.

There was an interesting sequel to this television programme. South African-born all-rounder Tony Greig, who had captained England before becoming Packer's agent, arrived in South Africa weeks later and was annoyed to hear of the treatment handed out to his protégé, Rice. An interview was set up between the eloquent Greig and the unsuspecting Locke. On this occasion, it was Locke who had not done his homework and he was uncharacteristically hesitant as Greig took over the role of interviewer, questioning him on his attitude to the right of the professional to be paid for his services. To his credit, and although it must have been embarrassing for him, Locke still screened the interview in its entirety.

After my run out of Allan Lamb in the 1982 Datsun Shield final at the Wanderers — an action I thought was acceptable at the time but later regretted terribly — I came off the field and was met outside the dressing-room by Locke who wanted a snap interview. Aware of his reputation, I turned to the camera-man and asked him what he was going to take. When he replied that he would just be filming the two of us from the waist up, I agreed to the interview, but added, 'If you ask any trick questions, Martin, I'll kick you as hard as I can on the shins.'

While the face of cricket has changed at higher levels, the game has been left untended at grass roots. The heavy emphasis on provincial and national success has resulted in club cricket suffering and the standard dropping. When Mike Procter took over the captaincy of Natal, he set high standards of physical fitness. We practised and trained at least three times a week, and Natal developed an exceptionally strong side. But the result was that we never attended club practices and played in very few league games that season.

I found a similar situation in the Transvaal. In my only year with Wanderers before retiring, I played in only two league and three one-day games for the club. At the annual dinner at the end of the season, I turned to the fellow next to me and asked him which team he had represented. 'I've been playing for your side for the past two months,' was his startling reply. And we had never met!

Transvaal administrators, aware of the dangers, have now taken the wise step of insisting that provincial players must attend at least two club practices every week. The influence of the province's leading cricketers at club level, their ability to attract new players and help them develop, is vital to the game. A couple of top names might bring short-lived Currie Cup success, but a strong club set-up will ensure that the province's cricket remains healthy.

During the last decade we have seen a sharp rise in the number of professionals playing at club and provincial level. These overseas players have helped enormously in coaching at schools and clubs while their presence has also raised the standard of league cricket at weekends. There has also been an increase in the number of young South Africans who are now earning a living from the game, coaching and playing in South Africa in the summer, and then joining English counties and clubs in the off-season. Their influence on the game is certain to grow.

Radical changes to the game over the past 14 years have brought a deep concern about the future of cricket in this country. Helped by sponsorship and the media, cricket has become a very popular sport, but important decisions now have to be taken to foster it and protect its traditions against too many alien influences.

CHAPTER FOUR

Procter and Richards in the Seventies

If Jackie McGlew, who led Natal to seven successive Currie Cup titles, was the dominant figure of the 1960s, then the next decade belonged to Barry Richards and Mike Procter.

Richards and Procter, schoolboy contemporaries in Natal, toured England with the South African Nuffield side in 1963, and their parallel careers continued until they both retired within a season of each other twenty years later.

They started their first-class careers with Natal in the mid-sixties, and both had a county trial with Gloucester in 1965, adding 115 for the fifth wicket in the match against the touring Springboks. They continued to parade their talents on the county stage during the South African winters, soon becoming world-class players, but were to enjoy only fleeting moments of international success, first against the touring Australians, and then when they joined Kerry Packer's troupe. Richards had one record-breaking season in Australia — scoring 1 538 runs at an average of 103,85 in 1970–71 — and was later to spend two more years there in semi-retirement. Procter spent the 1969–70 summer with Western Province and the following six with Rhodesia. But, finally, both returned to Natal where they ended their playing days.

My arrival in Natal coincided with McGlew's departure and for the next five years the province's fortunes waned. Eventually the captaincy of first Richards and then Procter, took Natal back to the top.

They were contrasting characters and leaders. Procter, energetic and enthusiastic, was a team man deeply revered in Gloucestershire and throughout South Africa. Richards, a master tactician and technician, was more of a loner, much misunderstood in the pioneering days of the professional.

The technical master at work. Barry Richards playing for Hampshire against the 1975 Australians. Richards made 96 and 69 retired hurt in the match.

Barry, uncertain of the feelings and opinions of the press, administrators and public, was wary of any intrusion into the players' domain. People outside his immediate circle were treated with suspicion. He was seen by many as being moody and withdrawn, but beneath the veneer was a warm, friendly man.

In the mid-seventies Barry began to feel that he was being badly treated, particularly by the media. Later he cited a lack of interest for his eventual disillusionment with the game, but I am sure that it was this mistrust which was a major factor in his disenchantment.

He could be abrupt, and his petulance occasionally took his team-mates by surprise. Not that he always got his own way. In a Currie Cup game against Rhodesia in Bulawayo, Barry was determined to build a long innings. It was a sweltering day and he came in at lunch on the first day, hot, tired and undefeated on 70. Leg-spinner Peter Albers was the Natal 12th man. He was to have played, but had stood on a sharp spike on the eve of the game and ended up having to carry the drinks. His mood was not improved by Barry's lunch-time demands. First Peter had to flap a towel in front of Barry to cool him down and then, as was part of his 12th man duties, he had to fetch lunch for Natal's two batsmen. Barry asked for a ham roll and fruit salad without juice. Albers forgot the latter instruction and arrived with the fruit swimming in liquid. There was an angry reaction from the tense Richards, 'I said no juice.' Albers grabbed the salad in his hand and squeezed every drop from it. 'There you are,' Peter said as he slammed the mashed fruit down in front of Richards. Barry thought it was as funny as the other players in the Natal change-room.

Had Richards allowed the sunny, smiling side of his personality to emerge more often, I believe he would have played far longer and with more enjoyment, and it is unfortunate that he did himself less than justice as far as the public was concerned.

Procter, on the other hand, was a more relaxed and tactful character, a popular figure wherever he played. He was a cricketer of great integrity and the only time I have seen him genuinely angry was following an unethical or dishonest act out in the middle.

During my last few years with Natal, Procter and I were heavily criticised for not fielding more young cricketers in the Currie Cup side and relying too heavily on 'the old guard'. The attacks on Procter increased after I had left the province and much of it was personal. At

Mike Procter, all-rounder supreme.

the end of my only season with Transvaal I was down in Natal and attended a farewell party for John Lever. During the evening a deeply disturbed Procter drew me aside. 'Do you think we were right in keeping with the older players?' he asked. 'I'm starting to believe our critics were right.' It was a typical reaction from Procter. He had served Natal, South Africa and Gloucestershire loyally and well, and had established a string of records, yet in the last days of his career he was still sensitive to criticism and honest enough to admit he might have erred. It was this humility which made him such a respected figure.

Richards and Procter, in their individual ways, made an enormous impact on cricket in South Africa. When they started making their living from the game, the public and business world did not fully accept or understand professionalism in sport. Richards, through outspoken comment and action, was considered the real mercenary and he caused resentment among many who followed the game. He often felt he was being singled out for criticism as a mercenary and his instinctive, stinging reaction did not endear him to many in the cricket fraternity.

Procter sought the same rewards, but he had a much better press and public image. Mike was never labelled a mercenary, yet he picked up the same financial benefits as Richards

Such was the esteem in which Procter was held that the Natal players initiated a testimonial month for him near the end of his career. He had spent six Currie Cup summers with Rhodesia and one with Western Province, and it was clear that he would not play in the 80 Currie Cup matches for Natal which were necessary if he was to qualify for a full benefit.

Richards, on the other hand, caused some problems when he returned to Natal from Australia in 1982–83 and was immediately granted his benefit by the Natal Cricket Association. Tich Smith had been due for a benefit in the same season and he had to wait another year.

But, in spite of their contrasting public image, both Richards and Procter succeeded in drawing the province out of the quagmire, transforming Natal into a positive and forceful cricketing unit.

An important factor in Natal's success in this period was the solid and loyal support of the administrators. There are two minor incidents involving Richards and Procter which highlighted the trust and respect that existed between them and the administrators. On one occasion, during Richards' three-year tenure of captaincy, Transvaal set Natal a winning target of 217 in 160 minutes. Richards scored a century in even time to take Natal to victory and, at the cocktail party that evening, I asked a beaming Dereck Dowling, president of the Natal Cricket Association, why he was so happy. 'When my captain is happy, I'm happy,' he replied. Years later, when Procter was in charge, he and I went to see Dereck about arranging bonuses for the players in the Datsun Shield final. He told us there would definitely be some financial incentive, but could not give any firm commitment. 'That's fine,' said

Procter. 'You've never let us down in the past and we'll be happy with anything you decide.'

The summer of 1972–73—the season prior to Richards' appointment—was a harsh, unhappy one for Natal with the A and B sides finishing last in their respective sections. At that stage there was a certain amount of player unhappiness with the administration. Inconsistent selection (19 players turned out for the A side in 1971–72 and 17 in 1972–73) was one of the causes of widespread discontent.

I had a chance meeting with Dave Dyer and Dougie Morgan at this time, and we decided to call the Natal players and the captains of the various league teams together to discuss the problems. A memorandum, listing our complaints and making a number of constructive suggestions, was drawn up and submitted to Dennis Dyer, who was NCA president at the time. The administrators could easily have ignored the criticism, but instead they reacted positively, negotiating with the players on a number of issues. And so started an open, healthy and happy player/administrator relationship in Natal which, I believe, later bore fruit out in the middle.

The period was not one of gloom for me. In January, 1973, I married the girl I had met during the Western Province game at the Oval in Pietermaritzburg a year previously. It was a match of incident and high drama. Natal had been bundled out for 76 on an Oval greentop as Robin Jackman picked up a hat-trick, but we fought back, dismissing Province for 121. Richards' second innings of 73 enabled us to reach 263, and Western Province then collapsed, making only 60 and leaving us victors by 158 runs. I took eight for 35 in the first innings and five for 18 in the second, a match analysis of 13 for 53.

Shortly after the Western Province first innings ended on the Saturday afternoon, I was parading the crowded perimeter, thinly disguised in my white shorts and size 15 tackies, and pleased with my eight wickets. I was trying to round up friends, and a bevy of beauties, for an impromptu party we had organised for the Province players at my nearby digs, the Establishment.

I thought I would be easily recognisable as the bowler who had performed such Herculean feats on the cricket field just minutes before. Not for the first time, I was mistaken. Walking towards me was a young, pretty blonde, Beverley Marshall. She turned to her sister, Shirley, who was with her, and said, 'What an enormous tennis player!'

Fortunately, Bev, a student at the local teachers' training college, had attended a number of parties at the Establishment and knew a couple of my house-mates. When the invitation came, she decided to accept. Arriving at the house, she asked for 'Vintcent van Wyk, the tennis player.'

During the party, puffed up by my own success and a couple of celebratory drinks, I asked her to dance. Bev had no idea why I was behaving in such an outlandish way. 'My, but you're conceited about your good looks,' she said. 'You're the first woman who has called me good-looking, and I'm going to marry you,' I replied.

It was only on the Monday, when my photograph appeared in the afternoon newspaper, that she realised I played cricket, and that my name was not Van Wyk but Van der Bijl. We went out dancing on the Friday evening, and her first words to me were, 'I thought your name

The highlight of the 1972–73 season.

was Van der Bijl, but now I believe it is Van Wyk and you play cricket.' Even I was getting confused at this stage!

Bev played a crucial role in my development as a cricketer. Her ability to keep my feet firmly on the ground whenever some heady success threatened to sweep me away — a trait which she showed on the first evening we met — has been particularly important.

So has her sense of humour. In 1976 I travelled up to the Wanderers with the Natal side. The previous weekend's pair in a club game against Tech was still fresh in my mind and my discomfort became even more acute when Transvaal opening bowler Clive Rice bowled me before I had scored. The next morning I telephoned Bev from the hotel, expecting some gentle words of sympathy, but she greeted me with, 'Good morning, Bradman, how are you feeling today?'

Like my mother, she has not learnt the intricacies of the game, but has always been perceptive about attitudes. When I was captaining Natal, I left my declaration too late, and Rhodesia, struggling with eight wickets down, played to a draw. I came off the field and Bev's first words to me were, 'Why did you declare so late?' Frustrated and angry, I snapped back, 'Mind your own business.' However, she took great delight in the newspaper headline the next day, 'Van der Boob,' and after that, whenever I hadn't played too well, she would introduce me as 'Vince van der Boob.'

She has also provided constant support when I needed it. When we moved up to Johannesburg, and I had my only season with Transvaal, I started slowly and was criticised for not being committed to my new province. Bev, as she had done in Middlesex in 1980 when I struggled initially with my form, was a source of endless encouragement and sound advice.

The lot of a cricketer's wife is not an easy one. To the outsider, it might appear glamorous and exciting, but it is not. Occasionally, of course, there are perks — our trip to Middlesex was one — but these are few and far between. During the season, the wife of a Currie Cup cricketer plays the role of a single parent. For the player in a successful team it is easy to forget the responsibilities at home and at work. This was brought home forcibly in 1981 when Bev and I were invited back to London as guests for Middlesex's opening match against the MCC at Lord's. As I was saying goodbye to our children, the eldest, Sarah, who was seven at the time, held on to me desperately, sobbing, 'Oh Dad, I wish you weren't a cricketer.'

When at times the kids misbehaved in company or in the crowd at cricket, Bev would remark loudly, 'What can you expect from a kid who has only one parent!'

Bev provided the right balance in my cricketing life, loyal support when I needed it and criticism, tempered with humour, when it was justified. And, as a single parent, she has done an excellent job with the children!

At the start of the 1973–74 season, Richards emerged from the shadows to take over the captaincy, immediately regaining the Currie Cup.

A toothy smile from skipper Barry Richards as we move to our Currie Cup win over Transvaal at the end of the 1973–74 season.

Success in Natal has long been attributed to outstanding captains. McGlew not only turned Natal into the dominant power of the sixties, but his tutelage profoundly influenced young players like Trimborn, Procter, Richards and Henwood. Richards always needed a challenge to bring out the best in him. His mother's birthday, the presence of the television cameras at a one-day game in England, or annoyance at ultra-defensive field-placing to him from the first ball of a club game, could provide an inspired display. At 28, he was at the peak of his career. In the two previous summers, he had scored 1 089 and 1 064 Currie Cup runs — no other South African has ever scored over 1 000 — but he constantly needed to set himself fresh goals. The captaincy of Natal came at the right moment and provided him with a new lease of life.

His determination and discipline on the field gave Natal a new confidence and, in his three years as captain, the Currie Cup was won twice and the Gillette Cup once. I have never seen him more motivated and he scored 898 in only 12 innings to average 82 in that 1973–74 season.

In the Currie Cup game in Cape Town, he and Dave Dyer had an opening partnership of 120 in 70 minutes. Morne du Plessis, later to become the Springbok rugby captain, was making his debut as an opening bowler for Province, and he came in for particularly heavy punishment. After stumps that evening, Morne told me that, given the choice, he would rather play rugby against Moaner van Heerden than bowl to Richards. At the height of the onslaught, Dyer and Richards were engaged in a mid-wicket conference when André Bruyns, the Province opening bat, interrupted. 'Barry, bite me on the neck,' he said. 'What are you talking about?' asked Richards. 'Just bite me on the neck.' Utterly bemused, Richards asked him why. 'I like a bit of passion when I'm getting stuffed,' Bruyns replied. Later, with Richards picking the gaps with monotonous ease, a frustrated Bruyns called out to his skipper, Eddie Barlow, 'Come on, Bunter, put the fielders in the gaps.'

Richards' attacking approach transformed his side. His simple philosophy was that a half-volley should be hit for four whether it was the first ball of the match or the last.

His knowledge and tactical understanding were remarkable. He developed a special field-placing for Pelham Henwood which turned the left-arm spinner into a major attacking weapon. Placing five men to the on-side and four to the off, Richards instructed Henwood to bowl at, or just outside, the leg-stump. This meant that a right-handed batsman, wishing to attack him consistently, had to hit across the line and against the spin. I used to field at deep square-leg to him and I caught numerous batsmen trying to sweep. In our match against Rhodesia in Bulawayo, three batsmen were dismissed in that fashion. 'I see I've just won the Rhodesian Sweep,' remarked Henwood.

Sections of the media, and several opposing captains, criticised Henwood and Richards for being negative, yet the Natal spinner had his best season ever, taking 32 wickets at 17,4 apiece, following it with 42 wickets in the next season.

Celebrations after our Currie Cup win over Transvaal at Kingsmead. Barry Richards and I douse Pelham Henwood with champagne after he had spun us to victory over Transvaal with his best-ever figures of seven for 34 in their second innings.

Richards was, in fact, a most attacking captain. In the first game of the season, against Western Province at the Oval in Pietermaritzburg, he declared Natal's first innings closed on 278 for four — he had 186 not out — in an effort to force a decision. It backfired, and we lost, but Richards had shown the flexibility and positive spirit which would ultimately bring success. We wrapped up the Currie Cup competition in the final game at Kingsmead, beating Transvaal by an innings and 48 runs. After the game, Ali Bacher, the Transvaal and Springbok captain who had just announced his retirement from first-class cricket, congratulated Natal and added, 'We have no excuses, we were outplayed in every department,' and then, almost as an after-thought, 'even in the captaincy.'

Because he set such high standards for himself, Richards was a demanding leader. I had my most successful season to date in that summer of 1973–74, taking 64 first-class wickets and equalling Joe Partridge's South African record, but Richards simply would not allow me to slacken. During the final game against Transvaal, I bowled Lee Irvine and Robbie Muzzell in rapid succession, beat new batsman Kevin McKenzie a couple of times outside the off-stump, but then bowled two half-volleys which he hit through the covers to the boundary to finish the over. As I was collecting my cap from the umpire, Richards came puffing up. Twice he had run the 70 metres to the fence to fetch the ball. 'You shouldn't even call yourself a bloody league bowler,' he shouted at me. 'Just jack yourself up!'

But, for most of that very happy season, his humour was never far from the surface. On the slow Newlands wicket, rarely a happy hunting ground for me, I had a particularly happy match that season, taking five for 40 and seven for 47 as we won by 221 runs. At one point, however, the umpire accused me of illegally using Brylcreem to keep the shine on the ball. It was a fairly tense moment and I called Richards up from first slip. 'What's up?' he asked as he joined us. 'He says I'm using Brylcreem,' I replied. 'What!' exclaimed Richards, turning to the umpire. 'Don't be silly, why would Vince use Brylcreem, he's almost bald.' The umpire found the comment as amusing as I did and dropped all charges.

Richards helped in my development by emphasising the importance of bowling to a field and of trying to out think the batsman rather than just concentrating on line and length.

Towards the end of his third year as captain—the 1975–76 season when we again won the Currie Cup—there were clear signs of wear and tear. Again the fact that there were no new horizons contributed to his decline in interest and enthusiasm, and it came as no surprise when he resigned to take up a coaching post in Western Australia. Later he had two series with Packer's World Series Cricket and played no more first-class cricket in South Africa until returning for the 1981–82 season.

As Natalians bade farewell to one of their most famous cricketing exports, they welcomed home another—Mike Procter. Mike could not have shown better timing in his return to Natal and his recovery from injury. Pat Trimborn had announced his retirement and Procter took over as my new-ball partner. The world's greatest batsman, technically anyway, had been replaced by the world's finest all-rounder.

With Richards' departure, the captaincy passed to me and I could not have had a better vice-captain than Procter. His experience, youthful zest for the game and fiercely competitive approach rubbed off on me. He was the perfect team member, a fast bowler with a remarkable strike rate, a more than adequate spin bowler, a safe catcher in the slips and an aggressive batsman capable of turning a match within an hour. He set a Currie Cup record that season, taking 59 wickets, and that was obviously a vital factor in our success. Natal won both the Currie Cup and the Gillette Cup that year to record the first-ever double.

We beat Eastern Province by seven wickets in the Gillette Cup, but were almost denied our Currie Cup triumph by the weather. We had to beat Rhodesia outright to take the championship and, by mid-morning on the final day, needed two more wickets for an innings win. Heavy rain started to fall, holding up play for five hours, and it seemed certain to prevent us winning the Currie Cup. When the rain did stop all the Natal players rushed out to help the groundstaff mop up and play resumed at 4.15 p.m. With rain again threatening, the ninth wicket fell and, in drizzle and poor light, I bowled Jackie du Preez to wrap up the double. Moments after we left the field heavy rain again drenched the ground.

Throughout that season, Procter's advice and the example he set were invaluable. In our first-round encounter against Rhodesia at Kingsmead, we desperately needed to win to stay in contention as we

The Rhodesian sweep? Heavy rain threatened to end our Currie Cup challenge on the last day of our game against Rhodesia at the Queen's Ground in Bulawayo in March 1977. Natal needed two wickets for outright victory but rain held us up for five hours. Finally, it stopped and the Natal players worked with the groundstaff to mop up the water. It took 27 minutes to take the two wickets and as we left the ground heavy rain again fell.

had suffered our perennial loss to Transvaal at the Wanderers in the opening match of the season. Duncan Fletcher was holding us up on the final afternoon and Procter was bowling his off-spinners to him. I decided to replace him with Henwood, though Procter argued that he should continue as he was turning the ball away from the left-hand Fletcher. With his second delivery, Henwood enticed Fletcher into sweeping a catch straight to Henry Fotheringham at deep square-leg. Procter ran up from slip and showered me with praise for my shrewd bowling change. He and I both knew there had been a huge slice of luck involved, but he wanted to show me, an inexperienced captain, and the rest of the team, that I had his wholehearted support.

Inspecting the Pietermaritzburg Oval wicket with Sarah before the Currie Cup game against Transvaal in the summer of 1976–77. We both look concerned but Natal went on to win by seven wickets.

The following two seasons were little short of disastrous. I retained the captaincy but we went through one stage in this period when in 13 successive outings we did not win a game. The reasons were not difficult to find. Pat Trimborn, Bob Woolmar and Gerald Katz had departed the scene with Richards and, after our double in 1976–77, Pelham Henwood, dogged by his leg injury, and Aubrey Lilley, due to business commitments, also stood down. I was the only member of the attack remaining from the previous summer and we ended last on the log. We might still have managed had Procter stayed, but Kerry Packer had launched his World Series Cricket in Australia and the Natal all-rounder was one of his first major signings.

My hat-trick against Eastern Province at Kingsmead on the last day of 1978. Geoff Cook is caught at slip by Chris Wilkins, Bob Whyte falls leg-before and Dave Brickett is bowled. Mike Madsen is amazed and Bruce Groves and Dave Pearse share my jubiliation.

South Africans seem not only to have given good accounts of themselves during the two years of World Series Cricket, but had good relationships with Packer himself. Tony Greig had been one of the instigators of the venture and Procter became a key figure, and was later part of the Packer team which defended their actions in the High Court in London. He also introduced the South African concept of having four players in the 30-metre inner ring throughout a one-day match.

I remember Procter recounting his first meeting with Packer in England. He was introduced to the Australian magnate, who examined Procter as if he was a thoroughbred he had just bought. 'You're going to have to lose at least 10 pounds,' Packer said. 'Why don't you strap them on and get into the nets,' Procter retorted. Packer laughed and they developed a close friendship from that moment.

At one stage word came back that Packer was trying to put together a Springbok side, and Procter mentioned to Tich Smith and me that, if this was the case, we would be going over. When Graeme Pollock and Denys Hobson were flown to Australia, but could not play a match — because, as non-county players, they were not regarded as professional — the plan fell through. I was obviously destined never to play cricket in Australia.

The season which followed (1978–79) brought me only slightly more cheer as we improved to finish third, but we did reach the final of the Datsun Shield before losing to Transvaal — and a Graeme Pollock century. The last day of 1978 saw my first Currie Cup hat-trick which I hoped would herald a change of fortunes for Natal the following year. Bowling against Eastern Province, I took the wickets of Geoff Cook, Bob Whyte and Dave Brickett, but this proved to be a false omen and Natal had to wait a further two seasons before the Currie Cup returned to Kingsmead.

The war between the cricket establishment and Packer over, Procter, Barlow, Le Roux and Rice returned to add some much needed sparkle to the end of the domestic season.

Procter made his presence felt in the match against Western Province just two days after flying home. We had batted first on a typically flat Newlands wicket, making a paltry 186. Garth le Roux, named Packer's Man of the Series — a remarkable achievement when one considers that such fast bowlers as Lillee, Holding, Daniel and Roberts were involved — took four for 65, but he was to be overshadowed by Procter. By 4.00 on the afternoon of the first day, the flag next to the Newlands scoreboard was flying at half-mast and Western Province were 48 for nine. Embarrassed by my meagre contribution of one wicket, I asked Procter what was happening. 'I don't know,' he replied with typical bluntness, 'they just seem to be missing them.' Western Province recovered slightly to finally reach 77 and Procter finished with six for 25.

We made 245 in our second innings, and I enjoyed my innings of 61. Ken Cooper and I, neither of us renowned for our courage against pace, added 62 for the ninth wicket in spite of the wrath of Garth. Procter, in devastating mood, then continued the carnage, taking five for 65 as Province were dismissed for 227 to give us a 127-run victory.

On that final afternoon, one wicket, in particular, underlined the Procter genius. When Adrian Kuiper, then only a tender 19, came to the wicket, Procter bowled him the inevitable bouncer which the young Province batsman bravely hooked in front of square for four. Procter stood in the middle of the wicket, hands on hips, scowling 'So, here we have one of those young hookers,' he called out. Procter swung round and, without consulting me at mid-off, started rearranging the field-placings. He positioned two men on the long-leg fence, another at deep square-leg, one at short-leg and moved mid-on wider. He strode back to his mark near the sightscreen, pointedly adding another five paces to it. He stood there for a moment, staring at Kuiper in the distance and then came charging in, hair flowing, a magnificent sight to all but the unfortunate batsman. Everyone in the Natal side expected another bouncer but, showing superb control, he produced a slow, swinging yorker. Kuiper, taken in by the Procter menace, was already ducking as the ball was delivered. Too late, he realised his error and was bowled.

Tich Smith, on his debut for Natal in the 1972–73 season, had a similar confrontation with Procter, playing for Rhodesia at the time. I was Smith's captain at university and, knowing he enjoyed hooking, I thought that some advice would not be out of place. I told him Procter would bounce him as soon as he went in, and added that it would be wise if he just ducked and refrained from hooking. He nodded in agreement, but the first ball he received was a Procter bouncer and he promptly hooked him to the boundary. Walking down the wicket, Procter snarled, 'Listen, son, there's a hospital down the road full of young hookers like you.' Smith went on to make 38, and he and Procter are now the firmest of friends.

The Natal Cricket Association's decision to award me a benefit in the 1979–80 season came as a complete surprise. The concept of the benefit was still fresh in South Africa — only Graeme Pollock, in the Eastern Province, had previously been honoured in this way — and we were all treading new ground. The result was a benefit of spontaneity and enthusiasm, a season which proved highly enjoyable, yet humbling as firms, businesses and individuals responded in most generous fashion. My conscientious committee, chaired by Julian Thornton, ensured that my benefit was financially rewarding while Peter Pollock, one time opponent and mentor, but now a close friend, organised the highlight of my year, a banquet at the Durban City Hall. Pollock and SATV caught me totally unawares with a 'This is Your Life' programme — bringing on to the stage close relatives and old friends from throughout South Africa — and it proved a wonderfully moving evening. Tony Greig, Charles Fortune and Chris Barnard were the

Dr Chris Barnard, one of the guest speakers at my benefit banquet in the Durban City Hall, telling me about fast bowling.

guest speakers. Dr Barnard, in his guttural accent, spoke of his youth in Beaufort West where 'we were taught three things — rugby, braaivleis and the Nationalist Party' and there was little time for cricket. But, he added, they had once played a match against my old school, Bishops. The locals were barefoot and clad in khaki while Bishops arrived at the ground in whites and tackies. 'I turned to one of my team-mates and asked him who the bunch of moffies (queers) were.'

Early in the season I telephoned Gary Player to ask if he would write an article for my benefit brochure. I had been introduced to him just briefly, and when he came to the phone he asked if we had met. I told him of our fleeting meeting. 'I remember,' he said, 'it will be a pleasure.' Four days later his article was on my desk. It was the willingness of people, some virtual strangers, to give of their time and money, which proved the making of a special year.

But on the field it was less satisfying. We again finished third in the Currie Cup and I was more than happy to hand over the captaincy to Procter at the end of the season. I would have done so two seasons earlier, but Procter, involved with Packer, was not a permanent fixture in Natal. I never really regarded myself as a good leader, being better suited, I thought, to the role of supporting vice-captain. I found towards the end of my tenure as captain that I reacted badly to criticism and was not bold enough, too often sheltering my decisions under accepted practices, and taking the easy options rather than exhibiting an enterprising and individual approach.

My batting, however, blossomed under this increased responsibility and, in one season, I scored four Currie Cup half-centuries, highlighted by my highest first-class score of 87 against Rhodesia.

Throughout these three disappointing seasons for Natal, the continued support of Tich Smith proved invaluable. The true test of a team-man comes in adversity, not when the side is riding a run of victories. Smith gave me outstanding support during these unproductive years, and his positive approach made the disappointments easier to bear.

Natal had been slipping back into a phase reminiscent of those lean years at the start of the seventies. We had not won anything under my captaincy since the double, four seasons previously, and the lack of emerging young talent was disturbing. But, just as Richards had done

Mike Procter leads his happy side off the field at Kingsmead after the 1980–81 win over Western Province which assured Natal of the Currie Cup. Tich Smith, Ken Cooper, Paul Parker and Chris Wilkins are the other players.

so effectively, Procter gave us new direction in that 1980–81 season.

A pre-season training programme, ruthlessly conducted by former Zimbabwean Martin Benkinstein — Hitler to us — lifted the Natal squad to new levels of fitness. And Procter, striving for perfection, helped give us fresh goals, both individually and collectively. His simple dictum was that we should go out to the middle and enjoy ourselves. Of course, there was an important rider — the only way we could do that was if we produced positive, winning cricket.

Procter was never a dictatorial leader. He was essentially a players' captain, a leader who encouraged his men to contribute and participate, a policy which built up the spirit in the side. Each player did not rely solely on the captain for direction. He knew where we were going and how we were going to get there. In this way, Mike was very like Brearley and I can pay him no higher compliment than that.

He seldom became flustered on the field, and his calm approach helped settle the inexperienced players in the side. And while he always demanded your best, he never attempted to mould or change your natural game. It is an approach which the West Indians use in both coaching and playing the game. Natural ability is encouraged, not curbed, strengths are developed and weaknesses are minimised.

Procter's handling of Brian Whitfield, a studious opening bat, and Neville Daniels, a relaxed, free-scoring batsman, underlined his approach. Whitfield was encouraged to play the role which came easiest to him and Procter never attempted to turn him into a more flamboyant

The Currie Cup winning team of 1980–81 celebrating in style.

batsman. Daniels was encouraged to play his shots and he grew in confidence as a result.

Fresh from my stint with Middlesex, I probably bowled better in that season than ever before, taking 54 wickets at less than 10 apiece, but Procter, a perfectionist, was never totally satisfied. One morning Bev, who was reading the newspaper, turned to me and said, 'What was Proccie going on about last night? He said you were not bowling well and yet here it says you're top of the averages.'

But the Natal player of the year was unquestionably Chris Wilkins, who had to play half his Currie Cup innings on a hard but green Kingsmead wicket prepared to accommodate our all-seam attack. Wilkins was the highest run-maker in the Currie Cup season scoring 585 at an average of 54,09. He had represented both Border (1962–66) and Eastern Province before moving to Natal in 1978, and this was the first time he had played in a winning Currie Cup team. 'I've waited 18 years to win the Cup,' he said in a moment of elation. 'I thought it was easy,' retorted his opening partner, Brian Whitfield, who was playing in his first season.

This was the happiest season I ever had for Natal, and the principal reason was Procter's captaincy. In spite of a long and hard career as a professional cricketer, he had the ability to make every game feel like the first of the season. Cricket was a job to him, but such was his enthusiasm that he always looked as if he was playing only for the sheer fun of it. He had the right balance between playing the game for its enjoyment, and tapping it for the financial rewards.

CHAPTER FIVE

The early tours:
An international flavour

While the cancellation of the Australian tour of 1971 finally slammed the door on international cricket in South African, it did herald a period of far reaching change. Insignificant though these changes might seem today, they were big steps forward at the time, and ones which had seemed impossible a few years earlier.

The principal motivation for change was a desire to regain South Africa's test status. The aim, therefore, was to appease the International Cricket Council and, window dressing or not, important advances were made.

The administrators were sure that by meeting the conditions laid down by the ICC — creating a single body representing South African cricket — the door would be re-opened. The players, however, were less optimistic, believing that South African cricketers would remain out in the cold unless the demands made by Hassan Howa, president of SACBOC, that cricketers must have equal opportunity from junior school level, were met. The players' assessment proved to be correct.

Later, when the door to test cricket remained firmly closed in spite of the ICC's conditions being met, changes continued to be made for moral and ethical reasons rather than merely to impress outside opinion.

September 28, 1973, saw the first major visible change. The 17-year-old Edward Habane and Edmund Ntikinca represented the South

Edward Habane with George Langa, one of the pioneers of Black cricket in South Africa.

African African team in the Datsun Double Wicket International at the Wanderers. The venture was planned by Springbok Lee Irvine and public relations man Robin Binckes, with two objectives in mind — to bring international cricketers to South Africa and to stage a multi-national event. Basil D'Oliveira, under a coaching contract with SACBOC, was due to partner Tony Greig in the England team, but was refused permission to play by his employers.

Habane and Ntikinca met with some success, beating New Zealanders Bev Congdon and Bruce Taylor, and going down narrowly to the Australians, Ian and Greg Chappell. But, more significantly, this competition heralded the first major meeting between White and Black players. It was only a small step but there was widespread reaction. The left saw it only as window-dressing, the right were aghast at this new liberal tendency while the centre, resignedly, accepted that the first move forward had been taken.

Australians Ian and Greg Chappell, the winners of the Datsun International Double Wicket competition at the Wanderes in September 1975.

Of course, there were different motives involved. Administrators and cricketers, grabbing at any crumb of change, hoped that the tournament would help us along the road back to test cricket. Politicians used it to shape their ambitions. Dr Piet Koornhof, the new Minister of Sport, said at the tournament, 'I am confident that we will get back into international cricket before long. I will do everything in my power to get you back, but I would ask for your co-operation and collaboration in this task.' Meanwhile, the Government was conducting a running battle with Pietermaritzburg's Aurora Club, later to become the first non-racial club to play under the auspices of the SACA. Dr Koornhof said that the Government would not allow 'its policies to be flouted through the establishment of multi-racial cricket' and said that Aurora were 'busy using cricket for political purposes and their concern is not for the game as such.'

The Nationalist Government's policy on sport was confused and confusing. Dr Koornhof was aware of this, and even joked about it. He told the story about a cabinet minister who was asked one afternoon what the South African sports policy was. 'I don't know,' replied the cabinet minister, 'I haven't spoken to Piet Koornhof today!'

In the same year that the Goverment allowed multi-national cricket for the first time, it also withdrew Mr Hassan Howa's passport, preventing the president of SACBOC making representations to the ICC in London. One step forward, two back, was the story of the seventies, a period in sport dominated by political considerations.

The advance of multi-racial cricket was given an important boost by Derrick Robins, an English cricket benefactor, who arranged a series of tours to South Africa. While providing international competition for local cricketers in the early years of isolation, his tours also proved a significant vehicle for political change.

He brought teams to South Africa for four consecutive summers from 1972–73, and his tours helped break down racial barriers. Early in 1973, he brought an all-White side, but eight months later, just three weeks after the multi-national double wicket tournament in Johannesburg, he arrived with a party which included John Shepherd and Younis Ahmed, the first Black cricketers to tour South Africa. By the time his third tour was over, South African teams had included Black players for the first time.

Every year the touring teams grew in strength and they played vital roles in this transitional period, advancing the cause of cricket while also adding spice to the domestic season. The Derrick Robins teams comprised mainly county cricketers with a liberal sprinkling of international players. The matches played against the pick of South Africa's cricketers on each tour were never billed as test matches, but they did provide local players with a goal.

The first touring team (in January–February 1973) was led by David Brown with J. T. Murray his vice-captain. Rupert Hanley, playing for Eastern Province, bowled magnificently against the tourists, taking six for 34, and, in the match against the South African XI at the Wanderers,

England test batsman John Edrich is caught behind by Tich Smith. A relieved Eddie Barlow joins in the appeal. Edrich, playing for the Derrick Robins' XI, had scored 180.

I found myself carrying the drinks for the only time in my first-class career. To rub it in, Hanley pulled a hamstring after six overs and I spent the next two days in the field, never my forte. The South African side, with a century from Barry Richards and an innings of 97 by André Bruyns, buried the tourists by an innings and 117 runs.

The two sides met in a 60-over game to wrap up the tour and, indicative of the attitude to one-day cricket at the time, the match was afforded only two terse lines in the South African Cricket Annual. We bowled the Robins team out for 146, but we then collapsed and, when I went to the wicket, the score was 117 for nine. In one of the most enjoyable partnerships of my career, Jackie du Preez, sprightly and enthusiastic, and I scrambled a one-wicket victory.

The next Derrick Robins tour, which started in October 1973, was to have a far greater impact on South Africa. Apart from Shepherd and Ahmed, the side, led by Brian Close, contained such players as John Edrich, Bob Woolmer, Roger Tolchard, John Snow, John Lever, and Australians John Gleeson and Bruce Francis.

Shepherd, the Kent all-rounder, was the first West Indian to play first-class cricket in South Africa and his was an inspired selection. Typically West Indian in his approach, he was a whole-hearted, amusing cricketer who played the game for the sheer enjoyment of it.

Almost instinctively, he understood the tenor of South African politics, and revelled in the role he was playing. Before the third and final 'mini-test' against South Africa, Shepherd and I walked out to have a look at the Wanderers wicket. A youngster ran up to Shepherd and asked for his autograph. Winking at me, Shepherd said, 'Sorry, son, I can't write.' The boy looked at me knowingly and then replied, 'Don't worry, Mr Shepherd,' and ran off, leaving a highly amused West Indian behind.

A true calypso cricketer, he opened many spectators' eyes with his whirlwind batting, exuberant fielding and lively bowling. We did feel he was susceptible to the bouncer early in his innings and decided at the pre-match team talk before the Wanderers encounter that we would test him. He had become a good friend on tour, but I happened to be bowling when he came in and my instructions were clear. He ducked under my bouncer and looked up the wicket with a pained expression on his face. After the second bouncer, he was clearly annoyed but wicket-keeper Lee Irvine's remark, 'Why the black look, Shep?'

John Shepherd, a key member of the Derrick Robins and International Wanderers touring sides of the mid-seventies, playing one of his favourite strokes.

brought roars of laughter from him and he proceeded to club 53 of the 60 runs scored while he was at the wicket. He hit one of my attempted bouncers cross-bat for six over extra cover and the ball never rose more than three metres above the ground. As happened so often on this tour, he had the last laugh.

In the three SA Invitation XI matches against the tourists, the national selectors picked their strongest team, and I was given a taste of what we were missing by being out of test cricket. The bubbling confidence of skipper Eddie Barlow, and the support of experienced Springboks, Barry Richards, Mike Procter, Lee Irvine and Graeme

Pollock, made a deep impression on me. In the first of the games, down at Newlands, I was nervous and unsure for my first couple of overs. Both Pollock and Procter came across and spoke to me before my fourth over, and that helped settle and relax me.

In a small way, my state of mind showed the influence isolation was already having, and even in those far-off days it was obvious that the departure of the core of Springboks would leave a void which would be almost impossible to fill. And so it proved with the second West Indian tour in 1983–84 when the Springboks, without Barlow, Richards and Procter, battled hard but lost.

The 1974–75 tour saw another important step towards 'normal' cricket. The Derrick Robins XI, again captained by Close, was further strengthened by the inclusion of Tony Greig (England), and Australians Terry Jenner and Max Walker.

One of the highlights of the tour was a remarkable match-winning innings played by Graeme Pollock for Eastern Province. Close had declared the Robins second innings closed at 288 for seven, leaving EP a formidable winning target of 259 in 197 minutes. Pollock, in majestic mood, dominated the innings, scoring 167 in 160 minutes. He scored all but 82 of the required runs and, when the defeated and disconsolate Robins team reached the dressing-room, captain Close asked them if they had learned anything from Pollock's brilliant innings. There was no response so he repeated the question. Finally, John Hampshire replied, 'Yes, you mustn't declare too early.'

The one mini-test was played at Newlands on 27 March 1975, and two players — Dickie Conrad and Edward Habane — became the first Blacks to play in a mixed South African first-class side. The tourists were eclipsed by the South African President's XI who won by 260 runs. Habane ended the game by bowling Terry Jenner, and was carried off shoulder-high by the elated crowd.

Looking back, many will say, with some justification, that the selection of Habane and Conrad was window-dressing. But it must be remembered that this Newlands clash was not a test match and the two were not representing a Springbok side. It should also be emphasised that to reach the ultimate goal of multi-racial cricket, it was essential that an example be set at first-class level. Their selection was part of the process of change and to see this match as an entity in itself would be taking it out of context. The changes taking place at that time were inconceivable five years previously and, anyway, would not have been allowed by the Government. Window-dressing or not, the inclusion of Blacks for the Newlands match was another advance in this important transitional period. The carrying of Habane from the ground was a symbolic gesture, an act which illustrated that the changes were welcomed by the cricket fraternity — the spectators included.

The Robins XI returned in January 1976 — their fourth and final tour — and played fixtures against the four major cricketing provinces. It was fitting that while they were involved in their opening first-class game — against Natal in Durban — the South African Cricket Association, the South African Cricket Board of Control and South African African Cricket Board met in Johannesburg to form one controlling body. SACBOC president Mr Rashid Varachia headed a nine-man motivating committee which was to steer South Africa through tricky waters to non-racial cricket.

In their desire to encourage mixed cricket, the administrators included an African XI in the Gillette Cup competition. Quite understandably, the newcomers were hopelessly outclassed, dismissed for 78 after Natal had made 361 for two declared (Alan Barrow 202 not out) off 54 overs.

But the highlight of the season came in March when Greg Chappell brought a powerful International Wanderers side to South Africa. Managed by Richie Benaud, the tour party included several world-class players and the bulk of the Australian test side. Only Jeff Thomson was missing from their attack and Alan Hurst, who was soon to play test cricket, was his replacement. Ian Chappell played in only the first game — being replaced by New Zealander Glenn Turner — and the other Australians were Dennis Lillee, Max Walker, Gary Gilmour, Ashley Mallett and Martin Kent while England provided Derek Underwood, Phil Edmonds, Mike Denness and Bob Taylor. John Shepherd was the lone West Indian in the side.

Almost before the tour had started, an ugly controversy had erupted over a subject considered taboo in cricket at the time — money. Barry Richards, Lee Irvine and Graeme Pollock, dissatisfied with the financial terms offered the South African players, refused to play in the first match against the Wanderers.

Richards and Pollock were widely recognised as the two best batsmen in the world at the time and they were unhappy that less

Graeme Pollock, one of the most devastating hitters of the loose delivery in cricket, heaves a short delivery over mid-wicket during the International Wanderers tour. Greg Chappell watches from slip.

talented players in the touring party were receiving far higher payment. This was the first time a clash had taken place over money and the public was outraged. The three were widely criticised in the media, accused of being unpatriotic and greedy. In fact, all they were asking for was a fair financial deal which the administrators at first were not prepared to give them.

They had asked me to join them in their boycott. I declined and, while fully respecting Barry Richards' right to earn a professional wage, I did not want to miss the opportunity (perhaps my last, I thought) of playing against the world's leading players. I also felt that as I was not in the class of Richards and Pollock, it would be presumptuous of me to join in their protest.

It was this type of adverse publicity which gave Richards a bad name. He was labelled as a mercenary who cared little for the game itself but was interested only in lining his own pockets. This was grossly unfair. Playing cricket was Richards' livelihood. He had played professionally since leaving school, and had a limited working life with no other trade to fall back on once his playing career ended. He believed — and it is an opinion which is universally accepted today — that he should be paid for his ability and performance, just as a business or professional man is remunerated. Professional cricket was still in its embryonic stage in South Africa in 1976 and, because Richards led the way, many of his actions were dismissed as being selfish money-grabbing.

The South African XI, without these three key players, went down by 185 runs in an extraordinary game at Newlands. We seemed to be coasting to victory when the Wanderers led by only 126 with two second innings wickets in hand. Gilmour, nursing an injured shoulder, was not going to bat, but told skipper Greg Chappell that, if the ninth wicket stand was at all successful, he would go in and swing the willow. Underwood (29) and Hurst (21) added 32 valuable runs before Gilmour, batting virtually with one hand, hit three sixes and 11 fours in making an undefeated 80 in a 10th wicket partnership of 96 in 64 minutes with Underwood. We had a disastrous second innings of 69 as Mallett took four for 24.

With fear an important motivating factor, Denys Hobson and I had a rollicking partnership of 54 for the eighth wicket in the South African XI's first innings of 290.

I have often been asked what a tail-ender feels about facing genuinely fast bowling. The answer is, very simply, petrified. I had joined Hobson, an old friend from university days, just before tea when the score was 234 for eight, and our lead on the first innings was 14. As we came out to bat after tea, I noticed that the number of overs bowled read 82. I pointed out to Hobson that, after a further three overs, the second new ball was due and Hurst would no doubt pulverise us. Fortunately, Lillee was only to join the tour in time for the second 'mini-test' and, with Gilmour injured, John Shepherd, a medium pacer, was sharing the new ball with Hurst, certainly the quickest bowler South Africa had seen since the days of the youthful Procter. 'What are we going to do now?' I asked Hobson. 'I don't know about

The early tours: An international flavour 85

you,' he immediately replied, 'but I'm not waiting around for that new ball. Let's have a slog.'

I wholeheartedly agreed, and we put on 36 frantic runs in the next three overs with Hobson, who finished with 49, hitting spinner Underwood for four sixes. When Hurst, scowling and menacing, took the new ball I had the misfortune to be facing. It was before the time of helmets and I was in fear of my life. I played and missed at his first, second, third and fourth deliveries, coped rather well, I thought, with the fifth, edging it over the slips for four, and then comprehensively missed the sixth ball. Shaken but alive and looking for some support, I walked down the wicket to meet the grinning Hobson. 'Well done, Vince, you're handling Hurst well. You stay down there and I'll look after Shepherd this end.' He saw out an over from Shepherd, but I was out to Hurst in the next, caught behind by Taylor for 14.

A light-hearted encounter with my old friend Denys Hobson during a Natal–Western Province Currie Cup match at Kingsmead.

86   Cricket in the Shadows

Three Black cricketers, Tiffy Barnes, Howie Bergins and Pinkie Carelse, played in the first match and were retained for the Johannesburg outing when Richards, Pollock and Irvine returned.

The second encounter at the Wanderers produced a classic confrontation between two cricketing greats, Australian fast bowler Dennis Lillee and Springbok batsman Graeme Pollock. The Australian lost the first round but won the second.

We dismissed the tourists for 134 and then the masterly Pollock, who fashioned a superb 124, and Richards (52) laid the foundation for our reply of 324. Lillee did not pick up a wicket in conceding 64 runs and some gloaters in the media foolishly dismissed him as an overrated bowler.

A rare meeting between two cricketing greats. Graeme Pollock ducks under a Dennis Lillee bouncer during the South African-International Wanderers XI encounter at the Wanderers in 1976.

Martin Kent's excellent contribution of 155 inspired a Wanderers second innings recovery of 466, and the match looked certain to end in a tame draw with just over two hours remaining and the South Africans needing 277 to win. But with the criticism no doubt rankling, Lillee ripped through our second innings, taking seven for 27.

When I went out to join Tich Smith, at 76 for eight, there were still 13 overs to be bowled. My friendship with Tich was immediately tried when I met him in the middle of the wicket. 'The only way we are going to save this game,' I said, 'is if you take Lillee and I try and keep the other bowlers out.' He gave me a wry smile but agreed, and then produced a gutsy, match-saving innings, facing Lillee's last seven overs, taking blows all over the body and only adding to his score when two runs were assured. We saw out play, Smith ending on 12 while I was on 5.

In the final game, which started in Durban the next day, Smith produced innings of 52 and 45, and Lillee later told me that of all the batsmen he had bowled to in South Africa, only Richards played fast bowling better than the Natal wicketkeeper/batsman.

Smith has always had immense sporting talent, playing flyhalf in the Natal rugby side in 1972, reaching the last 16 in the Natal amateur golf championships and playing provincial cricket for 12 years before being unceremoniously dropped just a couple of one-day games away from retirement in 1984. At the time of the Wanderers tour, he was one of the most attractive South African batsmen to watch, equally fluent playing back or forward.

In retrospect, it is depressing to think of other cricketers who did not get their just rewards, players who peaked during these early years of isolation when Springbok caps were no longer awarded. I was fortunate that my trip to Middlesex, and the rebel tours of the eighties, did bring some form of recognition. But players such as Chris Wilkins, Pelham Henwood, André Bruyns, Dave Dyer, Peter Swart, Lorrie Wilmot and Tich Smith will never be remembered as Springboks of the seventies.

So we went down to Kingsmead, one down with one to play. Of the SACBOC players, Tiffy Barnes had scored a brave 30 against Lillee and company at the Wanderers and Howie Bergins had taken four wickets at Newlands, and dismissed Bob Taylor twice at the Wanderers, to reveal some of their talent. But their performances were

One of the highlights of the International Wanderers tour was the contest between Dennis Lillee and Tich Smith. Here they are pictured together during the Durban game.

to be overshadowed by a 30-year-old left-arm spinner, Baboo Ebrahim, brought into the South African side for the Durban game.

We had batted first and collapsed to 99 for seven when I again went out to join the in-form Smith with Lillee in rampant mood.

During the second innings in Johannesburg, when Lillee was ripping through our batting, Hobson and I, both padded up, were waiting our turn at the crease. Hobson, was paging through the Wits University Rag Magazine when he suddenly burst out laughing. He had found a tale which related to our present predicament. Lord

Nelson, or so the story went, was sailing the high seas when the young boy in the crow's nest sighted four French frigates off the port bow. He scuttled down to Nelson and told him the news. 'Very well, my boy,' said Nelson, 'I want you to go down to my cabin and fetch my telescope and my red shirt.' The boy did as he was told. Lord Nelson turned the Victory round, and blew the four frigates out of the water. The boy was impressed, but puzzled. 'Lord Nelson, sir, I can understand why you wanted your telescope, but why did you call for your red shirt?' he asked. 'You see, my boy,' explained Nelson, 'if I'm wounded during battle, the colour of the blood won't show on the shirt and the crew won't be alarmed.' The boy was even more impressed. For day after day the boy continued his dawn to dusk watch, scouring the seas until suddenly, looming over the horizon, he sighted 150 French frigates. Down to the deck he slithered, 'Lord Nelson, Lord Nelson, 150 French frigates off the starboard bow, sir!' he panted. 'Fine, my boy,' said Nelson, 'just go down to my cabin and fetch me my telescope, my red shirt . . . and my brown corduroy pants.'

It became the team joke and whenever a batsman showed any signs of hesitancy against the Australian pacemen, the cry would go up from the change-room, 'send out his brown corduroys!'

Hobson and I discussed methods of avoiding opposition fast bowlers' bouncers. The first, obviously, was to make sure that you never face them, the second was to make friends with the fast bowlers. With some relief, therefore, I managed to have a couple of drinks with Lillee at the Wanderers, and felt that I had developed a fairly promising relationship with him. Of course, in those pre-helmet days you did go out to bat with the realisation that if Lillee wanted to take your head off, he could. But as I went to wicket at Kingsmead, I was hoping that Lillee had not forgotten our friendly chat a couple of days earlier.

As I reached the wicket, I was happy to hear Lillee call out, 'Give you one off the mark, mate.' But then, as I took guard, I suddenly started thinking. What does he mean? Will he give me a slow, comfortable delivery which I can hit to get me off the mark, or is he going to give me a bouncer off the mark? Being a natural pessimist in that type of situation, I prepared for the worst, and as Lillee reached his delivery stride, I started to duck. Which is as well because he bowled me one of the fastest bouncers I have ever faced and I saw only a blur as it went over my head. I looked up and there was Lillee, his follow-through completed, standing just a metre away from me. He fixed me with a steely stare and I tried to remain unmoved, certain that it would not be wise to jest with him at that moment. The tension out in the middle was finally broken when fellow-batsman Smith came down the wicket chuckling, 'Luckily, that was his slower one, watch out for his really quick one!' and then burst out laughing.

Tony Greig told me how, in a similar incident in Australia, Lillee had bounced him first ball, a delivery which cleared wicketkeeper Rod Marsh and went for four byes. His effort and momentum had taken Lillee up to the England batsman and he then dipped his finger in his mouth and marked the sign of the cross on Greig's forehead. Had Lillee done that in Durban, I might have retired hurt!

One of the lesser known players in the International Wanderers side was Alan Hurst. With a vigorous, rhythmical action, he was almost as fast as Lillee and he went on to make an impact at test level when he established himself in the Australian side in 1978–79.

Smith and I added 75 for the eighth wicket, a particularly satisfying partnership. The one emotion you cannot show in the middle is fear as it gives the opposition the upper hand. As Barry Richards said once, 'No one enjoys facing really fast bowling, but some batsmen hide their trepidation better than others.' Nothing is more rewarding for a lower-order batsman than to take on the quick bowlers successfully.

The South African XI scored a moderate 178, Lillee taking four for 42. We then proceeded to dismiss the tourists for 99 and, though I did not bowl particularly well, I picked up four for 20.

The drama in this match was still to come. Richards, in sparkling form, and Barlow had given us a start of 114 when the former, failing to pick up a Hurst bouncer, was struck a vicious blow behind the ear. He was taken to hospital for treatment and X-rays and, though there was no serious damage, he returned pale and still a little dizzy. Such was skipper Barlow's determination to beat the tourists, and level the series, that he insisted the shaken Richards return late in the innings. He added a further 10 runs before being out for 80 and, with Graeme Pollock hitting 63 and Smith 45, we set the Wanderers 349 to win.

The afternoon of the third day and the morning of the fourth belonged to Ebrahim. The small Indian spinner bowled with control and intelligent variation to take six for 66 in 29,1 overs and the tourists were dismissed for 226.

Surprise packet of the International Wanderers tour was little known Indian spinner Baboo Ebrahim who picked up six wickets for 66 in the tourists' second innings at Kingsmead. He was already 30 at the time and the nagging question remains: What would he have achieved had doors been opened earlier?

It was a fitting end to a season which had promised and produced an abundance of good cricket while also advancing the cause of multi-racialism.

Moves had been started to introduce one controlling body for cricket, but Government policy was still an obstacle. Finally, after long and tortuous negotiations between the Government and administrators of various race groups, the formation of a single non-racial body to control cricket in South Africa was announced on 18 September 1977. The new body, which did not include the Hassan Howa faction, was to be known as the South African Cricket Union (SACU) and Mr Rashid Varachia was unanimously elected president.

The founding of the SACU was the result of the past six years' activities. The changes which had taken place, the roles played by administrators and cricketers of all races, the support in some Government circles in spite of vehement right-wing opposition, and the influence of the Derrick Robins sides and the International Wanderers had combined to take South African cricket to its goal of one national controlling body. But the ultimate desire of gaining test status remained out of reach.

CHAPTER SIX

The Middlesex Venture

When I started in the first-class game, South Africans were just beginning to play regular county cricket. Tony Greig, Mike Procter, Barry Richards, Lee Irvine, Norman Featherstone and Hylton Ackerman were migrating north every South African winter, even though the venture was initially unprofitable. Featherstone told me at the time that a season's cricket with Middlesex would cost him R1 000.

In the early years of my cricket career, from 1968 to 1972, I was studying for a Bachelor of Arts degree at Natal University in Pietermaritzburg, determined to follow my father into teaching. At the time there was no real incentive to play county cricket. It still seemed likely that South Africa would play international cricket and there was no financial carrot to lure me overseas.

During those years there were occasional vague county offers brought back by Richards and Procter, but I never really gave them much thought. Later, when I was happily involved in teaching at Maritzburg College, I did not want to interrupt my career by playing professional cricket for a season or two.

But in 1979 I began to have grave doubts about continuing in teaching. I was still enjoying my work immensely, but the fact that I would be more secure financially if I turned to business was weighing heavily on my mind. I finally decided to join Wiggins Teape, an international paper company, and agreed to start with them in Durban in January 1980.

It was at this time that I received my first firm offer to play county cricket. Glamorgan contacted me in October 1979 while I was still teaching and for the first time I started entertaining thoughts of having a season in England. So much had changed since I had come into the first-class game and for a number of reasons the idea of playing county cricket was now more attractive. Not only would it be a refreshing change after 12 years of Currie Cup cricket, but I had always wanted to test my ability against the best overseas players. I also knew by then that genuine test cricket for South Africans was no more than a pipe-dream. Financially, too, county cricket had become far more lucrative and that would allow me to take my family across with me. There was also the nagging feeling that I was nearing the end of my career and, if I was to venture overseas, it would have to be soon.

But, of course, there were now other considerations and I was committed to start in business in January.

With more hope than good judgement, I approached Derek Smith, managing director of Wiggins Teape, and told him of the Glamorgan offer. He was sympathetic but, understandably, felt that I could not spend six months away in my first year with the firm, so I was forced to turn down the Glamorgan offer, convinced that I would never get the opportunity to play on the county circuit.

The Middlesex approach came from committee member J. T. Murray and coach Don Bennett at the end of January, 1980. I immediately turned them down, convinced that my firm's attitude would not have changed after I had been with them for just a month.

A couple of days later Mike Procter invited me to a braai at his house in Durban and there I bumped into Murray and Bennett again. We spoke about the Middlesex offer and decided that some behind-the-scene approaches might help my cause. It was Procter's idea that Murray should pay a visit to Derek Smith and try to twist his arm. Murray was to emphasise the fact that I would have 34 free days during the season which I could spend at Wiggins Teape's head office in Basingstoke, Hampshire.

What I did not know at the time was that my managing director, a Londoner, was a Middlesex man through and through, and had watched Denis Compton and Bill Edrich in the Golden Summer of 1947. I think he also realised that, although I had been with them only a couple of weeks, I was committed to the company and wanted to build a business future with them.

Derek also felt that as Middlesex's home ground was Lord's, the headquarters of world cricket, I might be able to assist in South Africa's fight to re-enter the world cricket arena. In this period, just prior to the 'rebel' tours, there was a growing feeling amongst administrators and cricketers that sufficient changes had been made to warrant South Africa's return to the international fold. Derek believed that I could assist Mike Procter and others in keeping the lines of communication open. He agreed to release me for the English county season, and it was only later that I told him that I had been party to Procter's machinations.

My acceptance of the Middlesex offer drew an irate reaction from Glamorgan and a sprinkling of adverse publicity. Glamorgan felt that I had been contracted to them and it took a number of telephone calls to convince them that I had refused their offer and they had no hold on me.

I travelled out with the family; Bev and our two children, Sarah (6) and Chloe (4). During the flight to England I felt very unsure of myself. Here, at the age of 32, and after making my mark in domestic cricket in South Africa, I was trying to establish myself on an international stage and against some of the great players in the world. It really was a question of having to prove myself all over again. The usual worries and concerns that precede a season were now greater. Would I take wickets, would I be able to adapt to the conditions and would I be able to justify other people's faith in my ability?

The Middlesex committee gave us a wonderful welcome. We were taken to a fully furnished flat in the City where we found the pantry stocked and flowers for Bev. The flat had an unusual situation, on the top floor of a block of businesses in the commercial heart of London, and within walking distance of St Paul's.

After-hours the area was like a morgue and on Sundays you had to use the tube to find bread, milk and the newspapers. On weekdays, in contrast, my shorts and size 15 tackies did not blend easily with the bowler and brolly brigade as I walked to the Stock Exchange parking lot to fetch my car.

1980 turned out to be a dream season, not only for me but for Middlesex as well.

I started painfully slowly and my anxiety lasted for a number of weeks as the pressure on me grew. My record in the Currie Cup had been greeted with a fair amount of scepticism at Lord's. Cricket writer John Thicknesse had been given my Natal benefit brochure and, as he mentioned to me soon after my arrival, he found articles comparing me to Joel Garner and Max Walker difficult to believe.

The chilly weather, my general lack of condition and a poor bowling rhythm did little to lift my spirits — or those of the Middlesex members who viewed my early form with growing dismay. In three pre-season friendlies against club sides I took only one wicket.

1980 and the migratory Van der Bijls in transit.

This inability to slip easily and quickly into a groove should not have surprised me. In South Africa I had never been a net bowler, relying rather on early club games, and spells of 20 to 30 overs, to find my form and fitness.

In desperation, I sought a solution in the Lord's nets and a week's prolonged practice helped me find some of my touch. It was the first time in many years that I had gone right back to the basics of bowling in an effort to perfect my action. Down at the nets on the fourth day, I remarked to the coach, Don Bennett, that I had not been able to bowl the away swinger consistently for a number of seasons. He immediately said: 'Your arm is too straight and the ball is being delivered straight over the top. You must bring your arm round a bit and cock the wrist.' I asked him why he hadn't told me on the first or second day of practice. 'You never asked me,' he replied.

It was my first lesson on being a professional cricketer in England. If you wanted advice or help, you had to ask for it. It was not bandied about as was the custom in South Africa.

Even Barry Richards, the classic stylist, appreciated unsolicited advice, even from the uninitiated. In the Natal nets, at the start of every South African summer, we would find Richards, fresh from another county season, batting with a very open stance, an approach he adopted to counter the many leg-side yorkers bowled in one day cricket in England. 'Forget about the French cricket you play overseas,' I would call, 'turn sideways and play properly.' In England you had to time your pearls of wisdom!

The first Middlesex team talk took me by surprise. In South Africa pre-match meetings are part and parcel of team sports and, at Currie Cup level anyway, they are elaborate affairs with field-placings and opposing players' strengths and weaknesses being discussed.

The Middlesex talk started with John Miller, the physiotherapist, who spoke at length on what action to take if a person's heart stopped beating out in the middle. It seemed a macabre way to start the season, but no one could doubt the usefulness or the seriousness of the lecture. During the fifth test at Adelaide in the 1978–79 series, John Emburey had, on the strength of a previous talk by Miller, saved Australian Rick Darling's life when his heart stopped beating. Darling, hit above the heart by Bob Willis, had swallowed his chewing gum which lodged in the back of his throat. He was revived by Emburey, who administered the 'pre-cordial thump' to start his breathing again.

I struck up easy friendship with the players and was lucky to have wicket-keeper Ian Gould, a bouncy and enthusiastic cricketer, as my room-mate. We shared rooms when we travelled away because we were considered untouchables — we both smoked.

A rainy day at Lord's and passing the time with Phil Edmonds on my left and (clockwise) Mike Gatting, John Emburey, Roland Butcher, Clive Radley and Ian Gould.

It was a happy union, too happy, I remember thinking at Hove, where we were forced to share a double bed and I awoke to find his arm and leg wrapped around me. That was taking our friendship too far! Gould's relaxed approach to the game was more South African than English, and he had a delightful sense of humour. In Middlesex's game against the touring West Indians, our tail-ender Wayne Daniel, the Black Diamond, donned my white helmet as he prepared to leave the dressing-room and go out to face his countrymen Holding, Garner, Roberts and Marshall. 'Look,' Gould called out to me, 'the Diamond looks like a pint of Guinness with your helmet on.'

My first county game was against Clive Rice's Nottinghamshire and I settled some of my fears by taking four wickets. At the end of the day's play I grabbed a beer and strolled into the Notts dressing-room. The surprised look on their faces told me that it was not the accepted practice, but I nevertheless sat down and had a couple of drinks with

Bowling at Lord's watched by umpire Dickie Bird.

Rice and a few of his players I had met previously. Of course, it was the custom in South Africa to have a drink together after stumps and it was often the most enjoyable part of the whole day. I think by the time we had finished that evening the Notts players also thought it was worth a trial.

What did surprise me in England was the professional jealousy which existed between the players. Perhaps it was understandable. County players are not playing the game only for enjoyment as most of us do in South Africa. They are employees and have to shoulder their way to the top in their chosen field. The jealousies came across in the form of disparaging remarks which would often be passed about another player's success; they emerged in the attitude of Mike Selvey, the former England pace bowler and my Middlesex team-mate.

Selvey had helped me enormously when I first arrived at Lord's and we had got along well. At the start of the season it appeared that I would open the bowling with Wayne Daniel with Selvey providing the seam support and the spin coming from John Emburey and Phil Edmonds. I went on to have a successful season, but Selvey struggled. He did not bowl with any penetration nor was he filling the role of stock bowler. And, because our roles overlapped, and I was taking wickets and keeping it fairly tight, Middlesex could afford to drop him and bring in the young Simon Hughes as a shock bowler.

So it was due to my presence that Selvey lost his place in the Middlesex side at various times during the season. It must have been difficult for him. He had been a key member of the Middlesex attack for a number of seasons and had helped them win numerous trophies. Now he was being done out of his job by a temporary worker and by the end of the season his animosity towards me was obvious.

Before going to England, I had been constantly told that many county cricketers' approach bordered on selfishness. But, of course, it is important to realise that in any team, or group of people, there are certain individuals who are largely concerned with their own well-being. This is symptomatic of life itself and not just cricket.

In the county game against Nottinghamshire an incident occurred which, at the time, I thought was selfish. In retrospect, though, I was too hasty in my judgement, too ready to jump to conclusions.

I went to the wicket with Middlesex struggling on 86 for six and joined another former England batsman, Graham Barlow. Barlow played a vital role in our successes that summer. His constant encouragement to the bowlers and fielders kept our enthusiasm high.

I was dropped, off Clive Rice, when I had 10, but Barlow and I then took the score along to 288 in a partnership which I thoroughly enjoyed. I actually tossed away a maiden first-class century, falling on 76 as I tried to rush the score along to reach 300 in the allotted 100 overs. Had I stayed, we would have reached that target easily, and I would have had my hundred. In the end, neither objective was attained.

When Barlow was in his nineties, our scoring did slow, and Mike Brearley sent out a message telling us to get on with it. Barlow was out on 97 as he tried to force the pace and returned to the dressing-room, angry at having been given an instruction which prevented him reaching three figures. I was surprised at the time, but I believe I misinterpreted the incident. Barlow's anger was temporary and a natural reaction to the intense disappointment he felt at not reaching his century.

What I did find in England was the widespread feeling that 'the game's the thing,' and there was a genuine desire to play cricket in the right spirit. In the 1982 Benson and Hedges final at Lord's, Essex seemed to be cantering to victory. Then came one of their inexplicable collapses and fast bowlers Norman Cowans and Wayne Daniel turned imminent Middlesex defeat into victory in the gloom of the closing minutes. After the game, television commentator Peter West was interviewing the two captains, Middlesex's Mike Gatting and Keith Fletcher of Essex. West mentioned to Gatting that the umpires would have been justified in bringing the players off early because of the poor light. Fletcher, the defeated captain, immediately interrupted. 'I think that the umpires were absolutely right to continue playing. The crowd had come to see a result and we had to play on.' It was a wonderfully sporting approach from a man who might easily have blamed the conditions for his side's frustrating loss.

The 1980 Middlesex team was beautifully balanced with 10 internationals in the side and no obvious weakness. Almost all the players had successful seasons, and we should have made a clean sweep of the four competitions instead of having to settle for just the county championship and the Gillette Cup.

Our bowling attack was undoubtedly the best I have seen in the first-class game. Emburey is widely regarded as the finest off-spinner in world cricket and Daniel, the West Indian, a potent, consistent strike bowler who could be frighteningly fast when the mood grabbed him

Daniel's presence in the side was, in fact, a bonus for Middlesex. They had signed me on only because they thought Daniel would be in the West Indian team which toured England that year and they wanted an international bowler to bolster their attack. In the end, and because of Daniel's inexplicable omission from the tour party, they had us both. The unexpected return of Daniel was such an important boost to our chances that Phil Edmonds rushed out to Ladbrokes and took a fairly large bet on Middlesex winning all four competitions.

Middlesex had an excellent start to the season and did not lose a game in the first two-and-a-half months. But then we went through a bad patch, losing five successive John Player Sunday League games and having one abandoned. It was a disastrous slump which ultimately cost us the John Player Trophy. We finished third, having won 10 out of 16 matches while Warwickshire ended top with 11 victories.

We lost to Warwickshire as a result of an extraordinary innings by Geoff Humpage, by far the most effective innings played against us all season. He came in when the score was 33 for three after 11 overs, chasing 216 in the 40 overs and they eventually won going away as Humpage made 108 not out. For the first and only time in the season Emburey was taken to pieces, conceding 55 runs in seven overs.

In our very next Sunday outing, against Derbyshire, we batted first and scored 185 off 38 overs. It was clear that the weather was going to interfere, but Brearley, instead of bringing on Daniel, bowled Emburey who was hit for 11 runs in the over. That took Derbyshire ahead of us on run rate as the rain came and, as far as I was concerned, it was the only tactical error made by Brearley all season.

We had no match commitments the next day, but Brearley asked us to come in to Lord's for a practice. While we were there, the players were called one by one to the committee room where Brearley and Mike Stirt, convenor of the selection panel, were waiting. They were concerned that the team's performances were starting to wane and we were all asked what we thought the reason was. It was the first time I had heard of players being counselled individually. We then went up to the dressing-room and Brearley spoke openly about our earlier discussions and gave what he thought were the pertinent reasons for our sudden lapse of form.

He gave credit to Roland Butcher who had said he believed everyone had already built the mantlepiece for all four trophies, that we were looking too far ahead and not playing each session and game as they came.

Brearley said he agreed totally with this view and we decided on a change of strategy. From that moment Brearley introduced team discussions before every session of play so that each player would know what was expected of him, and the team, during the next few hours.

This particular team meeting had an interesting sequel. Brearley released the story of the players' meeting to the Press and singled out

Butcher for the contribution he had made.

I am convinced it was this recognition which transformed Butcher that season. Richly talented but lacking in confidence, he could not command a regular place in the county side and his activities were usually confined to the one-day games. Brought into the side for the very next county game against Hampshire, he responded with a brilliant second innings contribution of 153 not out as we swept to an unexpected victory. The next county outing was against Yorkshire at Scarborough and Butcher produced another dramatic innings, cracking 179 to set up our win. Brearley's praise and inspiration had given Butcher the boost and the confidence he so badly needed, and at the end of the season he became the first West Indian-born player to be chosen for England.

In the fourth competition, the 55-over Benson and Hedges Cup, we were beaten by Northamptonshire in the semi-finals. They made a moderate 206 on a flat Lord's wicket and I, as much as anybody, was to blame for Middlesex not reaching that target. We had started well, and had reached 114 for three when we suddenly lost two quick wickets in the gloom.

I was next in and, though the spinners were operating, it obviously suited us to go off at that stage and resume the chase in the morning.

Arriving in the middle, I took guard and peered down the wicket at the umpire, a delightful fellow by name of Budd.

'What do you want?' he called up the wicket to me. 'I can't see you,' I replied, 'but if you can see my end please give me two-leg.' A ball later the umpires took us off.

The next morning I resumed with Mike Gatting, who made an excellent 91, and together we took the score to 165. We were only 42 runs short with five wickets in hand and really it should have been a doddle. Unfortunately, I was in a six-hitting mood and twice struck Richard Williams into the grandstand. I tried to do the same to a full toss from Peter Willey but was caught on the fence for 18 and, instead of a comfortable win, and a place in the final, we collapsed to lose by 11 runs.

A couple of days later Gatting took me to task for that stroke, blaming me for the defeat. I was angry with him at the time, but he was absolutely right. Had I stayed there we would have won at a canter.

The three-day County Championship is the premier competition and we secured the title in the penultimate match of the season, beating Glamorgan by 72 runs at Cardiff. It was one of our best performances of the summer with Brearley making a significant contribution, both as captain and opening batsman.

Rain had interfered and, with just over six hours' play remaining, we had to set Glamorgan a target and bowl them out. Brearley's brilliant 124 not out enabled Middlesex to declare at lunch, leaving Glamorgan four hours to make 235, and we finally won the match by 72 runs with six overs to spare.

We ended the season only 13 points clear of Surrey on the county table, though two startling performances by South Africans added to our tensions in those closing weeks.

The first came from Mike Procter at the picturesque ground at Cheltenham where he led Gloucestershire against us. In the first innings of the game I produced what I will always regard as my finest spell. We had scored 220, and that evening I picked up four wickets for 6 in five overs, including the wicket of Procter which gave me particular pleasure. In the space of two overs, I sent down six deliveries to my Natal team-mate, which he played at and missed, before finally bowling him through the gate with my seventh.

But it was Procter who finally buried us. We had set Gloucester 270 to get in the last afternoon and, when we broke through to have them 65 for three, it seemed we would have our victory. But Procter produced an extraordinary innings of 134 not out and Gloucester won the game with an hour to spare. His was a most uncharacteristic innings. He lifted only two strokes, both one-bounce fours over cover off the spinners, and he played Daniel particularly well.

The reverence in which Procter is held in Gloucester is quite remarkable. On the Gloucester centenary brochure there are pictures of two players depicting the old and new in the game. Procter was not captaining the county at the time of the celebrations, yet Gloucester used illustrations of him and W. G. Grace on the cover. To have honoured an overseas player, rather than one of the locals, shows the deep respect which Procter commands in that county.

The second South African to hold up our title charge was Kepler Wessels, the Sussex left-hander. At Hove, another Brearley hundred had laid the foundation for our first innings of 360 for four declared. I took six for 47 as we bowled Sussex out for 172 and victory, which would have settled the championship with two matches remaining, seemed a formality. But, with Sussex following on, Wessels produced a marathon innings of 254 — the highest individual score of the season — to prolong our agony until we met Glamorgan a week later.

A fitting climax to a marvellous season came at Lord's when we met Surrey in the final of the Gillette Cup and proved to a capacity Lord's crowd that we were indisputably the team of the season. We bowled tidily — I took one for 32 in 12 overs — to limit Surrey to 201 in their 60 overs and then Brearley, in outstanding late season form with his 96 not out, and Butcher, with a flamboyant and undefeated 50 which earned him a ticket to the West Indies and denied his captain a deserved century, took us home with seven wickets and six overs in hand.

The presentations and celebrations remained, but the adventure was over. It had been an unforgettable summer, liberally sprinkled with wonderful incidents both on and off the field.

Relaxing with Mike Brearley and the Gillette Cup.

While the passage of four years, and the enormous amount of cricket played in that season, have turned many of the matches into a blur, the characters have remained sharply in focus.

Probably the most entertaining character I met in 1980 was Middlesex team-mate Phil Edmonds. Highly intelligent, at times controversial, he has his share of critics, but I found him an engaging, unconventional personality who occasionally went out of his way to shock people merely to see their reaction.

Tradition often became the butt of his humour, and while some of the players found his remarks irritating, his sharp mind kept the dressing-room refreshingly alive. Possibly because he expected everyone else to have the same incisive wit and intelligence, he did not develop friendships easily. But I respected Edmonds enormously and, though I know others might disagree, I found him a valuable, loyal team man and a tremendous trier. He missed much of the 1980 season because of a knee cartilage problem but returned successfully towards the end.

Edmonds underlined his value to Middlesex in the Gillette Cup final at Lord's. He had been included in the squad of 12 but he was eventually left out of the side and carried the drinks. For a man who had played for England it could not have been easy. But, if he was disappointed about the decision, he never showed it during the game. Although he was not playing, his bubbling enthusiasm in the dressing-room helped us through several tight moments and kept our expectations high.

After Mike Brearley relinquished the Middlesex captaincy at the end of the 1982 season, Edmonds wrote a fairly scathing article about his former county and England captain. Brearley, who had led his country to their remarkable 1981 Ashes win over Australia, had received universal acclaim for his outstanding leadership, and Edmonds' criticisms were widely reported. Edmonds wrote that Brearley had not assisted his playing career and the fact that Middlesex now had a new captain in Mike Gatting would result in him playing better cricket. Edmonds' views were not news to me. He had voiced similar objections during the 1980 season, but he was the only cricketer I met who felt that he would not grow and prosper under Brearley's captaincy.

Brearley, too, would not have been surprised. He and Edmonds used to talk long and hard about it. I think basically theirs was a clash of personalities. Both men are very strong, intelligent characters. They enjoyed the challenge of each other's company, but Edmonds was adamant that his talents were not being correctly harnessed. He felt inhibited because he was not granted the field-placings he wanted, but Brearley, who had captained Edmonds for many seasons, was sure about what he required from his left-arm spinner.

Edmonds also felt that he was not being bowled sufficiently or at the right time, and I believe part of the problem lay with John Emburey. Edmonds and Emburey were very close friends. Emburey had always given Edmonds enormous credit for helping him adapt to test cricket and for proving a great source of inspiration. Almost overnight, however, Emburey replaced Edmonds as the number-one spinner, not only for England but for Middlesex as well. So Emburey would now get the turning end; he would have the wind in his favour and would be brought into the attack first. Though left and right handers usually complement each other, the second spinner is not bowled as consistently and he is usually the one to be omitted when an additional seamer is brought into the team.

Edmonds' assessment of Brearley's captaincy was not helped by the fact that, by his own standards, he had had a poor season. At the beginning of the summer there was more luck than design involved in the wickets he took. He went through a very difficult period — as most spinners do at some point in their careers — and was unable to bowl with any consistency. Full tosses and double-bounces entered his repertoire, yet Brearley bowled him regularly in an effort to help him find his form. Just as he was starting to unearth some of his form, he was sidelined by a knee injury which required surgery.

Edmonds probably did not have the accuracy and consistency of a world-class spinner. Not for him the hours of tight control which made Hugh Tayfield and Emburey masters of their trade. For him, bowling was a challenge, an opportunity to produce the perfect delivery, even at the risk of conceding a boundary.

I believe his personality is evident in his bowling which I find creative and lively, never dull and boring. A series of maidens for Edmonds would be meaningless, and the result was that he never developed the control which Brearley wanted as part of his armoury.

A delightful personality in the Middlesex side was former England off-spinner Fred Titmus. He had made his debut back in 1949 and is one of only two players—Wilfred Rhodes is the other—to have played county cricket over five decades.

Titmus had crossed the Thames briefly to play for Surrey but had now rejoined the Middlesex staff and, with John Emburey on duty with England and Phil Edmonds injured, he was recalled to the county side. Enthusiastic and lively, he was like a school kid in his first match.

Titmus was renowned on the county circuit for his dry wit and he used it to good effect on his former Surrey team-mates when we played at the Oval. Titmus was bowling when Pat 'Percy' Pocock, wearing glasses for the first time, came in to bat. 'Why're you wearing glasses?' an intrigued Titmus asked his old friend. 'So I can hear you better,' was Pocock's sarcastic retort. Titmus did not reply, but his very first ball knocked back Pocock's leg stump. As Pocock turned to start his long walk back to the pavilion, Titmus called after him: 'You didn't hear that one too well, did you Percy?'

At Scarborough, in the match against Yorkshire, Titmus was having trouble with Phil Carrick, another spinner, who was treating his bowling with scant respect. The end came, however, when Carrick leapt down the wicket and struck an on-drive with enormous power. It looked like a certain boundary but Roland Butcher, fielding at mid-on, took a couple of paces and then flung himself to his left, clutching the ball in two hands, just centimetres off the turf.

It was undoubtedly the greatest catch I had ever seen and I ran across to Titmus, threw my arm around his shoulders, and said, 'Great wicket, well bowled!' Titmus looked up at me and, with a twinkle in his eye, replied: 'Oh, I just gave that one a bit more air.'

Butcher, a West Indian who had settled in London, is easily the finest all-round fielder I have ever seen. He is a safe and, at times, brilliant catcher close to the wicket and an athletic outfielder with an excellent throw. I have never seen a fielder quite so adept at picking up the ball at speed. He was correctly dubbed 'Hoover' by his Middlesex team-mates.

Shortly before he left on the England tour of the West Indies, Butcher was asked which cricketer he admired most. 'Colin Bland,' he replied immediately. Here we had the first West Indian to play for England, about to leave on a tour of the Caribbean, talking about a White South African as his hero!

The other West Indian in the side was Wayne Daniel—the Black

Diamond as he is universally known. A magnificently built athlete, Daniel has been a consistent, penetrative opening bowler for Middlesex, though the West Indies have never fully recognised or exploited his talents at international level. On the Middlesex staff since 1977, he has done most of his bowling on the slow Lord's wicket, but he has given unstinting service to his county. In fact, of the overseas players involved on the county circuit in 1980 probably only Gloucester's Mike Procter was a more loyal import.

On a quicker wicket, such as at Hove where Sussex play their home games, Daniel is as fast as anyone I have seen. And, possibly because they also had Imran Khan in their line-up, Sussex had to contend with him at his most devastating.

Daniel, in one menacing over at Lord's and watched by Imran at the non-striker's end, bowled a series of bouncers which brought him three wickets and ended Sussex's aspirations in the Benson and Hedges.

But he was to have an even greater impact on the Gillette Cup semi-final at Hove two months later. We had made a modest 179, but Imran made a grave error in the closing stages by bowling several bouncers at Daniel. One delivery nearly took Daniel's head off, and he lost his helmet taking evasive action, but every bouncer was greeted with a roar from the Middlesex dressing-room. We knew what effect this onslaught would have on Daniel. And so it proved. With wicket-keeper Paul Downton standing nearly 25 metres back from the stumps, and taking the ball at shoulder height, a steamed-up Daniel ripped through the Sussex batting. He finished with six for 15, we won by 64 runs and Imran must still be rueing the poor timing of his bumper barrage.

For the most part, however, the good-looking Daniel is a friendly, amusing man. He often eased the tension in the dressing-room with weird and wonderful tales of his social encounters. And, after watching him in pubs throughout England for six months, I have no reason to doubt his sources of reference.

He enjoyed himself at my expense when Middlesex met his countrymen in a 50-over game at Lord's. We played really badly and made only 124. Wayne and I were both understandably nervous about having to face the full West Indian pace attack and when my turn came to bat — the score was 62 for seven and Holding was bowling — I could hardly get to my feet. As I reached the dressing-room door, Daniel called out: 'Vince, watch out for that Holding man. I told him you were the biggest South African racist I ever met.'

I hardly remember the walk to the wicket, but fortunately the West Indians were in genial mood—they could afford to be—kept the ball

1980 Gillette Cup semi-final, Middlesex v Surrey, at Hove. Wayne Daniel loses his helmet as Imran Khan bounces him. Simon Hughes is happy to be at the other end. The Black Diamond retaliates but, in spite of the no-ball, Imran is ready.

Wayne Daniel, who took six wickets for 15, receives the Man of the Match award from the late Ken Barrington after Middlesex's semi-final win.

up, and I made 15. But the total of 124 was no target for them and they won by nine wickets.

At the time Daniel spoke very seriously about coming out to South Africa and playing for Natal. While he would have been a popular and successful figure on the field, I believe he would have struggled to adapt socially in this country. Finally, however, the desire to regain his place in the West Indian test side proved too great and he decided against a summer in Durban.

As a family our summer in London was probably the happiest six months we have had. Obviously we enjoyed the new experiences and, as an ex-history teacher, I was particularly interested in the surroundings. The experience of having no pressures outside cricket was a new and welcome one. In between matches, or when the day's play was over, I could go home and be with the family. In South Africa any spare time during the season would be spent on trying to catch up with my work.

This was an aspect of South African cricket that really worried me and, ultimately, had an important influence on my decision to retire. The majority of Currie Cup cricketers are still amateurs who have to make their living outside a time-consuming sport. In the battle to do both, family life suffers, and I know this has led to the premature retirement of a number of our leading players.

It had been a marvellous six months, liberally laced with good, exciting cricket, and memorable moments on and off the field. The fact that it was also a successful one, and I was able to help in Middlesex's triumphs while also allaying some of the doubts I had about my own bowling ability, made it a very special season.

Bev has obviously heard this one before. At my Middlesex farewell dinner.

CHAPTER SEVEN

Mike Brearley — the pick of captains

My first meeting with Mike Brearley was outside a school in London where Middlesex were doing their pre-season training. Brearley came out to greet me and the early conversation was guarded but cordial. I found him to be strangely reserved and it was only later I discovered that, for a number of reasons, he was unhappy about my signing. The news that I had been contracted by Middlesex was broken to him while he was touring Australia, captaining the England side. John Emburey, who later became a close friend of mine, was with him when news filtered through that I had been signed by Middlesex. 'Who the hell is this Van der Bijl guy?' asked John. Brearley apparently replied that he had no idea but said he was going to put the matter right on his return to London.

There were a number of factors involved. Brearley was — and still is — strongly opposed to the Nationalist Government's racial policy and was understandably reluctant to have a South African in his county side; as part of my contract, I was to be provided with a furnished flat in London and this was the first time an overseas player had been afforded the luxury of free accommodation and finally, he, as Middlesex captain, had not been involved in the county's decision. He must have had reservations, too, about the signing of an unknown 32-year-old South African pace bowler, and the fact that he had not been consulted first must have aggravated the situation.

My first meeting with Mike Brearley — 'the Ayatollah' — in London. The conversation was stilted and formal. Brearley once wrote tongue-in-cheek that he had grown a beard to 'roughen my exterior for contacts with the rebarbative Australians'.

Two weeks before my arrival in London he had voiced these objections to the Middlesex committee but, of course, he had had to accept a *fait accompli*. I sensed his opposition, or at least his lack of enthusiasm at my presence, at this initial meeting. It made the challenge that much more difficult but, in the end, far more rewarding.

Even during this initial period, when Brearley had reservations about me, he still made me feel part of the side and tried to involve me as much as possible. He realised that whether he liked it or not I was part of the team for the season and he brought me constantly into the discussions and team talks during this early but crucial period.

My form in the pre-season friendlies, worrying enough for me, could have done little to set his mind at ease. Brearley must have thought his worst fears were being realised and certainly I did nothing in my first two weeks with Middlesex to make him feel any easier or happier about my ability.

Fortunately, a week of concentrated practice at the Lord's nets helped solve some of the problems before our first county game against Nottinghamshire at Trent Bridge. I was determined to justify the Middlesex committee's faith in me and, even though the weather was dismal and there were frequent breaks for rain, I was able to answer some of the sceptics.

My first ball was bowled to Patsy Harris, an opener who had also played for Eastern Province, and happily it was an almost perfect delivery, which pitched on leg and seamed away, beating the groping batsman outside the off-stump. Brearley's reaction brought me even greater satisfaction. He turned wide-eyed to the wicket-keeper and started chatting excitedly to him, as if realising for the first time that I had some ability.

Later I took my first wicket, bowling Tunnicliffe for 33, and the response of the Middlesex players was a further boost to my morale. West Indian fast bowler Wayne Daniel was fielding at long leg and he came sprinting in to give me a hug and a 'Well played, man'. That one

A cheerful Wayne Daniel and I relax after a day in the field.

single act meant more to me than any other during the season, particularly as Daniel is not given to extravagant actions on the field.

That first county day with Middlesex helped settle me. I had finished with four wickets, but it was the team's acceptance of me as a cricketer, rather than my individual success, which made all the difference.

What also helped break down the barriers between Mike and me was that our attitudes to the game were so similar. Politics and apartheid, inevitably, cropped up in this initial period and here again I think there was so much common ground that this also helped in the change of attitude.

Brearley was undoubtedly the greatest captain I played under. As Rodney Hogg, the Australian fast bowler, said: 'I think he has a degree in people.' Brearley understood people, how to motivate them and how to direct them. He set the players goals and continued to monitor their progress as part of a team effort. He ensured that everybody worked for the same ends and that his players were happy in what they were doing.

When he took over the captaincy of England, he felt that he had to uphold the conservative traditions of the game if he was to do the job properly. Awarded an OBE in 1978, he thought he had to be on his best behaviour. He was seen as totally pro-establishment and anti-Packer. It was a side of him the Australians found irritating and, as he wore a full beard during the tour Down Under, they labelled him 'the Ayatollah'.

As a conformist in these years, Brearley rarely allowed his natural exuberance to bubble over. The change came after the 1979–80 tour to Australia when he relinquished the captaincy of England.

By then he was becoming increasingly involved in psycho-analysis and during sessions was encouraged to be more open with his emotions instead of bottling them up inside. Occasionally he would do the most extraordinary things and then enjoy watching the reactions which followed. In a county game against Surrey he came under fire from the small crowd for his slow batting in an innings of 91. At one stage, after one of the spectators barracked him, he swung round and bellowed: 'If you're so bloody good, why don't you come and bat in my place.'

He also started showing emotion out in the middle. In the Benson and Hedges quarter-final against Sussex he brought me back into the attack with the idea of maintaining the very tight control we had over their batsmen. Gehan Mendis was batting and I decided to bowl a series of yorkers to limit his strokeplay. The first, unfortunately, was overpitched and Mendis hit me through the covers for four.

I turned to apologise to Brearley and then watched in disbelief as he threw his Middlesex hat to the ground and proceeded to kick it in annoyance. 'Mike,' I called to him, 'that was totally unnecessary.'

Typically, he accepted the admonishment and, as he stooped to pick up his hat, said: 'You're absolutely right, a bloody childish thing to do, sorry.'

There was also a much publicised clash with Imran Khan in the same game against Sussex. During the Middlesex innings, Imran had been continuously no-balled for breaking the rules governing one-day cricket by bowling more than one bouncer per over. With Imran batting, but at the non-striker's end, Wayne Daniel proceeded to send down one of the most devastating overs I had ever seen. Charging in off 25 metres, he unleashed a series of frightening bouncers. I counted five in the over and one struck the number nine batsman on the shoulder. The over also saw three Sussex wickets fall and, because the bouncers were producing wickets as the batsmen defended themselves, the umpire did not call them.

Imran, standing next to the umpire, started to criticise him openly for not no-balling Daniel.

Brearley, fielding at mid-off, immediately shouted at Imran: 'You tried to bowl bouncers at us but couldn't get it up. Now just keep quiet and leave it to the umpire.'

Imran made some angry retort and Mike walked up to him. Mike Gatting, fielding on the boundary in front of the members' pavilion, came charging in behind Mike and wrapped his arms around him, clearly giving the impression that he thought his captain was about to involve himself in an unseemly brawl.

Brearley actually ended up more annoyed with Gatting than with Imran when this whole incident received widespread publicity the next day. He was also upset at the sensational nature of some of the newspaper articles, but I nursed a sneaking suspicion that he was just a little pleased that people would now see that he had a spark of outward aggression in him.

In a typical, tongue-in-cheek comment to Fleet Street cricket writer Michael Melford, he described the clash with Imran as 'a friendly exchange of views.'

I admired his captaincy enormously but I can understand that he had his detractors — just as Tony Greig did, though for completely opposite reasons. Greig, the extrovert, annoyed the traditional, conservative cricket supporters. Brearley, in contrast, found critics amongst those who wished to see an outwardly more aggressive approach on the field. Greig had been popular in Australia because he responded to the crowds. When barracked, he would react by clamping his wrists together as if held by handcuffs. Brearley irritated Australians because of his apparent indifference.

In South Africa one could make a similar comparison between Eddie Barlow and Ali Bacher. Barlow's attitudes on the field were transparent to the crowd. One could almost guess what move he was going to make in the next few overs by his actions. But with Bacher you could not. People like watching the Barlow-type captain because their involvement in the game is that much stronger. This is not to say that Brearley and Bacher were any less aggressive. Both were uncompromising, but they were quieter and less demonstrative.

As I wrote in the previous chapter, Phil Edmonds was highly critical of Brearley's captaincy, though I believe that was a clash of personalities rather than an objective assessment of his qualities as a leader.

What I did find curious was that county cricket followers often found fault with Brearley because he epitomised the traditional England captain. Fielding on the boundary at Somerset where they have one of the most aggressive county crowds (the result, perhaps, of not having a leading local football side), I became involved in an argument with a spectator who was constantly hurling abuse at Brearley.

It emerged that this fellow admired Greig, who was largely colonial in his style of leadership, and rejected Brearley, a captain with a brilliant mind, but an introverted nature on the field. It was ironic that the captain with the 'typically English' approach could not find favour with sections of the English crowds.

While the outsider might have viewed Brearley as a tolerant, easy going leader, he in fact demanded an exceptionally high standard.

He always expected the very best from his players and, in this way, was similar to Mike Procter. Both aimed for excellence of performance, arguing that success would naturally follow. An example of this came in our game against Sussex when I was bowling to Imran Khan. I bowled one of my best overs ever, beating the bat with the first four deliveries and then finding the edge with the final two, both of which evaded the slips on the way to the boundary. Mike, excited and beaming, came up to me at the end of the over and almost hugged me. 'What a fantastic over,' he said. In my very next over I sent down an innocuous full toss and Imran was caught at mid-wicket. 'A bit lucky weren't you,' was Mike's reaction as we met in the middle of the wicket.

The over before, even though it had been unproductive, was to him a very special piece of cricket. The fact that I had picked up the wicket we dearly wanted in my next over was almost immaterial. It was this search for excellence, even if it resulted in defeat or failure, that was typical of his approach. The result, of course, was that a pat on the back from Mike was more sought after than praise from one of those gushing captains who heap credit on you, even if your achievement involved luck or bad cricket.

He also had a sense of fun, a fact which the Australians, in particular, might find difficult to believe. I remember having a soda siphon fight with him when we were in Scarborough for the game against Yorkshire. He was at one end of the bar, clutching a siphon, and I was at the other, similarly armed, and there we were rather childishly spraying each other. Watching the recently retired England captain behaving in this outlandish fashion, and receiving a thorough drenching in the process, was a delightful old lady of about 80. She was beautifully attired in a long dress, white gloves and pearls — but dripping soda.

We rushed to her side, profuse in our apologies, but she stopped us with her laughter: 'No, don't worry about me, you just go ahead and enjoy yourselves this evening.'

Brearley also had a touch of humility which I believe is essential in any leader. I remember a tense moment during the county game against Yorkshire. We had been on top for most of the game but David Bairstow was in the process of producing an amazing innings of 145 which seemed likely to save the game for Yorkshire. Mike was trying a variety of ploys in an attempt to dismiss him and at one stage, when I was at the end of my run, I asked him to move the third slip across to leg-gully. He refused and I remember saying to him: 'Mike, the problem with you is that you think all fast bowlers are bloody idiots.'

He thought about it for a moment and replied: 'You're absolutely right,' and with an enthusiastic 'good luck' he moved the slip across. The plan did not work, but it showed a flexibility and willingness to accept ideas which were important attributes in his make-up.

At Uxbridge, in the game against Derbyshire, I had more luck with one of my ploys. Peter Kirsten, who made 82, and David Steele, finally not out with 86, had taken Derbyshire to an imposing 185 for two. In a moment of desperation, I suggested to Brearley that he change his ultra-defensive field-placing to the traditional, attacking one. Brearley was enthusiastic, bringing in two slips and a gully in an effort to pressure the batsmen. I broke through almost immediately, bowling Kirsten, and Derbyshire collapsed to 220 all out. I finished the innings with five for 34 and my match figures (46-21-59-10) were my best of the season.

Clapped off by Mike Brearley, Clive Radley, Graham Barlow and Wayne Daniel at Uxbridge after Middlesex had beaten Derbyshire. I took five for 25 in the second innings and my match figures of 10 for 59 were my best of the season.

Over drinks, after the first day's play, Kirsten paid tribute to Brearley's captaincy. 'I always felt that Mike was one step ahead of me. I never felt comfortable.'

Brearley's innovative spirit was expressed in his own bowling. At Cambridge University — where he gained a first in Classics — he occasionally bowled underarm. And in 1980, faced by a stubborn partnership or the prospect of a grim draw, he would deliver a whole over of slow, dropping full tosses aimed at the top of the stumps. He had very little success, but it gave him great delight.

He welcomed constructive criticism and new ideas, but he thought about the game so deeply and we respected him so much, that when he did something unusual we were more concerned about why he had done what he did rather than the merits of the move.

In the county game against Yorkshire, Bill Athey, who had just made the England side, came in to bat in the second innings. I was bowling and was appalled to see Mike immediately move in a silly point for my first delivery. My reaction was that it was a waste of a fielder but

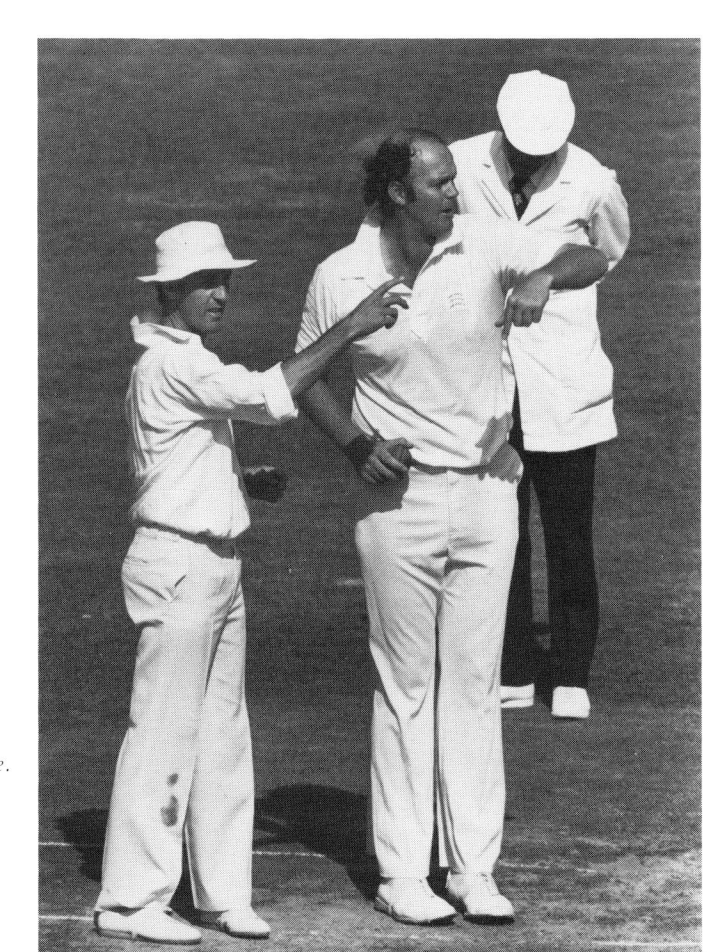

The photograph suggests that Mike Brearley, now clean-shaven, and I are at odds on the field-placing, but that was rarely the case.

I knew that Brearley must have had his reasons for crowding the batsman. I ran up and bowled a wide, swinging half-volley in the hope that Athey, feeling claustrophobic, would attempt to drive too early in his innings. He did just that and edged a catch to the wicket-keeper. Mike was excited by this success, not only because we had picked up a valuable wicket, but also because I had understood his plan and managed to carry it out without a word passing between us.

Respect for his captaincy was not confined to the players. During the 1980 season he cast a spell over Surrey. Middlesex and Surrey were unquestionably the two strongest county teams at the time, yet we never had any trouble against them. We played them in every competition—the John Player, the Benson and Hedges, the Gillette Cup and twice in the county championships—and the only game we did not win, the three-day game at the Oval, ended in a very favourable draw. But I believe the most important single reason for this dominance was Mike's captaincy.

And Ladbrokes, the turf accountants, agreed. Just before the Gillette Cup final at Lord's I was on my way to the nets and saw that the Ladbrokes' tent was open. I went in and was astonished to see that we were being quoted as 5 to 2 favourites, while Surrey were 6 to 1. I found those odds extraordinary for a one-day game between sides which were well matched and had finished first and second on the county table.

I told the fellow behind the counter that the odds did not seem right and his reply was that the difference between Surrey's Roger Knight and Mike Brearley as captains made Middlesex clear favourites. Even the betting men, who knew their cricket, saw captaincy in the final as crucial to the outcome. And so it proved. Mike's field-placing was superb, his bowling changes innovative and shrewd, and his batting controlled as he made 96 not out to shepherd us to a seven-wicket victory.

His cricket writing underlines the profound knowledge he has of the game. In addition to regular contributions to the London *Sunday Times* and various magazines, he has written several highly readable, informative books. His writings show his deep understanding and provide an insight into what makes him such a remarkable captain.

Brearley once wrote that 'the captain of a county team is, all at once, managing director, union leader and pit face worker.' I found he filled all of those roles in the Middlesex side.

Brearley and I spoke long and hard about South Africa and politics. He was well read on the subject and was not one of those critics who had never seen the country for himself. After the 1964 tour he had stayed on in South Africa, visiting the homelands and Soweto, talking to leaders of all race groups and generally taking a look at the problem firsthand. He was obviously not impressed with what he saw and, while we agreed in our opposition to apartheid, we disagreed about the methods of combating it.

My point was simply that history had shown that sanctions and isolation could take you only so far along the road to reform. Continued too long, the effects are counter-productive. But, once the atmosphere for change is right, communication should be established in the hope that involvement and dialogue will produce further change.

I also felt that South Africans, historically, react badly to outside criticism and pressure. Our inclination has been to retreat into the laager when we feel threatened, to fight it out rather than involve ourselves in negotiations and compromise.

I believe that for a period Mike actually agreed with me. He produced a magazine article in favour of a mixed tour to South Africa with players coming from various major cricketing nations of the world as a first step towards open dialogue. My feeling is that the controlling bodies missed an opportunity of really furthering change in this country, not just in cricket but perhaps socially and even politically.

Time, in fact, has again altered Mike's point of view as I discovered when I last saw him in 1983. I spent the day with him at Lord's, watching India playing the West Indians in the World Cup final. We dwelt briefly on politics, and it was clear that his dislike of South Africa's racial politics made it impossible for him to come to terms with the prospect of renewed cricketing ties. A morally sensitive man, he believed he could not reject South Africa's social and political activities, and then play sport against us.

CHAPTER EIGHT

After Middlesex

The temptation to return to Middlesex the next year was immense. Just before the end of the season a wealthy London businessman and loyal Middlesex supporter approached me with an extraordinary offer. He asked me how much compensation Wiggins Teape would require to release me for another year.

But there were a number of factors which made it impossible. I had given a commitment to my firm that the Middlesex contract would be for only one season. In addition, they could not, with justification, release me again when they had Henry Fotheringham and Dave Brickett, two other Currie Cup cricketers who also wanted to play in England, in their employ. Also I was nearing the end of my cricketing days and had to give serious consideration to my new business career.

All the speculation was ended by the fact that Bev had fallen pregnant. Had we returned to England in 1981, she would have had three children, one a baby, to care for in a London flat, and that prospect did not appeal to either of us.

I was fortunate, however, to be invited back to play for Middlesex at the start of the 1981 English summer. As county champions, they met the MCC at Lord's in the traditional pipe-opener to the season. The game ended in a dismal draw and, while I only took one wicket, I was happy with my form.

I spent an enjoyable 10 days with Mike Brearley and renewed many old friendships. Brearley, though pleased to see me, was honest enough to admit that he had not been in favour of my inclusion in the side to play the MCC. He again had not been consulted and my invitation had come from Middlesex secretary Alan Burridge. Brearley, as he pointed out to me, was more concerned with planning for the new season than remembering the past, and my inclusion meant that one of the young players he wished to blood in this match was omitted. It was typical of Brearley to have mentioned this openly. Outstanding leaders do not take the easy options.

It was during my season in England in 1980, and in the South African summer which followed, that my bowling peaked. I was helped at Middlesex by the captaincy of Brearley and the fact that I operated in harness with two world-class performers in Daniel, a genuine strike bowler, and Emburey, an off-spinner whose control and variation kept the pressure on the batsmen for long periods.

There is also no doubt that a change in attitude helped me attain these new heights. In isolated South Africa I had become tired of the humdrum routine of the Currie Cup and my edge was blunted. Every season the same teams, the same faces would do battle and, without international cricket to provide any relief or perspective, provincial cricket was losing its appeal.

I was taking Currie Cup wickets regularly, but success merely blinded me to the fact I had lost much of my ambition and drive.

My six months with Middlesex, with its fresh challenges and new experiences, rejuvenated me and I found my youthful enthusiasm returning. The only adjustment I had to make was to bowl a fuller length on the slower English wickets. Initially, I became frustrated when I sent down what I considered a perfect delivery, just short of a length, and the batsman would have time to withdraw his bat or adjust his stroke. Now, for the first time in at least five years, I was able to swing the ball consistently, and this allowed me to try and beat the batsman, both in the air and off the wicket.

Ironically, the need to operate defensively in one-day matches turned me into a more attacking bowler. I now started to concentrate on producing the accurate yorker, a standard delivery at the end of every one-day innings when the objective is to give the batsman as little room as possible to play his strokes. I would bowl a series of yorkers at the leg-stump with six fielders on the leg-side and three to the off, and this experience sharpened up my bowling enormously.

I returned to South Africa fitter and better-equipped than ever for a new Currie Cup season. Instead of my usual pedestrian start to the summer, I found myself among the wickets from the outset, picking up 54 from eight outings at an average of 9,5. It was a most gratifying season as I never honestly believed I was capable of bowling so consistently well over a whole season. But the Middlesex venture had also a negative consequence. I believe, as a result of my success in England, I started becoming slightly big-headed about my cricket.

There is no doubt that my character changed during my career. My father's influence had given me an excellent start, and for years I followed his traditional, conservative example, steering free of controversy, playing the game as it should be, and enjoying it.

With close friend Allan Lamb in happier times.

Later, as I improved and became something of a figure, I grew more confident and possibly even arrogant. For a time, starting in England in 1980 and crystallising in the dreadful run-out of Allan Lamb in the Datsun Shield final in February 1982, I behaved as if I was more important than the game.

The Lamb run-out finally brought me crashing back to earth forcing me to sit back and reassess my actions out in the middle. I did not like what I found. I had become more cantankerous towards umpires and opposition batsmen and my 'chirping', an accepted part of the game in South Africa, had become personal. I remember Jimmy Cook saying to me once, 'You know, you have always chirped, but in the old days you used to smile at the same time. You don't any more.' Warning bells should have been ringing, but they were not. I was enjoying my success too much.

I have sat for hours and thought about what prompted me to run out Lamb in the Natal-Western Province final at the Wanderers. I was bowling to Adrian Kuiper with Allan Lamb, incidentally a very good friend, at the non-striker's end and helping Western Province re-build after a poor start. Kuiper played the ball down on the leg-side, I fielded it at silly mid-on and, turning to go back to my mark, saw that Lamb, backing up, had yet to regain his crease. I threw down the wicket and Lamb, still out of his ground, was run out.

I have watched televised recordings of that incident a number of times, once together with Lamb in Roy Pienaar's home in Johannesburg in 1983, and my reaction is always one of acute embarrassment.

What worried me was that I took two steps back towards my bowling mark before throwing at the wicket. At the time, unaware of the delay, I thought the run out acceptable, and in the spirit of the game, but it was wrong. Others have pooh-poohed it by saying that it was in the laws, though possibly not in keeping with the spirit of cricket. But I have serious doubts about that, and I am beginning to believe that the ball was dead once I had taken those two steps back towards my mark, and that Lamb should not have been given out.

Those initial steps have continued to haunt me. At the time I thought my action spontaneous, indeed it was, but what had driven me to react in that way? Had the heat of the moment got to me, or had a new competitiveness, a hidden killer instinct, suddenly surfaced?

John Emburey, who was watching at the time, remarked immediately after play ended — in a narrow Western Province victory — that I would not have reacted in the same way had I been playing in England. At the time I argued with him, but when I eventually saw the replay on television I was convinced he was right. It is strange that only Chris Wilkins, of the Natal side, thought that I was wrong and Mike Procter, captaining Natal on the day and renowned for his fairness, firmly believed at the time I was right.

The incident had its sequel in the Natal innings and again I was involved. We were just a couple of runs short of victory and I was facing Stephen Jefferies. He beat me outside the off-stump and there was the sound of the ball hitting something as it passed through to wicket-keeper Stephen Bruce. The Western Province players were convinced I had been caught behind, but I was equally certain that I had not touched the ball and it had just nicked the off-stump, without dislodging a bail,

My instinctive reaction to the Lamb run out incident in the Datsun Shield final at the Wanderers in February 1982 was to be delighted to have had a hand in his dismissal. After seeing television replays of the run out weeks later I was to change my mind.

as has happened to me on two other occasions. There was pandemonium out on the field and Lawrence Seeff, who hardly ever says anything on the field, ran up and swore viciously at me for not walking. While this was going on the ball went through a couple of hands on its way back to the bowler. Kirsten, receiving the ball in the covers, strolled across towards the non-striker's end where Paddy Clift, with his bat grounded behind the crease, watched him approach. Certain that the ball was finally dead, Clift walked down the wicket for a mid-wicket conference with me, and Kirsten ran him out.

A couple of deliveries later, it was all over. We had made 176 for eight in reply to Western Province's 178 for eight — and the law of the jungle had come to the Wanderers.

It was undoubtedly the most depressing game of cricket I have ever played in. Natal's initial anger was born out of the belief that not only was the run-out of Lamb legal, but it was also within the spirit of the game. We never doubted it and an enraged Procter, usually the most diplomatic of captains, said testily in his speech at the presentation that there were ways to win cricket matches and Natal would not have wanted to win the way Western Province had. Lamb told the media that he thought I had been 'clowning' when I aimed at the stumps and that was why he had made no attempt to make his ground. Such is our friendship that at the cocktail party that evening we were able to discuss the incident. I asked him whether he really believed I was joking when I threw at the wickets. He just smiled, yet I believe he knew I was serious in my intentions.

I was vulnerable to attack in the weeks that followed, and the outcry over the match was understandable and justifiable. But Kirsten's remarks to the Press in the Western Province dressing-room after the game were particularly painful. He said he had run out Clift in retaliation for my dismissal of Lamb and added that 'everybody thought Van der Bijl was a gentleman but his true colours came out today.'

What did save me in the weeks that followed was that deep down I knew my behaviour, regrettable though it was, had been totally spontaneous. Other actions taken that day were not.

It was two weeks after the final that I saw the incident re-played on television for the first time, and I understood only then the reason for the deep anger of the Western Province players. I realised that I had been

The tension of the controversial and deeply disturbing final is mirrored in the faces of the players of both sides at the official prize-giving. The Western Province players (below) are Lawrence Seeff, Peter Kirsten, Roy Pienaar, Graham Gooch and 12th man Paul Rayner. There is no outward joy at having won the Shield.
Standing with me is Ken Cooper while (above) the expressions of Paddy Clift, Chris Wilkins, Barry Richards, Darryl Bestall, Les Taylor and Mike Procter also reflect the anger of the Natal players.

at fault and, totally shattered, I immediately telephoned Procter, and told him I was going to make a public apology.

Procter had been appointed Springbok captain for the matches against Graham Gooch's England side on that same day, and he asked me to delay any statement until after the tour was over. Procter felt that to highlight the incident again would disrupt the Springbok side which contained a number of the Wanderers' protagonists, including Kirsten and me. So my apology, and the acceptance that I had been in the wrong, only came once the season was over.

It was the darkest period of my career, but Procter did lift the gloom briefly in the first one-day international when Gooch took a sparkling century off us. As we were leaving the field, Clive Rice, who had not bowled because of his neck injury, turned and asked why I could not get Gooch out. 'How did you expect him to?' Procter butted in. 'Gooch didn't leave his crease once all day.'

The Wanderers blunder was, however, the greatest cricketing lesson of my life, causing me to reassess my approach to the game and consciously to control my competitive, 'killer' instinct which for the first time in my career had become visible. There is no doubt that bowlers, even successful spinners, require that instinct, an aggressive determination to get a batsman out. In the early years of my career, I was often accused of having no killer in me, and Barry Richards and Dennis Gamsy used to berate me for not bowling more bouncers. I believe I always had this aggression, but it was kept deep inside, and only in the later years did it surface for outsiders to see.

It is probably true to say that the pressures out in the middle combined with this intense competitiveness produced that moment of aberration.

What is worrying is that my 14 years of experience did not help me control myself, and today I am genuinely concerned about our young players who are starting off under totally different conditions.

Administrators do not accept that the modern cricketer has to contend with greater demands and outside influences than in the past. I believe they are wrong. The pressures, even during my years in the game, increased significantly. It took some six years of playing in the Currie Cup before I was recognised as I walked down the street, Today's youngsters, the Roy Pienaars and Adrian Kuipers, are turned into instant heroes (or villains) by television, a trend accentuated by the

Roy Pienaar (left) and Adrian Kuiper, two of South Africa's most promising players. How will they handle the new pressures?

swing to one-day cricket, with its mass appeal and widespread publicity.

The outstanding young player is public property, media interest in him is greater and he must be on his best behaviour, on and off the field. It is difficult for a youngster, who is playing the game largely for fun, to adapt to dealing with the problems — but not the benefits — of professional sport. In this age of the instant television replay, his actions on the field must be impeccable.

As a schoolboy, at Newlands in the early sixties, I remember watching Eddie Barlow showing dissent when he was given out in a Springbok trial match. The Press did not comment, and there was no television in those far-off days. So, apart from the few hundred spectators at Newlands that day, no one knew of Barlow's behaviour. Today, if the Press did not highlight such an incident, television would — probably in slow motion.

Golf, in spite of the vast sums of money involved and the enormous individual pressure, is one of the few sports that has come through this ordeal by television relatively unscathed. The Prices and Watsons conduct themselves with as much dignity today as the Players and Palmers did 25 years ago. But, for the rest, the tennis and rugby players, the footballers and cricketers have been found wanting.

CHAPTER NINE

The men in the middle

I have often wondered why lyricist Noël Coward did not mention umpires when he wrote about his 'Mad dogs and Englishmen go out in the midday sun'. I have never envied the umpire who stands for hours, often in boiling heat, unnoticed while the game runs smoothly. Suddenly, though, this unobtrusive offiical will find himself thrust into the limelight, his sound umpiring of the past forgotten, as one mistake turns him into a villain.

The pressures out in the middle are colossal. Throughout a long day, the umpire cannot once lose concentration, and often he has to make an instinctive decision in a tight moment while the television viewer, in the quiet of his lounge and with the aid of the slow motion action replay, waits to judge him.

When I ran out Allan Lamb, the ball could have been dead, but having watched the replay I am still not sure. It was long debated by the critics, yet umpire Perry Hurwitz had to make a judgement of Solomon instinctively and instantly.

Later that day, with the game at fever pitch, he was again embroiled in controversy when Paddy Clift was run out. I believe, on that occasion, he was wrong, and that the heat of the moment influenced his decision. The umpires are put under the same pressures as the players, and they will naturally make mistakes as the players do.

It was refreshing to read that umpire Barrie Meyer admitted to being wrong in the second test between the 1984 West Indians and

England when he gave Viv Richards out leg-before. That honesty, and the willingness to admit that he had erred, was respected by the West Indians.

It is easy for a player to say 'Sorry captain' after dropping a catch or playing a bad stroke, but the umpire is in a far more difficult position. He is expected to be the perfect arbitrator, yet he is human, susceptible to pressures and likely to make mistakes.

I enjoyed an exchange between Syd Moore and Mike Procter during a Natal–Western Province match. Procter was complaining about a leg-before appeal which had been turned down. 'If that had been in

An unnecessarily extravagant appeal.

England, it would have been given out,' he said. Moore turned and said to the irate Procter, 'Stop behaving like an overgrown schoolboy and bowl!' Procter swung round angrily and stomped back to his bowling mark. Walking away from Moore, he was grinning broadly. He wanted to keep the pressure on the umpire and did not let Moore notice that he had seen the funny side of the exchange.

It is difficult for umpires to treat players in a relaxed and easy manner, yet sometimes they take the mickey out of us cricketers.

England test umpire David Constant tricked me beautifully in Middlesex's match against Essex in 1980. I was batting with Mike Selvey, and we trotted through for two comfortable runs as he played the ball wide of third man. Believing the ball would be thrown back to the wicketkeeper, I was ambling towards the bowler's end when I saw umpire Constant suddenly scurrying off to the side of the wicket, as if the ball was being thrown in his direction and he was preparing himself for a run-out attempt. I took fright, tried to build up a gallop and then dived full-length to make my ground. Lying prostrate on the wicket, I looked up to find Constant—and the Essex fielders—doubled over with laughter. The ball had been lobbed back to the wicketkeeper!

During the SAB English tour of South Africa early in 1982, Graham Gooch, Geoff Boycott and John Emburey all told me that I had the umpires in South Africa in my pocket. Knowing the umpires as I do, I believe this is not true.

But I would be less than honest if I did not admit that, in my way, I tried to influence umpires, just as Trevor Goddard had done in my formative years. The crowd would see it in its most obvious form. When a batsman was struck on the pads, and I thought there was a possibility of it being out, I would appeal enthusiastically, hoping that my conviction would swing the umpire in a marginal decision. Usually it was more subtle.

Even when watching someone transparently obvious, spectators rarely understand the intricacies and the delicacies of the contest out in the middle. The purists might disagree, but attempts to influence or control umpires by those out in the middle have long been part of the game. And this is true not only of cricket.

Springbok rugby captain Morné du Plessis told me of one incident when Western Province were struggling to overcome a lively, typically abrasive Eastern Province side in the semi-final of a knock-out competition. Western Province were losing by a fairly substantial margin and, after one particularly torrid loose scrum, du Plessis called the referee aside and told him that Western Province had an important fixture — the final! — the next week and could not afford any injuries. If Eastern Province did not cut out the rough stuff, added du Plessis, he would lead his side off the field. The referee, shaken by this threat from the Springbok captain, immediately awarded a string of penalties against Eastern Province for their robust play and Western Province won by slotting over their kicks.

During my 1980 season with Middlesex, we were playing Sussex at Hove. I had bowled fairly well, taking five wickets, and we had them nine down. Their last pair had been resisting stubbornly and I was keen to end the innings so that we could enforce the follow-on. I was tiring and Mike Brearley came up at the start of a new over and told me he thought I should have a break. 'Hang on,' I replied, making sure that umpire Barrie Meyer was within earshot, 'let me just have another over at this fellow (Alastair Pigott). It's easy, I'll just throw one wide down the leg-side to open him up, and then I'll fire one straight at the middle stump and catch him in front.'

This I did and, though I have a shrewd suspicion that my second delivery was going just down leg-side, I let up a raucous appeal. 'Well bowled,' said Meyer after he had given him out. It was a close decision, and Barrie might dispute my view, but I believe he had been caught up in the moment because he had prior knowledge of my plan.

An almost identical incident had taken place just a fortnight earlier when we had beaten Nottinghamshire by an innings at Lord's. The eccentric Derek Randall, a lively, amusing and committed cricketer, was the batsman involved. I had bowled him in the first innings and he was determined to keep me out in the second, while delighting in the challenge of playing John Emburey, who finished with 12 wickets in the match, on a turning wicket.

Randall was consistently moving across his stumps to allow the ball to come on to him and he was particularly effective in dealing with anything pitched on middle and leg, hitting me through midwicket on several occasions. He was on 49 and I decided on the old ploy in an effort to get him to leave his leg-stump exposed. The umpire at my end was former England fast bowler Arthur Jepson and, standing next to him, I explained my plan to Brearley. My first ball I pitched on off-stump, the next was slightly wider, the third and fourth wider still, and slowly Randall was drawn across his stumps. The fifth delivery I bowled fast and pitched it up on middle-and-leg. Randall, moving well across, was hit on the pads and the umpire gave him out. I felt that the ball had cut back just enough to beat leg-stump, but the umpire had no hesitation in giving him out. I honestly believe that he, too, had unwittingly entered into the conspiracy.

There is no doubt that additional pressure has been placed on provincial players since the isolation of South African cricket. Matches between Transvaal, Western Province and Natal, in particular, have been given almost mini-test status since the sporting blockade. This pressure has been felt on the field and, as a result, a more uncompromising attitude towards the umpires has developed.

During the seventies in particular, players, administrators, spectators and sportswriters were more 'province-conscious' than a decade earlier when the common cause was to play cricket, and develop talent, for South Africa.

South African umpires obviously do not have the same experience and opportunities as those standing in England, and their standard, understandably, is not as high. In England, an umpire will usually stand in some 15 three-day and 18 one-day matches in the course of a season, and in four or five years he gains more experience than his South African counterpart could accumulate in a lifetime.

South African cricketers are often heavily criticised for not taking up umpiring when they retire, as many former players do in England, but the circumstances in this country are totally different. Nearly all Currie Cup cricketers are amateurs and very few retire from the game because they are too old. Usually they quit, often prematurely, for business or family reasons, and these considerations obviously prevent them returning as umpires. County cricketers are professionals who usually play for as long as possible and a number of them turn to umpiring as a livelihood when they leave the county circuit.

The poor standard of South African umpiring came to a head in the early seventies. In one Currie Cup match in Cape Town against Western Province, England test cricketer Bob Woolmer told me he counted 11 poor decisions, more than he saw in an entire county season.

Pressure on the umpire from two sources. Stephen Jefferies and Ray Jennings believe Graham Gooch is out. The batsman, in turn, feigns indifference. Who would want to be the man in the middle?

The umpires were not equipped to handle the pressures of what was generally regarded as the toughest domestic competition in world cricket. To lighten their burden, Natal skipper Barry Richards introduced 'a walking agreement' during the 1973–74 season. Mike Procter, captaining Rhodesia at the time, and Graeme Pollock, the Eastern Province skipper, were happy with the idea, but Eddie Barlow (Western Province) was not.

Barlow's attitude to walking was similar to that held by my father and others of his era. My father and I used to argue long and hard about it, but he (and Barlow) firmly believed that the umpire was there to do a job and the players should accept the rough with the smooth. In my

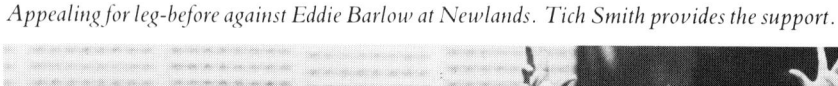

Appealing for leg-before against Eddie Barlow at Newlands. Tich Smith provides the support.

father's day, batsmen did not walk. He told me how he had scored 204 against Natal in Durban and had been given not out when caught behind on 8. The only time the incident was mentioned during the four days he spent in Durban was at the railway station when the team was leaving. The Natal wicketkeeper, Bob Williams, had come to see them off and, as he shook hands, he said, 'Well played, Pieter, bit lucky though, weren't you?' And my father replied, 'Yes, I did get an edge.'

Barlow would not commit Western Province to the agreement, but he did ensure that his players did not show dissent if a poor decision was given against them. This, of course, also eases the pressures and tensions out in the middle, and helps the umpire. Ironically, in the first game against Western Province after Barlow had declined the walking agreement, he was adjudged run-out when well in his crease. We watched his reaction closely, but he showed no sign of the displeasure he must have felt. He had kept to his agreement.

The other provincial captains felt, however, that if the batsmen were instructed to walk for catches either behind the wicket or for the bat/pad ones at short-leg, it would take some of the pressure off the umpires. The catch down the leg-side, when the ball hits both bat and pad or brushes the glove, is the most difficult decision for the umpire to make. It required a certain amount of intuition, whereas the leg-before decision is not as taxing as there are certain rigid guidelines in the law book. We believed that if the umpires were helped by the players in that one area, they would be able to concentrate on other aspects of the game.

The agreement worked for a number of matches, but eventually fell away amongst the other provinces when several players failed to keep to it in tight situations. Natal and Rhodesia continued implementing it for a couple of seasons and our matches were some of the happiest and most enjoyable I ever played in.

But to compare South African umpires to those in England is hardly just. As professionals the latter have very obvious advantages. It would be fairer to compare our standards with those found in Australia, New Zealand or the West Indies where cricket is run along similar lines. I am told our umpires are at least the equal of their counterparts in these countries.

Umpires who are committed, efficient and ensure the game is trouble-free, are held in high regard. Barrie Meyer, who has umpired in some of the toughest Currie Cup matches over the past two seasons, is a prime example. He has had the support of cricketers and sportswriters alike. Yet umpires who are incompetent and officious are simply not respected — just as inept players, administrators and sportswriters are not — and occasionally this will become apparent out in the middle.

Top professional sportsmen want referees or umpires to be equally proficient, but naturally the occasional human error is expected and

Appealing West Indian style. Franklyn Stephenson bellows vociferously and successfully.

accepted. When mistakes are the result of incompetence, however, problems arise.

It should be remembered that not only the players abuse the umpires. Spectators, of course, do also and so, too, do the cricket writers. Time and again you have certain scribes, usually sitting some 100 metres from the action, passing judgements on the umpire. In one game against Eastern Province, one of the local sportswriters wrote, 'Russell Fensham was given out leg-before to the first ball he received from Van der Bijl which cut back and looked like missing even a second set of stumps erected on the leg-side. Gradwell, too, was unlucky. Van der Bijl slipped one through the gate and Gradwell was given out caught behind when it nicked his pad.'

That, too, is putting pressure on the umpires. The written word is more damning than the spoken one which is often uttered in the heat of the contest.

The umpires are what players consider the uncontrollable factor in any match. Players going into an important game can plan their physical and mental preparation, but they cannot anticipate an exceptional performance from one of the opposition, or a wrong umpiring decision, and matches are often turned by these two factors.

For the welfare of South African cricket, it is vital that more respect be shown to the umpires. I also believe their status in this country must be raised.

While the natural movement of retired players is away from umpiring, former players would, I believe, consider standing if it were made a worthwhile pastime. Umpires should be paid and paid well, perhaps even twice the amount received by the players. If there is a financial incentive and the umpire, at the end of a season, can show his family a swimming-pool or caravan, then umpiring would be more attractive. Badges should be awarded to only the best, just as the pick of the players receive their provincial or national colours, and not just handed out to fellows simply because they have been umpiring for a number of years. The umpiring panel should be limited to the very best and, if they were paid enough and their status raised, I believe five or six former provincial players, all that are really needed, would take up umpiring.

Often umpire manipulation goes hand in hand with gamesmanship. Intense competition and rivalry will breed a certain amount of psychological warfare between player and player, and sometimes the umpire is involved. As long as gamesmanship is controlled and stays within the spirit of the laws, I believe it adds to the game of cricket.

There is a very distinct line between gamesmanship and cheating. Gamesmanship, the skill in using ploys to gain an advantage over an opponent, usually contains an element of fun. But in Australia, before and during the Packer World Series, gamesmanship sank to new lows. Tony Greig tells how he went out to bat in front of 70 000 baying Australians at Melbourne. As Dennis Lillee was charging in to bowl, with the crowd chanting 'kill, kill, kill' a short-leg fielder was spitting on the wicket in front of him.

Gamesmanship in cricket is all about understanding an opposing player and finding out what you can say to him which might put him at a disadvantage. I learnt in my first Currie Cup game against Eastern Province the value of a well-timed comment. Facing Neville Mallett, the left-arm spinner, I was playing out a succession of maidens as we fought a rearguard action. Peter Pollock at mid-off berated me continuously from mid-off. 'Can't a fellow your size hit the ball?' he would ask. He went on and on, and finally I tried an ambitious stroke off Mallett and hit a catch straight to Pollock. As I walked out he smiled at me, 'No luck,' he said, a twinkle in his eye, and it was only then I realised I had been had.

Against Rhodesia, in my first season, it was decided at the team discussion that when Peter Carlstein, the Springbok batsman, came in we would not talk to him. Carlstein, an extrovert and a delightful fellow, enjoyed chatting incessantly with those around him when he was batting. We felt that if we could put him off initially, he might lose his concentration and start playing his strokes too early. One of the players admired most by Carlstein in the Natal side was Mike Procter and they were close friends. Soon after Carlstein arrived at the wicket, he walked up to Procter and said enthusiastically, 'Proc, are you enjoying yourself out here?' Procter, as instructed, replied abruptly, 'Carly, stop talking and get on with the bloody game!' and stormed off. This so upset Carlstein that he played and missed at a couple of balls before being bowled having a wild slog at Norman Crookes.

Carlstein, because he reacted so strongly, was involved in many similar incidents, but occasionally the ploy would backfire. Shortly after moving up to Rhodesia from the Transvaal, he played against his old team-mates in a Currie Cup match. Going in at number three, he went to pad up and found a rubber duck in his kit-bag, planted there by a Transvaal player. Grimly determined, he went out and made 80.

The next time the two teams met, Carlstein played three successive defensive strokes. Wicketkeeper Lee Irvine, standing up, said, 'Typical Carlstein, has never developed any shots during his career.' Carlstein swung round and prodded Irvine quite hard in the chest with the bat. Irvine fell back and Ali Bacher came running in from mid-off shouting, 'What's going on here, leave my players alone.' Carlstein turned on him. 'Come one step closer and I'll whack you over the head with this bat.' The Transvaal players left him alone for the rest of his innings.

As the years went on I know my remarks to opposing players became more personal and cutting. In the 1978–79 Datsun Shield final against Transvaal, Natal were chasing an enormous target of 311. We were never really in with a chance, but I managed to club 43 near the end

The finger game. Eddie Barlow finds the umpire in full agreement.

to loosen Transvaal's hold briefly. Gordon McMillan, the Transvaal left-arm seamer, had been married on the previous day and had delayed his honeymoon to play in the final. During my innings I managed to hit him for probably the biggest six of my career — it bounced in the top row of the grandstand at the golf course end — and, as the ball soared away and he stared at me in amazement, I called up the wicket, 'That's your wedding present, Gordon.' It was said in jest, but it was an arrogant, unnecessary remark, and fortunately McMillan burst out laughing, saving me any embarrassment.

But after the Allan Lamb run-out incident I changed my approach and for the next two years tried to go back to my old behaviour.

It is important for the top players to set the example out in the middle. They have a moral responsibility not only to children watching, but also the impressionable youngsters entering the first-class game.

Captains often practise a form of gamesmanship, to lift their players to greater heights. A good captain has to know his players. The sensitive require coddling, the brasher ones react more positively to a heavy-handed approach. Mike Brearley would use the rapier with Bob Willis but the bludgeon on Ian Botham. Most of the captains I played under adopted the hoof-up-the-backside method to liven up my bowling, though I don't quite know why. 'Get that piano off your back,' was Trevor Goddard's usual comment, Procter would ask whether I wanted wicketkeeper Tich Smith to stand up, and Brearley threatened once that he was going to bring off-spinner John Emburey on 'because he is bowling faster than you'.

To be honest, I found that the gamesmanship out in the middle added spice to the contest. I could think of nothing more dull and boring then plodding back to my mark without saying something to the batsman, or having the occasional chirp with the umpire. I believe that the banter and chit-chat out in the middle is essential to the game, and I certainly would not have played for as long as I did had it not taken place. But it is up to the umpires and captains to see that gamesmanship never becomes unsporting.

CHAPTER TEN

The first rebels

While the Derrick Robins tours in the early seventies had encouraged change, both politically and socially, they also left South African cricket fans living in a fool's paradise. The advances that were being made convinced many that international cricket was just around the corner. The administrators, conservative and trusting in those days, were looking no further than the ICC to fulfil their part of the agreement and allow South Africa back into the test arena. But their faith was misplaced, and year after year their delegates were sent packing from London, empty-handed and frustrated.

Their preoccupation with the ICC also meant that a golden opportunity of solving South Africa's cricket problems went abegging. In 1977–78, Kerry Packer signed the world's leading players for his Australian Circus — yet South Africa should have beaten him to the draw.

Packer, seeing some ready takers among the world's disillusioned players, transformed cricketers' pay packets overnight, and Australia became the hub of world cricket. But the entire cricketing future of a South Africa desperate for international competition was at stake, and a Packer-type series could, and should, have been developed in this country.

Our rebel tours also came three years too late. Not only were the pick of the world's cricketers better off by then, but controlling boards had taken steps to tie their leading players to contracts from which there was no escape but banishment. The cricket authorities, caught unaware by Packer, reacted strongly to South Africa's attempt to break the blockade, and cricketing rebels from England, Sri Lanka and the West Indies were heavily punished as a result.

The changes on the playing fields of South Africa were an obvious indication that the cricket fraternity was opposed to apartheid and the internal policies of South Africa. The players and administrators did everything in their power to ensure that, at club and provincial level, selection was on merit alone. Accordingly the frustration felt by the top players during the seventies, when it was realised that genuine test cricket was little more than a pipe-dream, was high.

Local officials, born into the traditional game, sought only to play the game by the rules, and the idea of a rebel or Packer-type tour was abhorrent to them. They toed the line throughout the seventies, believing that if they fulfilled ICC demands South Africa would be re-admitted to test cricket. Behind closed doors, leading cricket men encouraged them and promises were made, which only delayed the inevitable moment when South African cricket had to break away and go it alone.

Cricket players and administrators have a dual loyalty — first to the welfare of the game in its broadest context, the second to the game domestically. There was no desire on the part of the South African administrators to cause turmoil and chaos in world cricket, and one of their most taxing problems was whether they should risk splitting international cricket to save the game on the domestic level. The ICC made up their minds for them.

In 1979 a fact-finding mission was sent to South Africa by the ICC and, in 1980 at Lord's, Mr Rashid Varachia, president of the SACU, addressed the Conference for 45 minutes before being asked to return in 1981 with fresh evidence to back his call for South Africa's re-admission. Mr Varachia and a four-man delegation, Messrs Wallace, Pamensky, Dowling and Dakin, duly travelled to London in 1981 and presented South Africa's case at Lord's. Though the matter was discussed at length, all that emerged from the meeting was a bland ICC statement to the effect that everything would be done to encourage mixed cricket in South Africa in the future. The South African problem had been shoved under the carpet for another year. The ICC's attitude finally convinced the SACU delegates that ICC countries, pressured by their governments, were merely stringing them along. In previous years the SACU had been determined not to compromise their delicate position with the ICC by stepping out of line, but now they decided to meet their responsibility to South African cricket.

By the 1980s, isolation was having a telling effect on South African cricket and an overseas tour was essential if the game in South Africa was to survive.

There is no doubt in my mind that the ICC's strategy, aimed at producing change in South Africa, should have been modified in the late seventies. Initially, isolation and sanctions had unquestionably pushed South Africans along the road to reform. After the formation of

Rashid Varachia welcomes members of the International Cricket Conference fact-finding mission on their arrival in Johannesburg in 1979. They are (from left) Bob Parish, Murray Chappie and Walter Hadlee.

the SACU the impetus would have been maintained, perhaps even accelerated by a fresh approach based on compromise and negotiations. The timing would have been perfect, but instead the procrastinating ICC lost a crucial opportunity.

Rashid Varachia and Joe Pamensky now took a back seat as moves began to attract England's leading players to South Africa. Mike Brearley, leading England to their extraordinary 1981 Ashes win over Australia, was asked by John Edrich if he would lead a near-test team to South Africa. As he wrote in his excellent book *Phoenix from the Ashes*, 'I could, I gathered, have virtually named my price. Many other players were similarly sounded out. My answer was no. Despite recognising that the cricketers of that country have done virtually all they can to make the game multi-racial, I have no inclination to play cricket in South Africa. In my view, it is only by the ban on international sport with that country that these desirable changes have taken place. And, despite the apparent injustice in sportsmen being almost alone in bearing the brunt of the protests against South Africa, my view is that the evil of that system and the opportunity that sportsmen have to dent it outweigh such considerations.'

But there were others keen to accept the offer and Peter Venison, an independent agent working on behalf of a South African hotel group, made initial contact with the England team playing in India. Venison was the ideal man for the task because he could invade the international cricket world incognito. It was only when key players in the English side reneged on their agreement, that the sponsors stood down. Peter Cooke, a managing director of a Johannesburg record company, and the ubiquitous Martin Locke, a freelance television personality, then picked up the pieces and mounted a clandestine operation on behalf of the SACU in England and India. Deceitful and secretive it was, but did the SACU have any option?

On 28 February 1982, days after the tour of India ended, seven of England's top cricketers, Graham Gooch, Geoff Boycott, Alan Knott, Derek Underwood, Dennis Amiss, John Lever and John Emburey, flew into Johannesburg. Three other test players—Mike Hendrick, Wayne Larkins and Peter Willey—arrived the next day, and Les Taylor, under contract to Natal, and Chris Old, with Northern Transvaal, made up the original 12-man party. They were later joined by Geoff Humpage, Bob Woolmer and Arnold Sidebottom, all coaching and playing in South Africa at the time. The venture was made possible by South African Breweries who agreed to underwrite the tour.

Sadly, Mr Varachia was not at the airport to meet the tourists. The president of the SACU had suffered a heart attack and died two months previously. Paying tribute to him, Mr Jack Bailey, secretary of the ICC, said revealingly: 'Cricket everywhere has lost a servant of wide vision and considerable stature ... he strove untiringly as the first president of the SACU for multi-racial cricket in South Africa, and for South Africa's acceptance at international level in the world of cricket. That his first objective should have been achieved speaks volumes for the tenacity of purpose of him and his colleagues.'

There was the predictable outcry against the tour from the rest of the cricket-playing world. The decision to come to South Africa could not have been easy, particularly for players such as Boycott, Gooch, Emburey and Larkins, who were assured of regular test cricket in the years ahead. But the players argued that as professionals they had the right to sell their services wherever they pleased. The ban of three years imposed on them afterwards was extremely harsh, and the England cricket team has been hit where it hurts most, suffering grievous losses in New Zealand and Pakistan before their first-ever whitewash at the hands of the 1984 West Indians.

But it is the double standards adopted by overseas countries that is particularly galling. During the SAB English tour, the famous English cartoonist, Giles, depicted two businessmen standing on a London wharf, watching one of their cargo ships being loaded with containers labelled 'Goods for South Africa'. One businessman, turns to the other and says, 'Isn't it disgusting that our cricketers have gone and toured South Africa. All just for lolly.' That says it all.

Mike Brearley would argue that you cannot compromise your principles, implying that if sanctions are to be enforced, they should be across the board. Yet South Africa trades freely with nations involved in the sports boycott, and all but four African countries.

The Springboks ran out comfortable winners against the SAB English tourists—taking the one-day games 3–0 and the 'tests' 1–0 with two drawn—against a side of considerable talent, but not possessing the bowling and batting depth required in international cricket.

While Gooch's men failed to win a game, they nevertheless showed that South African cricket was decidedly rusty, relying too heavily on the services of the older players, such as Mike Procter, Barry Richards and Graeme Pollock. The help the older Springboks gave the younger,

The Springboks' first toss in 12 years. Graham Gooch and Mike Procter at the Wanderers.

Graham Gooch, upright and arrogant, at the crease. A characteristic solid blow from the England opener.

inexperienced players during the series was invaluable and, at the end of the tour, we were left with the uneasy, nagging feeling that the retirement of these three players would leave a void impossible to fill. Their contribution was crucial in our victory in the first 50-overs game in Port Elizabeth when we won by the comfortable margin of seven wickets, but with only 16 deliveries to spare. Procter took two for 20 in his 10 overs, Richards stroked an elegant 62 and Pollock accelerated the scoring rate with 57 not out at the end — causing Chris Old to say that he was still batting as well as he had for the Rest of the World in England in 1970.

But the innings of the day had come earlier from Gooch, a Jekyll and Hyde character, quiet and charming off the field, confident, even arrogant on it. His 114 that day (14 fours and four sixes) was a superb effort, allowing the tourists to score 240 for five. He dealt very harshly with le Roux (10 overs for 70) and me (10 overs for 56).

It was the first time I had bowled to the dynamic Gooch. In 1980, in England, injury, first to him and then to me, had prevented our meeting. I had two ways of trying to get him out. The first was to try and lull him into playing a rash stroke by constantly complimenting him; the second was to exploit what I thought was a small chink in his technique. Gooch had adopted the bat-in-the-air, upright stance, invented by Tony Greig. He does not use this method to combat the fast bowlers, as most people think, but believes that it cuts down on the movement of his head as the bowler delivers while also giving him a 'two-eyed' horizontal view of the ball. My distinct impression, however, is that his first body movement is parallel with the wicket, either straight forward or straight back onto his stumps. I feel that the upright stance makes it difficult for him to get across, and into line, for deliveries outside off. So I tried the old routine of trying to draw him across his wicket by bowling progressively wider of the off-stump. It worked twice on tour, but on the first occasion he already had a century!

I wore a Springbok cap for the first time in the one-day game in Port Elizabeth. It had been 11 years since that day at Newlands when the last representative South African side had been announced, and walking on to the field in front of a capacity St George's Park crowd, excited at seeing the Springboks again, was a very proud moment.

The rest of the cricketing world, of course, was scoffing at our version of international cricket, but I found it a most invigorating experience. Suddenly provincial loyalties had vanished and support of the Springboks was the common cause. If it achieved only that, the tour was a success.

We moved on to the Wanderers for the 'test', the first played by a South African team since the tour of Bill Lawry's 1970 Australians.

I was making my test debut just one week short of my 34th birthday, and was as nervous as a 14-year-old on his first day at high school. I was given the honour of bowling the first ball but, to my horror, delivered a wide. 'I didn't realise what 12 years of isolation had done to South African cricket,' was Graeme Pollock's poker-faced comment.

My acute embarrassment was tempered, to a degree, by the wickets of Geoff Boycott and Wayne Larkins in my first spell, but that first delivery still haunts me.

I ended the test with 10 wickets — five for 25 in the first innings and five for 79 in the second — and the Press claimed that I was only the

Leaving the Wanderers with Garth le Roux after taking 10 wickets against Gooch's men in what was purportedly my 'test' debut.

third South African to achieve this feat on his international debut. To be perfectly honest, though, at no stage did I have the feeling that it was a true test match. Since that game, I have never worn my Springbok blazer for anything but team functions and official photographs. If I may be immodest, it is not that I do not feel I deserve my blazer. But, as something of a traditionalist, I believe a test match is a contest between two sides chosen by the controlling bodies of the countries involved. The series between Gooch's side and South Africa did not fill the bill. Others will, of course, disagree, but I feel the games against the SAB English, and the subsequent encounters against the West Indians, were not genuine test matches. If someone asks me how many test wickets I have taken, my reply is none. And how ironic that is. Kippy Smith has already taken two!

I nevertheless gained an enormous amount of enjoyment playing in the Springbok side and, of course, it was the next best thing to test cricket.

The Wanderers encounter, which we won by eight wickets, produced the only result in the three-match series. With the South African top-order in brilliant form—Richards (66), Cook (114), Kirsten (88) and Pollock (64 not out)—we compiled 400 for seven declared and bowled the English XI out for 150 and 283, in spite of a responsible innings of 109 by Gooch.

I had a particularly pleasing opening spell in the second innings and, although I did not take a wicket, I beat Boycott consistently outside the off-stump. Later I was a shade lucky to have him given out leg-before for 39 in the second innings. He felt, with some justification, that the ball might have been going down the leg-side. He and Gooch had added 119 in an opening stand as the tourists battled to save the match, and he was more than a little annoyed at his dismissal.

Some 25 minutes later we went to tea, and I was having a rub-down in the physiotherapist's room when a disgusted and angry Boycott came in with a bucket filled with ice and water, and threw the contents all over me. I shouted at Gooch to remove 'this maniac' from the room which he duly did. Five minutes later Boycott was back, but this time to tell me that he thought my opening spell 'had been a great piece of bowling'. That contradictory behaviour was typical of him.

I found Boycott an intriguing personality. I first met him when he was playing for Northern Transvaal, and Natal went up to Berea Park for a Gillette Cup match. He made 45, but he was later overshadowed by Natal's Barry Richards who struck a splendid century in 80 minutes. As Northern Transvaal were leaving the field at tea, with Richards in his seventies, Tiger Lance, playing for Northerns at the time, said to Boycott, 'This Richards is going to be a bloody good player when he grows up.' Boycott, not one to hand out unnecessary plaudits to a batting rival, replied, 'Well, he only played two good shots.' 'Yes,' retorted Lance, 'I thought you would like the two forward defensives he played at the start.'

There was much debate in the seventies about who was the best

The Wanderers during the first 'test'. A disconsolate Geoff Boycott starts the long walk back to the change-rooms after I had trapped him in front in the second innings. He was unhappy with the decision as I found to my discomfort minutes later.

opening batsman in world cricket — Boycott or Richards. The dedicated Boycott is committed to staying at the crease and, as the record book shows, his achievements are remarkable. Richards, the perfect technician, played with a relaxed charm and grace, but lacked the single-mindedness of Boycott when it came to methodically accruing runs.

The series gave belated recognition to many of our leading cricketers of the late seventies. Ray Jennings was rated by a humble Alan Knott as the best wicket-keeper in the world, and Alan Kourie, an accurate left-arm spinner, an obdurate middle-order batsman and a superb slip fielder, confirmed his prowess as an all-rounder supreme. Jimmy Cook, too, looked a world-class player with three half-centuries and one hundred in seven innings against the tourists.

But it was the emergence of Stephen Jefferies, undoubtedly the most exciting fast bowling prospect we have seen in this country for many years, which particularly pleased me. Stephen is a very ambitious bowler. Not for him the shackles of containment, the desire to simply bowl line and length, and the patient wait for the batsman to err, but rather the sheer enjoyment and joy of bowling the perfect swinging yorker or the testing bouncer. He is energetic and strong, but perhaps lacks one quality — tight control. Apart from Mike Procter, South Africa had no swing bowlers of any note in the seventies, and Jefferies' movement through the air has been particularly effective in domestic cricket.

We won the second limited-over outing at Kingsmead by the comfortable margin of 79 runs, and the real excitement of the tour was crowded into the last few minutes of the third and final game at the Wanderers. South Africa made 243 for five, but after lengthy breaks for rain, the English XI's target was reduced to 112 in 23 overs, irrespective of how many wickets they lost. With two overs to go, the match was reaching a wonderful climax. Wayne Larkins and Dennis Amiss were at the wicket with 21 wanted off 12 balls and seven wickets in hand. Le Roux, in the penultimate over, bowled Larkins with his first delivery and Geoff Humpage took a single off the next. I was fielding at long-leg and Amiss flicked the third towards me. I lost it in the gloom, vaguely moved five metres to my left, and then watched the ball cross the ropes where I had just been standing. Amiss then cracked two sixes off le Roux and 17 runs had come off the over.

A gleeful Arnold Sidebottom, with Alan Knott making a considerable contribution, picks up the prize wicket of Graeme Pollock for 3 in the 50-over international at the Wanderers.

The tourists wanted only four for victory off the last over and, it seemed, they would win with a couple of deliveries to spare. I was determined to make amends for my fielding lapse but the ball was wet and all I could do was attempt a series of yorkers on the leg-stump. Humpage missed the first two and was bowled by the third. My fourth delivery was rightly called a wide and the fifth brought a leg-bye off Knott's pad. Two balls remained, two runs were wanted. Amiss swung at the first, top-edged it and Jennings made 30 metres towards third man to take an excellent pressure catch over his shoulder. Arnold Sidebottom, needing two runs off the last ball of the match, squeezed it down to third man and turned for a second run, but Richards, who had come off the fence before the ball was bowled, threw in well and he was run out. South Africa had won by 0,03 of a run.

I was feeling rather pleased with myself as I walked up the long Wanderers steps to the dressing-room. Waiting at the top was my wife, Bev, and her first words were, 'You couldn't even let them win one game, could you.' And down to earth I came with a bump.

The tour proved a wonderful success, but it ended on a disquieting note with the English players banned from test cricket for three years. Mike Procter made a telling comment: 'Billy Beaumont leads the British Lions rugby side to South Africa and gets an OBE; Graham Gooch brings out an English cricket side and gets banned for three years.'

We did not get the expected capacity crowds during the tour, but widespread television coverage ensured that cricket was taken into homes throughout South Africa, and this did much to heighten interest generally.

When my father retired from teaching, he took up the post of director of coaching in the Western Province. It was just after the whitewash of the Australians by the 1970 Springboks under Ali Bacher, and interest in cricket was at fever pitch. In the space of a few weeks he was telephoned by 14 different Afrikaans schools in the Western Cape, all wanting to introduce their pupils to the game and asking for assistance. Four years later only two of those 14 schools were still playing cricket; a sign of what isolation had done to quash enthusiasm at a time when South Africa had arguably the strongest side in the world.

Isolation hits cricket at every level. At the top, the removal of a Springbok cap takes away some of the burning ambition which helps many cricketers attain new heights. No longer is there the incentive to encourage the struggling player through the rough period of his career. The general apathy pervades the whole game as fewer young cricketers continue playing after school, club attendances suffer, and crowds dwindle at club and provincial matches. At grass-root level, the lack of interest is felt by the young boys who have no heroes to emulate, no inclination to stage their own Currie Cup games. Test matches in the backyard also feel the effects of isolation.

The ICC countries, happily gorging themselves on a feast of test cricket and careful not to drop South Africa a crumb of encouragement, were outraged that the SACU should dare to go out in search of their own sustenance. The rebel tours have left South Africa further than ever from international acceptance, but the SACU did achieve its objective — to rejuvenate cricket in this country.

The tour ushered in a period of cricket mania in South Africa which hit a high-water mark with the arrival of the West Indians.

In 1982 the SACU made their annual pilgrimage to Lord's, but it came as no surprise when the delegates were refused a hearing. The

Practising my breakdancing with Les Taylor in a Johannesburg nightspot.

The first rebels 161

reaction of the new president, Mr Pamensky, was equally predictable. He declared that South Africans would go ahead and fend for themselves.

The cloak-and-dagger method of recruitment entered its second phase almost immediately when Tony Opatha, a former Sri Lankan bowler, who was playing his cricket in Holland, approached Pamensky in London and offered to bring a party of his countrymen to South Africa. Pamensky, with Bacher and Dakin who were also in London for the ICC meeting, flew to Rotterdam to meet Opatha and details of the tour were hammered out.

The tour was later to be overshadowed by the dramatic arrival in South Africa of Lawrence Rowe's West Indians. But, as a number of West Indians later admitted, the Sri Lankans paved the way for their tour.

On the eve of the planned six-week trip, the story broke in Colombo that 14 players had signed contracts to visit South Africa and, with the news that the cricketers' passports were to be impounded, Pamensky announced that the tour had been cancelled. The threat was

Former Springbok spin bowler Atholl McKinnon, the fun-loving liaison man of first the Arosa Sri Lankans and then the West Indians, was a highly popular and amusing personality. Here he shakes hands with Jerry Woutersz at Jan Smuts Airport as Anura Ranasinghe, Ajith de Silva, Bernard Perera, Lanthra Fernando, Lalith Kaluperuma and Bandula de Silva look on. McKinnon died suddenly of a heart attack in Durban while accompanying the second West Indian tour.

162 *Cricket in the Shadows*

not carried out, however, and the players slipped out of the country, flying via Hong Kong to South Africa and a warm welcome.

The party included five regular test cricketers, and three other top players were to join up after the official Sri Lankan tour of Zimbabwe. Even after a 25-year ban of the tourists had been announced by their Board of Control, the three were still keen to come to South Africa. However, they wanted to be paid in full for the tour, although they would be in the country for only three weeks, and the SACU, already suffering a considerable financial loss, refused to meet their demands.

The tourists, led by Bandula Warnapura, were not a strong side, winning only one of their 15 matches and that against a social side in the opening match. They lost all four limited-over encounters and both four-day 'tests'.

The Sri Lankans battled to come to terms with the Springbok pace attack. Here skipper Bandula Warnapura is uncomfortable against a short-pitched delivery. Warnapura, the most experienced and technically capable of their batsmen, had a disappointing tour.

South African opening batsmen, in particular, enjoyed the tour, hitting 10 of the 13 centuries scored against the Sri Lankans. Jimmy Cook struck four hundreds in six innings and Lawrence Seeff compiled centuries in each of his three matches. One was scored in the four-day international, and Seeff, under contract not to make statements to the Press, was fined by the SACU for modestly pointing out that it was not a genuine test.

Disappointing though the strength of the opposition was, it enabled the Springboks to start moulding a side. The Sri Lankans, even though they had lost the opportunity to play test cricket, were well satisfied with the tour, their financial terms and the experience of playing against top-class opposition. Opatha told me that, apart from the money, one of the deciding factors in touring was the opportunity of playing against the likes of Barry Richards and Graeme Pollock, household names in Sri Lankan cricket.

Ajith de Silva arrived in South Africa with a reputation as a world-class spinner. He was the pillar around which their attack was to be built, but the heavy reliance that the Sri Lankans placed on him, and the daunting prospect of having to contain several world-class batsmen on his own, proved too much. He had a disastrous tour, at times even refusing to bowl.

Not surprisingly, the one-sided matches were not well-attended by the public, but it was a happy tour, free of incident and the Sri Lankans proved popular and charming visitors.

Pamensky said, 'the tour will prove a milestone in South African cricket history.' He must have known something—in January the West Indians arrived.

The men behind the West Indian tour. Dr Ali Bacher, Gregory Armstrong and Joe Pamensky in discussion.

The exuberance of the West Indians. Ray Wynter slips as he is about to deliver his first delivery in the second 'test' at the Wanderers. Emmerson 'ET' Trotman is delighted while umpire Mitchley appears more concerned about possible damage to the wicket.

CHAPTER ELEVEN

The West Indians

I made my Currie Cup debut for Natal in the summer of 1968–69, only weeks after the South African Goverment had cancelled the England tour because of Basil D'Oliveira's inclusion; 14 years later, in my last season in first-class cricket, teams from first Sri Lanka and then the West Indies were welcomed with open arms to South Africa. The unthinkable had happened.

For five weeks in January and February, 1983, South Africa went cricket crazy as a party of 16 West Indians caught the imagination of the public, breaking through the clouds which 12 years of isolation had left hanging over our cricket. And, just as the gifted American Negro sportsman and musician had softened racial attitudes in the United States, so the West Indian cricketer made an impact on traditional South African thinking. The tourists were in South Africa to play cricket and earn a living, but in doing so they helped in the battle against apartheid. Appropriately, they ended their tour with a social game in Welkom, in the heart of Afrikanerdom, and the heavens did not fall.

The tour was a massive break-through for the SACU; the realisation of an impossible dream as the cavalier West Indians, with their extravagant, flamboyant style, delighted the crowds, and severely taxed the cricketers who opposed them. And how ironic that a tour, impossible during South Africa's test-playing days, had become a reality through a combination of isolation and money.

The tour was masterminded by Joe Pamensky and Ali Bacher, in conjunction with Barbadian Gregory Armstrong who accompanied the party as manager. Armstrong had visited South Africa secretly in 1982 to examine the situation first hand. The pioneering tour of the Sri Lankans, and the happy summer Alvin Kallicharran had spent with Transvaal the previous year, were important factors in convincing him that the West Indians could tour successfully.

Coming to South Africa was a courageous step for the West Indians. Their captain, Lawrence Rowe, told me of a visit he had from one of his friends in government who tried to persuade him from going to the land of apartheid. When Rowe indicated his intention to continue with the planned tour, his friend said, 'Lawrence, I urge you not to go. There's a possibility that when you land, you'll be shot on the runway.' Rowe told of the hush which fell over the players an hour before they reached Jan Smuts Airport, and the immense relief on landing when they realised that their fears were unfounded.

The man who held the West Indians together, respected skipper Lawrence Rowe.

The West Indians

Rowe, influential and respected, was the key player in the West Indian team. West Indian success had always been dependent on a captain who could weld individual brilliance into a cohesive unit while also overcoming inter-island rivalries. Sir Frank Worrell and, later, Clive Lloyd succeeded in generating team spirit while Gary Sobers, the world's greatest all-rounder, never created the same harmony.

The task facing Rowe was arguably the most taxing ever faced by a West Indian captain. Not only had he to marshal men uncertain of their future, ostracised by their governments and condemned by their friends, but he had to do so in foreign territory, under an independent flag, without the support of his controlling body or the rallying call of nationalism. Rowe did this with dignity and direction, and the tourists shared the series in 1983 and returned the next summer to beat the South Africans convincingly. Rowe showed only glimpses of his immense batting skills. He had scored a century and double century in his test

Beating and bowling a bemused Lawrence Rowe (0) in the first innings of the Wanderers test. Umpire Mitchley and Alvin Kallicharran look on.

debut against New Zealand and, as one of the few West Indians to play in the classic mould, he was rated by some of his countrymen as technically the most correct batsman to come out of the islands. Later in his career, a problem with eyesight, injury and a strange allergy to grass hampered his progress.

The West Indians were not a test team, but they were of test standard and, had Desmond Haynes and Malcolm Marshall joined them, as was widely anticipated, the team would have been exceptionally powerful.

Their determination to succeed was obvious, and they took tremendous pride in their cricket. Colin Croft, who has the greatest test strike rate of any West Indian bowler and is not given to showering praise on other pacemen, described Sylvester Clarke's spell of seven for 34 in the second test at the Wanderers as 'the most devastating I have ever seen'.

This was not a team thrown loosely together, and the spirit under Rowe remained excellent throughout. Individually, the players were keen to reveal their skills, and they cared deeply about their performance. Bernard Julien, warm and friendly, admitted to Bev and me at a cocktail party after the first test at Newlands that he had actually cried in private when he heard he had been omitted from the test side.

Though banished by their board, and disowned by their friends, Rowe's men proved splendid ambassadors for West Indian cricket. Their style is unique. Had South African cricketers rushed around hugging each other and rolling on the ground, there would have been disapproving murmurs about exhibitionism. With the West Indians, it was part of their magic. When they arrived 30 minutes late for the start of one game — 'the heavy traffic!' — it was accepted as 'typically West Indian' and quickly dismissed.

With the exception of Julien, Croft, Kallicharran and Rowe, the tourists were shy and reticent off the field, which contrasted sharply with their wildly flamboyant approach out in the middle. At cocktail parties, they were expected to be lively and amusing, and people found it strange that they should keep to themselves. These cricketing extroverts were social introverts. The tour was hurriedly put together which meant that an enormous amount of cricket was played in a short space of time. There were 10 one-day games — six against the Springboks — and two four-day tests in less than a month.

It was hectic, exciting and exhausting, both physically and mentally. It was also incident-free, though on one occasion, at least, luck and a quick-thinking young lady averted a potentially ugly occurrence. A West Indian was seeing a White girl to her car after a function one evening when she discovered she had locked her keys inside. With the aid of a wire coat hanger, he opened the car door. While he was busy with the hanger, a member of the South African Police arrived and after the keys had been handed over, he turned to the West Indian and said, 'Okay, now get to bed, tsotsi (mischief-maker).' 'What's a tsotsi?' the West Indian asked the girl. 'It means mate,' she quickly replied.

While the West Indians were constantly followed by doting crowds and besieged by autograph-hunters, nothing could be taken for granted in South Africa. Dave Dyer, the former Transvaal captain, was helping Trevor Quirk with the television commentary. Franklyn Stephenson, the talented West Indian all-rounder, was signing autographs across the fine-leg fence between overs when the cameras panned on him. 'I see Stephenson is being kept busy signing autographs,' said Quirk, and Dyer, spotting an attractive blonde in the group around Stephenson, added, 'And I'm sure picking up a few phone numbers.' SATV's telephone lines were busy for the next half-hour as irate viewers called in to object.

Alvin Kallicharran was the first West Indian I bowled to in South Africa. It was at Kingsmead the previous summer when Natal beat Transvaal on a greentop for only the third time in my Currie Cup career. The highest individual score in the match was Mike Procter's 55, but Kallicharran had batted well in making scores of 24 and 29 in difficult conditions. In his second innings, he was showing his particular penchant for hitting deliveries of a good length over mid-wicket for one-bounce fours. The third time he did it to me I said, 'You can't do that. That was a good ball,' he gave me a big grin. 'It's the bad balls that normally get me,' he replied.

His style of play epitomises the West Indian approach. Without the shackles of traditional coaching manuals, they allow their natural individualism free rein. Kallicharran produces shots which few South Africans would ever think of playing and does so with regularity. He told me how he had learnt his cricket in the streets with a rubber ball and a bat carved out of a tree branch. He and his friends had no coaching and used to listen avidly to John Arlott commentating on their test heroes, Gary Sobers and Rohan Kanhai. (The first time he saw Kanhai bat was when he joined him at the wicket on his test debut.) He and his friends used to try and visualize the shots Arlott was describing, and then rush out into the streets and attempt to reproduce them.

I asked Kallicharran who had taught him to play his defensive strokes. He explained that with the high-bouncing rubber ball on tarmac, and numerous fielders clustered round the batsman, it was natural and essential to angle the bat, in classic defensive manner, to keep the ball down. For the first time, the logic of cricket was brought home to me. Here was a man who had never been coached, yet he performed all the basics of the game correctly, and never at the expense of his own individual flair.

Kallicharran revolutionised my thinking on coaching. We had travelled to Welkom for a double-wicket competition and spent the previous day coaching local schoolchildren. I had a youngster in my net who could play a magnificent square-cut, but constantly backed away to leg to play it, and he was obviously in trouble against any ball pitched

A typical Alvin Kallicharran stroke, working a delivery of good length through mid-wicket.

up on the stumps. I was at a loss as to what to do with him and called Kallicharran across from an adjacent net. He immediately praised the youngster for his square cut and encouraged him to play it more often. Then, almost in passing, he mentioned that if the ball was pitched up he should move into line. He was nurturing individual flair but, at the same time, teaching some of the basics.

There is that old expression, 'conformity breeds mediocrity'. In South Africa we have always been inclined to follow the English pattern of coaching and have not produced the variety of cricketers that flow endlessly from the West Indies. Kallicharran's style of play, his method of coaching and his uninhibited approach to the game are typically West Indian, natural and invigorating.

Media speculation during the Sri Lankan and West Indian tours centred on who should captain South Africa. Mike Procter, who had suffered a severe head injury in a fall, was out of contention, and Peter Kirsten and Clive Rice were the leading challengers. They both had short track records as captain, yet both had enjoyed early success. Rice had just led Nottinghamshire to their first county championship title in 53 years, but his previous season with Transvaal had been largely unproductive, with victory achieved in only one of the five major competitions, the Benson and Hedges Night Series. Kirsten, by contrast, had taken over the captaincy of Western Province from Eddie Barlow, had guided his side to their first Currie Cup and Datsun Shield double.

For the one-sided 'tests' against the Sri Lankans, Kirsten was appointed captain — I thought deservedly — and retained for the series against the West Indians. Rice, of course, was to go on and lead Transvaal to their historic five-trophy, grand slam that season, and that fuelled the captaincy controversy for the second West Indian tour in 1983–84.

Rice is an uncompromising player, a fierce competitor and a highly respected opponent. I remember him once beating me outside the off-stump with a magnificent delivery and, as he followed through, I said, 'Well bowled.' 'Too good for you,' he muttered and stalked back to his mark. His next ball cut back sharply and hit me painfully on the inside thigh. 'That's better,' he chuckled. There was humour in his remark, but there was also a hint of toughness, a competitiveness which I respect in an opponent. He seems to delight in provoking a love/hate relationship with the crowd, particularly at Kingsmead and Newlands, and often, when bowling, harnesses their vocal reaction to unsettle the batsman.

A neck injury prevented Rice bowling against the Sri Lankans and the West Indians in 1982–83, and there were calls for his head from critics who thought he did not deserve his place on his batting ability alone. He was dropped after the two tests, missing the first four limited-over internationals, but returned for the fifth at the Wanderers, making a typically gritty 35 before being run out.

He has the ability to turn a match, revitalise a dying game and, as an all-rounder in the Eddie Barlow mould, he always leads from the front. He does, however, hide his sensitivity under a hard outer shell — reacting to press criticism as though he has not even read the morning newspaper. He keeps his thoughts to himself and, as a player under him, I occasionally found this disconcerting. I would want to understand, not only what he wanted me to do, but his intentions also. The inner 'feel' in a relationship between captain and player is, I believe, crucial.

I also found that Rice, as a bowler himself, had very firm ideas on my field-placings. At times I was uncomfortable bowling to fields that I thought did not suit me. He always knew when I was unhappy about it, but possibly felt my anger would lift my performance. He will no doubt remember a game against Eastern Province when I was bowling to Mike van Vuuren. He came up and told me he was moving from mid-off into a second gully position, and instructed me to bowl a ball short of a length on off-stump. I did as he asked, and Rice took a good catch to end the game. As we walked off, Rice laughed at me and said, 'I'm not so bloody stupid, am I?'

Rice drives his players hard, forcing them to compete at all times, and he never gives anything away to the opposition. This, simply, is his philosophy as a captain. I occasionally found his authoritarian approach unsettling, though he always put the team first. I do believe, however, that individual needs and aspirations have to be encouraged in the team effort.

Peter Kirsten is another gutsy and uncompromising player, but is quieter than Rice, possibly because he cannot show his raw aggression by bowling fast. His batting is neat and compact; the rapier and not the bludgeon is used. His agility, quick eye and full range of strokes make him a superb batsman. If he had been a golfer, he would have been known as a 'touch player'. His courage was tested by Sylvester Clarke and Ezra Moseley on numerous occasions during the two West Indian tours, and was not found wanting.

The task that confronted Kirsten was a tough one. Taking over a side which contained older, far more experienced players, such as Richards and Pollock, could not have been easy. They gave him full support, but captaining boyhood heroes did place him in a vulnerable position.

Results are often taken as the true test of a captain. But judging an event with the benefit of hindsight is often unfair. Mike Brearley once remarked that a decision is often criticised because it did not produce the desired result. But, as he points out, the alternative available to the captain at the time could well have had far more disastrous consequences. The captain must have an overall strategy and work towards it, and tight decisions must be taken with this plan in mind.

The danger to a young captain is that he might be swayed in his decision-making by the people he respects. Sometimes this will deflect him from his match strategy, and I believe this occasionally happened to Kirsten.

He was thrust into the hot seat without the apprenticeship necessary to bolster his confidence. The responsibility was awesome, and it was with trepidation that he took over command. His normal confident approach became tentative. He was honest enough to realise that he was a relatively inexperienced captain, but this seemed to weigh heavily on his mind.

The last afternoon of the first test at Newlands was a difficult one for the Springboks and Kirsten. The two previous rebel tours to South Africa — by the SAB English and the Sri Lankans — had produced one-sided cricket, and the crowds came to watch the West Indians in the hope of seeing an even contest rather than a Springbok walk-over. In addition, the West Indians, who had effectively put an end to their international careers by undertaking the tour, enjoyed enormous public sympathy and support. The atmosphere at the games was not one of a home crowd willing their team on to victory and, as far as I am concerned, it was this factor which helped distinguish these games from test matches. The result was that when the Springboks overcame West Indian opposition, the crowds did not acknowledge a fine victory and this left the side feeling deflated.

Years before, Procter and Pollock had told me of the thrill of playing in a test match, the excitement as you walked through the

The changing faces and moods of Peter Kirsten:

Happy and genial, he and Lawrence Rowe prepare to toss before the first test at Newlands in Cape Town.

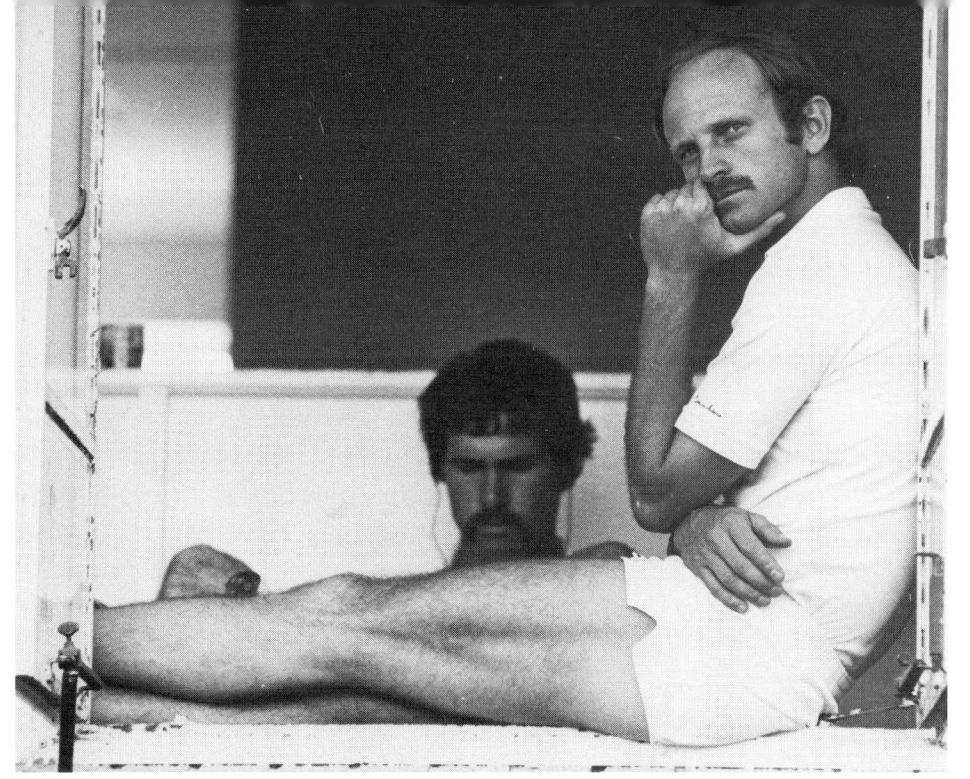

An anxious Kirsten in the Wanderers change-room while Jimmy Cook listens to his music.

The pressure tells? Kirsten kicks a stump after an attempt to run him out in the day/night game at the start of the second Windies tour.

mingling throngs outside the ground, the nervousness as start of play approached and the roar from the elated crowd when you took a wicket or struck a boundary. They also spoke of the packed dressing-room at the end of a successful test, when everyone who was linked to the Springbok side, from administrators down, came in to celebrate victory and drink champagne.

For the Springboks, those moments after the Newlands match were a massive letdown. We were already disappointed by the lack of support from the rows of spectators while we were out in the middle, and then we did not see an administrator for at least an hour after play ended. Our change-room was certainly not the bubbling, happy place it would have been after a test match victory. This impression was confirmed less than a week later when a top administrator came into the dressing-room after we had lost the second test at the Wanderers and said that he was glad the West Indians had won. 'It's good for cricket,' he added. He would never have said that after a genuine test. In the post-match interview with the Press at Newlands, skipper Peter Kirsten voiced our feelings. He said that the Springboks were not getting the credit and encouragement from the Press and public which they deserved. His remarks were judged to be untimely and selfish, particularly as the tourists had sacrificed so much in coming to South Africa.

Perhaps a Procter or a Bacher would have been more diplomatic, but the tenor of their remarks would have been the same. From this moment, pressures on Kirsten increased and the road to his eventual demise as Springbok captain had begun. Kirsten was in an invidious position for, by expressing the feelings of the Springboks, he further alienated public and media support. He continued to bat with great courage and emerged from the West Indian tours as a more confident batsman, but an uncertain captain.

It was a tough year for him and, by the end of the season, the pressures on him were almost unbearable. I do not believe that he was quite ready for the task, or that he was ideally suited to it, but he was the best man available at the time.

The controversy over the Springbok captaincy continued the following season (1983–4) when the West Indians returned.

I had retired but felt very strongly at the time of the second West Indian tour that there was only one man who could lead the

Springboks — Mike Procter. He was indisputably the most experienced captain in South Africa and, with the increased strength of the West Indians, the Springboks needed the best available captain to marshal their forces. I did not agree with the argument that the appointment of Procter would have been a backward step, and that the selectors had to build for the future. The captain should be the best available at the time, and the man being primed to take over should fill the role of vice-captain. Of course, in the South African context, we did not know where the future lay. I believe in the English system of picking a captain first, and then the rest of the team. The wisdom of this had been shown in 1981 when the England selectors recalled Mike Brearley — with telling effect — for the series against Australia. The Australians, in contrast, pick their 11 players first and then look around for the most suitable captain. South Africa needed the strength and confidence of Procter, and his appointment would have allowed both Kirsten and Rice to concentrate on their own performances which were crucial to a struggling Springbok side.

After leading the Springboks to their impressive 10-wicket win at Newlands, Kirsten was axed as captain. It was a severe blow for him. The pressure to drop him as captain had increased since Rice had led Transvaal to their unprecedented clean sweep of the major trophies. This inspired doubt in the selectors' minds whether they had made the right choice from the very beginning. Rice took over, and the strong drive of the Transvaal skipper seemed to give the Springboks more urgency.

It was a testing two seasons for both Kirsten and Rice and, while they came out with individual credit, the captaincy problem has still to be satisfactorily resolved.

The two four-day games against the West Indies in 1982–83 were the closest I came to the real thing — test cricket.

The Springboks overcame intense West Indian pressure to win the first four-day match at Newlands by five wickets. Again it was the presence of the old guard, Barry Richards and Graeme Pollock, which gave the whole side confidence.

Richards, at 37, and Pollock, who was to turn 39 a fortnight after the tour ended, were under close surveillance during the tour. How would they cope with genuinely fast bowling after years in the wilderness? Their response was characteristic, and typical of the world-class players they had become. Both had the same approach, to carry the game to the West Indians and prevent their fast bowlers dominating. This aggressive attitude rubbed off on others in the team, Alan Kourie, in particular.

In making 49 in an opening stand of 85 with Jimmy Cook, Richards gave his opening partner an invaluable boost and set the mood for the innings. The sharp edge had returned as Richards hooked, cut and drove with precision. But the day belonged to Pollock who produced an amazing innings, considering he had not faced bowling that fast for many years. His hooking of Moseley as he strode to a superb century was devastating. In the second test at the Wanderers, I had moments of doubt about Pollock. South Africa were eight for three, Clarke was cutting the ball viciously away from the left-hander, and I thought Graeme would never reach double figures. I should never have doubted him and he batted with great courage and charm to make 73.

Richards and Pollock take pride in their ability, and the opinions expressed by some in the media that they were too old to handle the West Indian quick bowlers were enough to spur them to several remarkable innings. The pressure on them was colossal with the public expecting consistently high scores every time they went to the wicket. One evening Pollock said to me wearily, 'I'm getting too old for this game.' Yet he and Richards continued to set a wonderful example to the rest of the side throughout the series.

The other hero on the opening day of the first test was Cook, who went on to make 73 and survived what can only be termed a 'death' ball. Ezra Mosely bowled a vicious bouncer which Cook, without a helmet, did not seem to pick up, and only a quick and late movement of his head —the reflex of a first division footballer? — enabled him to evade a delivery which seemed certain to strike him on the temple. Cook batted on resolutely, but never again was he to go in against the West Indian pacemen without a helmet. Kourie chipped in with 69 and South Africa made 449. I picked up four wickets and Kourie three as we bowled the Windies out for 246 and then Jefferies (four for 58) did most of the damage as they reached 309 in their follow-on innings.

The Springboks needed only 107 to win, but there were signs of rough seas ahead when barrel-chested Sylvester Clarke bowled throughout the innings to take two for 22 in 15 overs. A stabilising innings of 43 not out by Pollock took us through to a five-wicket win.

There was some marvellous cricket played. The first shots in a fascinating duel between Jefferies and the unorthodox hitter Collis King were fired in this match. Jefferies bowled King with a swinging yorker for 13, and the Springbok opener was to dismiss him a further three times during the tour with this type of delivery. Near the end of the tour, Gregory Armstong told me of a night when he was sharing with King and awoke to hear his room-mate shouting, 'I'll hit you for four, man, I'll hit you for four, Stephen.'

Newlands during the first 'test'. Collis King is yorked by Stephen Jefferies. The clash between these two provided one of the highlights of the tour — and gave Collis nightmares.

I had one particularly pleasing spell in the first innings at Newlands, dismissing Kallicharran, Rowe and King in the space of four overs. King had come in and scored 19 in just six balls and, with the first delivery I bowled to him, he attempted to hit me over extra cover, edged it and was caught behind by Ray Jennings. It had been a brief but belligerent innings, full of violent blows. I walked down the wicket and said to Jennings, 'With that approach, I'm not surprised he has not played in more tests for the West Indies. He's just a slogger.' Unprophetic words, those, as King alone stood between the Springboks and victory at the Wanderers three days later when he held us up with a magnificent 101 in the first innings and a brave 39 despite a high fever in the second.

Sport does have the nasty habit of making you eat your words. Neil Adcock tells how, in the 1960 series against England, he consistently dismissed Colin Cowdrey. In the final test he had bowled Cowdrey and, as he walked out, Adcock tapped him on the shoulder and said, 'You're my bunny.' In the second innings Cowdrey made 155! Mike Brearley recalls how, at the start of the England-Australian Series in 1981, Ian Botham disparagingly referred to Lillee as 'only a medium-pacer now'. Lillee was to take Botham's wicket five times in the tests.

Clarke had worried the Springbok top order in the second innings at Newlands, but none of us was prepared for the devastation he was to cause on the high-bouncing Wanderers wicket.

Like Les Taylor in the SAB English side a year previously, Clarke grew in stature as the tour progressed. Kirsten, already having problems with the Press and the public, had his confidence further undermined by Clarke, who seemed to delight in bowling the Springbok captain a series of unplayable deliveries. But, of course, Kirsten was not the only South African to be troubled by the brooding West Indian.

Clarke was deceptive throughout. His shambling, almost unathletic run-up disguised the aggressiveness and ferocity of his bowling. He had the uncanny ability to swing the ball in prodigiously at great pace, and then bowl a vicious leg-cutter at will. He had the added knack of bowling at three different paces without changing his approach to the wicket. Alan Kourie, who made 69 in the first test at Newlands, waited patiently for 45 minutes to ensure that he had the pace of the wicket and the bowling before attempting to hook. Unfortunately, he chose

Clarke's quickest delivery to hook, and had just started his stroke when the ball whistled passed his ear.

Clarke's extra pace, which he is able to generate seemingly without effort, had led many in England and South Africa to believe that he threw his quicker delivery. Not that anyone would want to say that to his face!

Barrel-chested Sylvester Clarke during his remarkable, match-winning spell at the Wanderers.

The second test was a great disappointment to the Springboks. It was a fluctuating contest, but we played ourselves into an excellent position on the last day only to have Clarke, in a dynamic spell of seven for 34 in 22 overs, snatch a 28-run victory. Alan Kourie, with six for 55, destroyed the West Indian first innings, and only a splendid King century enabled them to reach 267. Clarke struck back immediately, dismissing Richards (0) and nightwatchman Jennings (0) while Stephenson grabbed the wicket of Cook, also before he had scored, to leave South Africa 8 for three. Kirsten (56) and Pollock (73) bravely added 114 for the fourth wicket and we eventually reached 233.

Pollock again batted beautifully and showed his great worth to the side. He had a wonderful run of scores in the series — 100, 43 not out, 73 and 1. He was highly respected by the West Indians who referred to him as 'The Man'. That evening Clarke said to me, 'I just wish I had seen him play in his prime.'

The West Indians collapsed to 77 for seven in their second innings before an indisposed King with 39 lifted them to 176. South Africa needed 201 to win and, when Richards (59) and Cook (27) added 87 for the first wicket, it looked a doddle. But Clarke, bristling with menace, tore through the Springbok batting line-up and eight wickets were down for 124. Jefferies (31), before he was run out, and Kevin McKenzie (26 not out) took the score to 179, but we finally lost by 29 runs and the series was squared at 1–1.

The West Indians travelled down to Durban, where Mike Procter plotted their 84-run defeat in a one-day game against Natal, and we then embarked on a whirlwind nine days which included six limited-over internationals spread throughout the country.

A century by Richards, and Pollock's 66 not out, including 20 off Clarke's final over after he had been struck on the forearm, gave us a 91-run win in Port Elizabeth. Cape Town brought us a 43-run victory, but we squeaked home by only 12 runs in Pretoria. We made only 179 and the tourists were well-placed at 152 for seven with Stephenson on 35 and Murray on 12. I managed to trap Stephenson in front and then enjoyed bowling Clarke with a yorker for 0 after saying to him as he arrived at the wicket, 'I hope you can hook.'

We failed dismally in the night game at the Wanderers, losing by seven wickets, but the next day won by 51 runs to take a 4–1 lead in the one-day series. The match produced Rupert Hanley's startling hat-trick. Looking at his beaming face and listening to the acclaim of the crowd, I remember thinking that cricket justice was being served, and that he had finally been rewarded for his unstinting efforts. For many years he had been the backbone of the sides (Eastern Province, Griquas and Transvaal) he played in, often underrated by public and opposition, and yet a constant threat.

Mentally and physically drained, the players were whisked off to Durban for the final game — the third in a night and two days — and we were soundly thumped by 84 runs as Stephenson returned the incredible figures of six for 9 to bowl us out for 71.

So ended the historic tour, a remarkable five weeks which briefly turned many South Africans colour blind. The wheel of South African cricket had turned full circle since those early days of the walk-off. Gone was the all-White South African Cricket Association, gone was the window-dressing, gone was selection purely on race.

Sir Stanley Matthews, the legendary England soccer player who now coaches in Soweto, said after the West Indian tour, that for the first time young Black children were throwing away their soccer togs and taking up the game of cricket. The West Indian impact in South Africa was enormous. Cricket fever returned, kids were out playing in the streets, the bowlers charging in off long runs, 'like Sylvester'. The West Indians had stimulated interest in the game to a level last seen during the 1970 Australian tour.

Sport has a unique ability to cross barriers, whether they be religious, political or racial. My greatest moment as a spectator was watching Errol Tobias, the Coloured flyhalf playing in the Springbok rugby team, score his lovely try in the corner during the second international against the 1984 English tourists. It was a moving, emotional experience and one I will never forget.

Fitting, perhaps, that the last word on the tour should come from a West Indian. Al Gilkes, editor of *The Sun*, in Bridgetown, Barbados, was the only West Indian newspaperman to accompany the tour party.

He called the tourists '18 black missionaries', not the mercenaries the world was calling them.

'What the South African journalists and public dubbed a miracle had its most telling effect in the very last match.

'In the mining town of Welkom which, despite its name, is one of the strongest Afrikaner strongholds of the rightest wing, the barriers of

Hanley's hat-trick. The Spook is congratulated by Ray Jennings after his hat-trick in the one-day international at the Wanderers.

No disguising Hanley's delight.

racial discrimination fell down hard that day under the feet of the West Indians.' He concluded, 'The eighteen sad faces that boarded the aircraft at Jan Smuts Airport when it was all over, were glum, not because they were leaving South Africa, but because they knew that the world outside, having not been there to witness their miracle, would never believe or understand.'

An encouraging sign for the future. Youngsters followed the West Indians wherever they went. Here Alvin Kallicharran is greeted by his fans at the Wanderers.

CHAPTER TWELVE

The end of the road

The 1981–82 season — my last in Natal — was a see-saw affair; the pleasure of several excellent victories mixed with the despair of severe setbacks.

Our moments of unbridled joy were crowded into one week when we beat Transvaal three times — winning the second-leg Datsun Shield semi-final by eight runs to cancel out our first-round Wanderers loss, the mid-week play-off by three wickets and the Currie Cup encounter by two wickets. These tense, entertaining matches, played at Kingsmead in front of huge crowds, were low-scoring affairs, only three half-centuries — by the two skippers, Clive Rice and Mike Procter, and by Chris Wilkins — being compiled in eight innings.

In the Currie Cup game, I saw for the first time the competitive side of the usually quiet and impeccably-behaved Paddy Clift. Seeking 187 for victory, Natal were battling on 149 for six, and with Rob Bentley, nursing a damaged arm, retired hurt, I joined Clift at the wicket. With 38 still needed and a rampant Rice operating in the gloom, I did not rate our chances too highly. Rice's first delivery to me flew over the middle stump as I backed away slightly to square-leg. Clift, a close friend, came down the wicket and, prodding me hard in the chest with his finger, said tersely, 'Get into line and show some guts. You're playing for the team now,' and then walked back to the non-striker's end. It gave me a severe jolt and after that I played Rice far better, adding 29 with Clift, finally seeing us home by two wickets. Clift has since taken over the captaincy of Natal—Procter stood down a couple of weeks before the end of the 1983–84 season—and the determination he revealed at the wicket suggested to me that he would be the right man to succeed Procter. Within two weeks of the appointment, Clift's Natal side had won the Benson and Hedges Trophy, beating Eastern Province in a one-sided final at the Wanderers, so following a trend set by Richards by winning the trophy in his first season as captain.

Transvaal went into this fateful week, which buried their 1981–82 Datsun Shield and Currie Cup aspirations, without the services of the injured Graeme Pollock. His sheer presence is an inspiration to his side. Acknowledging this, Mike Procter said to me after our Currie Cup win, 'If Graeme had played in these three matches, and not scored a run, I think Transvaal would still have won two of them.'

The popular Transvaal batsman Kevin McKenzie had a dreadful run in these three matches, failing to score in the two limited-over games, and making 7 and 4 in the Currie Cup game. On the final evening, as Bev and I went into the cocktail party, we found McKenzie smiling and

Kevin McKenzie enjoying his cricket against the West Indians.

joking with a couple of the Natal players. 'Look at Kevin over there,' said Bev. 'You'd have thought he had just scored 150.' That reaction of McKenzie to defeat and failure was typical. With Robbie Muzzell and Jackie du Preez, he is one of the finest sportsmen I have met. A dedicated, brave cricketer, who tries extremely hard, he never allows the pressures out in the middle to get him down. Modest and sensible, he is an outstanding ambassador for the game. When he was eventually picked to play for the Springboks against the West Indians in Cape Town, he had a disastrous debut, twice being dismissed leg-before for 4 and 0 as he swept at off-spinner Derek Parry. Both decisions looked marginal, yet Kevin never complained or showed his disappointment.

In spite of the aggressive and eager captaincy of Procter, Natal failed to wrap up victories against several of the weaker provinces and we ended third on the 1981–82 log. We failed to beat Northern Transvaal at home — the match was played at the Jan Smuts Stadium in Pietermaritzburg — and had to follow on in the drawn game against Eastern Province in Port Elizabeth. Ironically, two former Natal players frustrated us in these drawn matches, army trainee Brian Whitfield scoring 100 and 58 not out for Northern Trasvaal, and paceman Clive Wulfsohn picking up six for 18 in our first innings in Port Elizabeth.

I did not bowl well in the Northern Transvaal game, taking only one wicket, and it was felt by many Natal camp followers that I had lost too much weight. Three times during my career I went on crash diets to slim down, usually from about 115 to 105 kg, for the start of a season. On each occasion I bowled badly, and my team-mates said I was having difficulty reaching the wicket. The result was that I systematically built up my weight during the course of the season and found a corresponding improvement in my bowling form.

It was a disruptive season for me with my job taking me from Durban to Johannesburg midway. For the first three months of 1982 I lived in a hotel before the family joined me. Work pressures, and the Datsun Shield final with the Allan Lamb run out, did little for my peace of mind, and my form slumped. With the arrival of the SAB English XI in South Africa, and a heavy programme of matches scheduled for the last month of the season, my branch manager kindly told me to keep away from the office, and I found that being able to concentrate only on my cricket helped enormously.

My 100th Currie Cup game for Natal — the penultimate outing of the season — was against Northern Transvaal, in Pretoria, shortly after the arrival of Graham Gooch's men. Procter promised to rest me as much as possible before the exhausting tour matches ahead. He gave me 50 overs in two days, explaining it away by saying he wanted me half a metre shorter by the time I joined Transvaal the next season. However, those long spells did me good, and I found my old rhythm returning as I took six for 64 in Northerns' first innings and eight for 47 in the second for career-best match figures of 14 for 111. The final Currie Cup match of the season was an exciting encounter against Transvaal at the Wanderers, and it came just two days after our third and final 'test' against the English tourists. I bowled 51 overs in the match and, for the first time in my life, I went after a bowling record — Mike Procter's haul of 59 Currie Cup wickets in a season. I had to take 11 wickets in the match — my last for Natal — but picked up only nine as Transvaal, set a target of 270 runs in 200 minutes by caretaker captain Barry Richards, were steered to a three-wicket victory by a glorious Clive Rice century.

It was with a heavy heart that I saw out those last few weeks of the season. I had been involved with the province's cricket for so long that, although born in the Cape, I considered myself wholly Natalian. It was a period of farewell cocktail parties and presentations. Natal had awarded me a benefit two seasons previously, and yet, after our last home game against Eastern Province, the president of the Natal Cricket Association, Dereck Dowling, generously presented me with a cheque for R1 000. It was after this match that Bev asked me when I was going to announce my retirement. 'You're not thinking of playing for another province are you?' Such was the closeness of the Natal cricket family.

Two years later — early in 1984 — I was to hear with deep regret of the problems in the Natal camp, the retirement of Mike Procter and Tich Smith, and the disruption of the previously happy player/administrator/media relationship. Throughout his career, both in England and South Africa, Procter has been such a force in cricket. The zest, dedication and genuine love of the game that he exuded deserved more than a departure in unhappy circumstances. He should have left to a fanfare of trumpets, and not been allowed to slip out quietly, just weeks before the end of the season, citing a lack of motivation as the reason for his retirement. Smith, in his benefit year, also left on an unpleasant note, dropped after 86 Currie Cup games, a couple of one-day games short of his retirement. It was typical of these fine sportsmen that they accepted their treatment as simply part of the game. They were both at the Wanderers to watch Clift lead Natal to their Benson and Hedges triumph, and they were as excited as I was at the happy ending to what had obviously been a traumatic season.

At 34, I still thought I had at least one, and possibly two, seasons left in the game. I was to be based in Johannesburg, but thought I could best serve South Africa's cricketing interests by playing for Northern Transvaal and not Transvaal. Transvaal will always be an extraordinarily strong cricketing province because of the gravitation of people to the Reef. The province has an exceptionally large circle of cricketers to choose from and my feeling was that I had more to offer a young, struggling province like Northerns than well-equipped,

Divided loyalties? Wearing a Natal jersey at a Transvaal net practice. Alan Kourie, Graeme Pollock and Jimmy Cook in attendance.

immensely powerful Transvaal. Even TCC managing director Dr Ali Bacher, hearing of my transfer to Johannesburg, said that while he would be pleased to have me in the Transvaal team, the imbalance moves like mine were creating in the Currie Cup was not benefiting South African cricket.

Northern Transvaal had approached me many years before and offered me a contract which included the captaincy, but I had declined. Before the start of the 1982–83 season I asked if I could turn out for them, but the request was refused by the TCC.

My brief affair with Transvaal cricket (the summer of 1982–83) coincided with the most successful season in the province's history. We won every available competition — filling the Wanderers' mantelpiece with the Currie Cup, Datsun Shield, Benson and Hedges Night Series,

Jimmy Cook and Clive Rice try to cheer me up during a tense moment with Transvaal.

Computer Sciences and Protea Challenge trophies.

I found it fascinating to compare the approach and attitude of Natal and Transvaal. In the successful Natal sides I knew, there was a heavy reliance on team spirit. Teamwork was a feature of the sides led first by Barry Richards and then Mike Procter, a sense that the other ten fellows in the side wanted you to do well, which lifted your level of performance. Within the Transvaal side there was an air of confidence and cool professionalism. Their attitude at the nets and out in the middle was very similar to that found in England. As a fast bowler, I was expected to get five wickets every match. And that was the spur to greater effort. In Natal, it was less professional, but I could feel the other players willing me to take a wicket; in the Transvaal, I was simply expected to perform.

It may be that Natal's approach was the result of their youth, and professionalism develops later as a team becomes more successful and experienced. Ideally, if one could balance these two attitudes, one would have the perfect atmosphere in a cricket team.

My first outing for Transvaal was in the Computer Sciences Triangular tournament on my old home ground at Kingsmead, and I had to make an unfamiliar right turn at the top of the pavilion stairs to the visitors' dressing-room.

The Kingsmead crowd saw Clive Rice's machine roll to fairly easy victories first over Western Province and then Natal. My most testing moment came on the Sunday night at the end of the tournament. A couple of the Transvaal players had joined the Natal side for a few drinks at Durban Collegians. Returning to the hotel, and with Kevin McKenzie driving the team combi, we pulled up at a red traffic light. It was late, and the streets deserted, so I foolishly suggested to Kevin that he treat it as a yield sign and filter through into the left lane. To our horror a car with a blue flashing light came up behind us and instructed us to stop. 'Let me try and handle this, Kevin,' I said, but from the look on his face I could see he was prepared for the worst. As I emerged from the combi the Durban traffic policemen came round to my side. 'Oh, it's you Vince. I thought it was a bunch of ruffians. On your way now, but just be careful.' This was greeted with laughter and derision by a relieved McKenzie who started calling me 'The Mayor'.

'The Mayor' made way for 'Mickey Mouse' as I started the season badly. One Transvaal official even went as far as to telephone my

'Mickey Mouse' becomes 'Mighty Mouse' after I finally enjoy some success with Transvaal. Kevin McKenzie, Ray Jennings, Alan Kourie, Neale Radford, Jimmy Cook and Henry Fotheringham attend the ceremony.

managing director, Derek Smith, with the request that he should not make such heavy demands on my time as it was affecting my cricket. Derek politely told him that I had been brought to Johannesburg to work and not play cricket.

McKenzie, who had labelled me Mickey Mouse, promised me that I would become 'Mighty Mouse' once I took five wickets in an innings. It was only in February, nearly three months later, that I satisfied him.

One of the most remarkable innings I have ever seen came from Alvin Kallicharran that season — watched by fewer than 2 000 spectators. Kallicharran fashioned a masterly 120 in just 80 minutes as Transvaal made 315 for four in the annual Protea Challenge clash against Western Province. He revealed an inventiveness that transcended the match itself, vividly demonstrating the difference in style between the West Indians and the rest of the cricket-playing world. The West Indians tend to play the ball according to its length — if it is short, they hit it square; the pitched up delivery is usually played

Relaxed Rupert Hanley and a pensive Alvin Kallicharran, who had just been dismissed for 0 by Northern Transvaal, in the Transvaal changing-room.

Unorthodox but even on his back he looks in control. Alvin Kallicharran slipped as he played his favourite hook.

straighter. Most cricketers are schooled to play line and length, and so their stroke-play is restricted immediately. West Indian flair was never more evident than in this glorious innings by Kallicharran, and no field-placing could stem his flow of runs as he tore the strong Province attack to pieces. That evening Graeme Pollock, who had watched Gary Sobers's famous innings of 254 for the Rest of the World against Australia in 1971–72, solemnly shook Kallicharran's hand and told him his century was one of the greatest he had ever seen.

The depth and strength of Transvaal's batting had allowed Kallicharran to blossom. Without the shackles of responsibility, and with an abundance of batting to follow, Kalli was able to play his natural, exuberant game, and he revelled in the opportunity.

Western Province, incidentally, came agonisingly close to winning the 55-over game as Graham Gooch cracked a superb 131. Province's final wicket fell with five runs required for victory and four deliveries remaining.

As the scoreboard in this game indicates — 628 runs were scored off a couple of balls under 110 overs — the Wanderers wicket was a batting paradise and hardly a ball deviated all day. South African one-day wickets favour the batsman exclusively. While I accept that the crowds come to see runs scored, the traditional balance between bat and ball is spoilt. One-day cricket has become a contest between two batting sides. I believe just a little encouragement in the wicket for the bowler would add to the variety and reward the better attack rather than only the stronger batting side. My stint in that Challenge clash — two for 30 in 11 overs — I rated as my best spell for Transvaal all season, far better than the one which brought me seven for 42 in the Currie Cup match against Eastern Province in Port Elizabeth four months later.

An unexpected bonus for Transvaal was the return to form of Henry Fotheringham. One of Natal's most exciting batting prospects in the seventies, Fothers had struggled to realise his potential when he moved to the Transvaal in 1978. The success of the Transvaal middle-order forced him to bat up the order, either opening or going in at number three, but his inconsistency led to him being dropped. In the 1982–83 season, he missed the first few games, but then returned, as an opener, against Western Province at Newlands. He produced classic innings of 61 in each innings in difficult batting conditions and ended the season top of the first-class averages (77,91). Almost overnight he and Jimmy Cook, became one of the most successful opening pairs Transvaal have fielded. In nine opening partnerships at the Wanderers, seven produced centuries and one was worth 96. Fotheringham's remarkable fight back was eventually rewarded when he was selected to open the batting for the Springboks against the West Indians in the next season.

It was during the Benson and Hedges night final — Transvaal beat Western Province by six wickets — that I saw for the first time that home crowds can become bored by constant success. While Province were on their way to a commanding 275, spectators, one wearing a Transvaal hat, hurled endless abuse at us; they wanted to see the top dogs beaten. With several world-class players in their line-up and in spite of producing positive, winning cricket, Transvaal attracted disappointingly small crowds, and it was only when closer games were anticipated that spectators turned out again.

Henry Fotheringham, elbow up, square drives against the West Indians. He and Jimmy Cook form a highly effective and successful Transvaal opening pair.

During the night final, I again exhibited ratty tendencies. I had not taken a wicket as I came up to bowl the final over of the Province innings with their total on a formidable 273 for five. My third ball of the over was a wide and then, to make matters worse, I bowled a no-ball. Chris Gibbons, the radio personality who was doing the live commentary at the match, boomed across the ground, 'Nice one, Vince.' I reacted by stupidly making a rude gesture, but regained some face by taking three wickets in the last four balls and narrowly missed taking a hat-trick in my last over for Transvaal. Nevertheless, the signs were there that I should start thinking about getting out of the game.

Transvaal's batting line-up was awesome. In fact, after my first two matches at the Wanderers, I used to leave my batting gear in the boot of my car, and on only three occasions in the entire season did I have to go and fetch it. So prolific was the top order that Clive Rice and Kevin McKenzie, particularly in the one-day games, gained few opportunities to play long innings. Yet their presence was fundamental to the team's success. On the few occasions that we were in trouble, and in spite of little match practice, they batted well. The top five places in the Currie Cup averages were filled by Transvaal players — Cook, Fotheringham, Kallicharran, McKenzie and Rice. Kourie, with 45 wickets, was leading wicket-taker and I finished with 41.

Our most rewarding victory came at Newlands where we played Western Province on a typical turner in the Currie Cup game. They had an advantage with Denys Hobson and John Emburey in their line-up while we fielded only one specialist spinner in Alan Kourie. But it was Alvin Kallicharran who proved our wild card, taking five for 45 with his off-breaks, as Province were bowled out for 202 in their first innings. We had made 196 with Emburey also taking five wickets, but then Fotheringham (61), Rice (62) and McKenzie (70) took our second innings total to 326 for six. Kourie, spurred on by Kallicharran's earlier success and dressing-room ragging that he was Transvaal's second spinner, then bowled us to a 122-run win, taking seven for 79.

It was the most successful season I had ever experienced, as Transvaal made a clean sweep of the five trophies, and the Springboks beat the West Indians in the one-day internationals and drew the two four-day 'tests' 1–1.

My retirement on the eve of the 1983–84 season came as a surprise to even my closest friends. I had, in fact, already started training in

A friendly clash with Lee Barnard.

The long and short of it. A tender moment with Alvin Kallicharran.

preparation for the second West Indian tour when I decided to quit the game. There were three reasons — my family, business pressures and lack of commitment.

During the previous two years, I had spent a total of seven days at home during the months of March. I had seen little of my three young daughters, and cricket was playing havoc with my family life. After weeks of indicision I finally decided to retire late on a Sunday night. Our eldest daughter, Sarah, heard about it only the next day. When I returned home from work that evening, she was waiting at the gate. She came running up, threw her arms around me and said, 'Thank you, Dad, for giving up cricket.' I realised then I had made the right decision.

At the back of my mind was the feeling that my cricket career had brought me more success and contentment than I had expected. To prolong it would, I thought, only have increased pressures on my family and my job. And, finally, I realised that I was becoming increasingly short tempered out in the middle. I had lost the necessary zest and, once that happens, it is time to depart the scene.

The decision to retire was not easy to make. Cricket had been part of my life for 16 years, but the fact that I did not miss the game at all in the season that followed confirmed my belief that my decision had been the correct one.

Many people have since said that I retired at the right time — at the top. But I alone realised that I had reached my peak two years earlier — for Middlesex in 1980 and Natal in the summer of 1980–81 — only experience had enabled me to keep on taking wickets and remain reasonably successful to the end.

I did have one final game — for Transvaal against the Rest of South Africa at the Wanderers as part of Clive Rice's benefit season. I ran up and bowled the first two balls and they were both wides. Lee Barnard, sitting next to Tich Smith in the dressing-room, remarked 'This looks like a classic case of a man playing one game too many.' I felt that, too.

CHAPTER THIRTEEN

The Characters

The eminent cricket writer Neville Cardus once described the contribution to test cricket made by Australian batsman Neil Harvey. To review Harvey's career statistically, he wrote, was worth about as much as adding up all Beethoven's notes to prove he was a great composer.

Cricket's appeal is that it is not centred on victory and defeat, nor bowling and batting averages. The heart of cricket is not the centuries or great bowling spells, but its players, their styles, eccentricities and quirks.

I was fortunate to be a contemporary of two of the world's truly great batsmen, Barry Richards and Graeme Pollock. Both prolific scorers, they were so different in style, attitude and approach.

When Richards was in the right mood, it was almost impossible to get him out. One could gauge his attitude from the pavilion. If his chin was tucked hard into his left shoulder as he took his stance, then the bowlers faced the prospect of a long day. He was technically perfect, but so often a nonchalant approach would disguise his genius.

I bowled to Richards only twice in first-class cricket. The first time was for South African Universities against Natal at Jan Smuts Stadium. He was batting on a greentop and had about 15 when I bowled him an almost perfect delivery, just short of a length and swinging away. As he aimed to cover drive me on the up, the ball cut back sharply. I had started to leap into the air, already anticipating his leg-stump tumbling out of the ground, when he casually adjusted his stroke and clipped me over square-leg for a one-bounce four. As I followed-through, frustrated, he looked up and with a friendly grin said, 'Well bowled, Vince.'

Where Richards differed from Pollock was that the longer he batted, the greater was the chance of getting him out. Early on, when determined to see off the new ball, he was almost immovable. When he reached a milestone, 50 or 100, he might become more vulnerable, boredom causing him to play a rash stroke.

Barry Richards, who showed many of the old masterly touches against the West Indians, lofts his pull to leg. Derek Parry follows the flight of the ball.

In an inter-town game between Pietermaritzburg and Durban, he was going through one of these periods. Durban were coasting to a comfortable win with openers Richards and Trevor Goddard still at the wicket. Neville Ireland, one of the fielding side, suggested to Richards that he would enliven proceedings by nominating which stroke should be played before each ball was bowled. Richards, eyes lighting up at the challenge, readily agreed, though he was not aware that the bowlers knew of the arrangement. After telling Richards to play a cover drive, Ireland would signal to the bowler that he wanted the ball pitched short. The call for a hook from Richards would bring a yorker from the bowler. This continued for two overs — from provincial seam bowlers Ravenor Nicholson and Neville McDonald — yet the score still mounted rapidly. It was then suggested to Richards that he face an over using just the edge of his bat. Again he agreed, and after playing five deliveries from Nicholson back safely, he turned the last ball down to

All power and placement, Graeme Pollock launches into his pull through mid-wicket watched by Natal wicket-keeper Tich Smith.

fine-leg to keep the bowling — with the edge of his bat! At times he had the game by its tail and could make a mockery of his opponent's ability.

Pollock, by contrast, was more susceptible to dismissal early on, having a left-hander's weakness outside the off-stump. Yet, as his innings developed, it became increasingly difficult to dislodge him. It is accepted that you have 20 minutes to get Pollock out. Once he reaches about 30, you have had your chance.

When Pollock played that excellent innings in the first one-day international against the SAB English in Port Elizabeth in 1982, he started to accelerate after he had reached 25. We needed about 6,5 runs an over at that stage and, sitting next to Alan Kourie, who had played provincial cricket with Pollock for many years, I remarked that it was vital that Pollock did not lose his wicket. Kourie, surprised at my naïvety, said, 'You haven't played much with Graeme, have you? He just doesn't throw it away. He'll be not out and we'll win with a couple

Lee Irvine, unorthodox and effective, goes on the sweep to Pelham Henwood at the Wanderers. Tich Smith is the wicket-keeper and Barry Richards is at slip. The purist might balk at the sight of Richards with his hands on his knees, but that was his customary position and so quick were his reflexes that he very seldom dropped a catch.

of overs to spare.' Pollock ended with an undefeated 57 and we won by seven wickets with 16 deliveries remaining.

Graeme loves scoring runs, but he also realises that he has a responsibility to his team and the game. He will give his wicket away only in a social match, and after playing a substantial innings. His record in the many Wilf Isaacs games against school and invitation elevens bears testimony to this. On almost every occasion he made more than 50 to delight the crowd, sparse though it might have been, and provide a challenge for the opposition. He might then give his wicket to the bowler he considered the most deserving.

A blend of Richards and Pollock would have produced the perfect batsman — unyielding at the start and yet gaining in strength as the innings was built, a classic stylist with a full range of glorious, perfectly-placed strokes. The way that both, in the twilight of their careers, rose to the fearsome challenge of the West Indian pacemen was a tribute to their genius and character.

There were a number of other batsmen who regularly troubled me during my career. Left-hander Lee Irvine, audacious and inventive, was exceptionally difficult to contain. Naturally gifted, and an effortless timer of the ball, he was able to hit exactly the same type of delivery through the covers or over mid-wicket. If Lee was not testing the bowler with his wide range of strokes, he was frustrating him with his sharp running between the wickets. He was another casualty of isolation, playing in only four tests.

Many batsmen do not realise that they can dictate line and length to the bowler. Keith Fletcher, the Essex and England captain, is one who does. Fletcher is an underrated but highly effective batsman. Bowling to him in 1980, I found that he would leave any delivery just outside off-stump. Anything pitched on middle or middle-and-leg, he would 'work' through the leg-side field. If the wicket was providing bounce, he would even leave the ball short of a length in the knowledge that it would clear the stumps. He forced me to direct my attack at him which he wanted as he moved into line well and was exceptionally strong to the on-side. He began to dictate terms to me, forcing me to bowl at one stump and keep the ball up.

In my early days, the successful Transvaal opening pair of Ali Bacher and Brian Bath used to provide a similar test. They accumulated runs, not by a brilliant strokeplay, but by merely pushing the ball into the gaps and running well between the wickets. Again anything wide of the stumps was ignored. Batsmen such as Bath, Bacher and Fletcher irritated me most because I had to slow down and cut my swing simply to make them play.

One batsman who could never adopt that approach was the effervescent Eddie Barlow. Confident and aggressive, he would carry the battle to the bowlers. The Springboks had a good but not a winning team when he arrived on the scene. Though not captain, his positive attitude rubbed off on others and transformed the side. At the age of 36 Barlow was invited to captain struggling Derbyshire and was paid what was then an unusually high salary of five figures. His inspiring leadership and the high priority he placed on physical fitness lifted the club to fresh heights, taking them to a Lord's final and helping three members into the England test side.

Eddie Barlow, pugnacious and dynamic, played a major role transforming a good Springbok side into a great one.

Whether batting or bowling, Barlow was at the hub of the action. When he took the ball, and stalked back to his mark, an expectant buzz would go through the crowd. Something was bound to happen. In one match in Cape Town, Pelham Henwood and I had added 35 for the ninth wicket when Barlow decided he would break the partnership. A roar from the Newlands crowd greeted him as he paced out his run. I walked down the wicket to Henwood and said, 'Whatever happens, Bunter isn't going to get us out.' Henwood agreed. I was facing and the very first ball I received was straight and pitched on middle stump. I missed it and walked back to the pavilion fuming while the Newlands crowd roared their approval. I expressed my annoyance to Barlow that night and, eyes twinkling behind his spectacles, he said, 'There is nothing more underrated than the straight ball.'

South Africans did not see the best of Glenn Turner on the International Wanderers tour in 1976. Turner, the best player to emerge from New Zealand since John Reid, was also the most professional. As Barry Richards had done in South Africa, Turner broke new ground for the professional in New Zealand and clashed frequently with amateur administrators as he fought for his right to earn a decent living playing cricket. When he came to South Africa he was a disillusioned young man and later he relinquished the captaincy of New Zealand. Labelled a mercenary, Turner returned to the international scene only in 1979 when his professional approach had become acceptable.

Glenn is a remarkable player. When he started out on the county circuit for Worcestershire in 1967, he lacked attacking strokes, but the demands of one-day cricket turned him into a glorious attacking player. His batting grip is unusual and commands the attention of the bowler.

From grip and stance, a bowler can usually ascertain a batsman's strengths and weaknesses. Turner's hands, for the purists anyway, are too far round the back of the bat handle. This should preclude him playing straight or driving with any freedom — or so I thought in 1980 when I ran in to bowl to him in the Worcester second innings when they were chasing 275 in 210 minutes. My first ball was a good length and he calmly hit it over the covers for four. The second I dropped shorter and he hit me on the up through the off-side field for another boundary. He hit a 100 in even time, scoring freely on both sides of the wicket, and my preconceived ideas of his weaknesses were quickly buried. Elegant and upright, he commands the utmost respect, proving yet another exception to the coaching manual.

The true test of greatness in a batsman is whether he appears to have time to play his shots and is able to hit the good ball for four. Allan Lamb has these hallmarks. He rarely appears flustered or hurried, but his almost carefree approach hides an inner determination to succeed.

Lamb plays through midwicket with immense power. For two years he almost cast a spell over me, frequently hitting deliveries on a length to the boundary, and I felt that I could not penetrate his defences. He dominated me psychologically and this was reflected in my bowling.

Lamb's bold approach to batting has been sorely missed on the South African domestic scene. His one failing was his impetuosity and, while at the crease, he rarely played the percentage game, which occasionally brought his downfall and left him open to criticism. Occasionally he did try. In one vital match against Natal at Kingsmead, he was determined to build a long innings for Western Province and decided not to talk to any of the Natal players. It was most unusual to see the normally cheerful Lamb studiously ignoring his friends out in the field. Finally, Natal wicketkeeper Tich Smith could take no more of it. 'Are you just taking this game seriously, or don't you want to talk to me?' Smith asked. Lamb burst out laughing and lively conversation ensued.

His 1984 success, three centuries for a struggling England side against the Clive Lloyd's West Indians and another against Sri Lanka, seem to indicate that he is finally curbing his impulsiveness and starting to assert his authority at the highest level.

I never had the opportunity of bowling to West Indian Viv Richards, but his countryman Alvin Kallicharran proved enough of a challenge. Kallicharran is a most difficult player to contain. His lack of height encourages him to play square of the stumps and he can hit deliveries fractionally short of a length through mid-wicket. A delivery on a length to Graeme Pollock is a couple of centimetres too short to Kallicharran, and it will be punished. Bowling when Pollock and Kalli are batting together can be a most painful experience. Pollock plays almost conventionally straight, but with immense power, while Kallicharran is quick to hit similar deliveries square. Balls pitched on the right line and length are hit to the boundary, and the bowler's confidence is quickly undermined.

Behind the batting styles of the masters are years of hard work and dedication. I have often been told that a player like Barry Richards was naturally gifted and never had to work for his success. The spectator has, of course, not seen the many hours Richards has spent in the nets, working at problems and eliminating weaknesses. For four years after leaving school, Richards would spend hours in the nets every day, having balls thrown at him and sheer repetition enabled him to perfect every stroke. The ease of his batting out in the middle was deceptive, and concealed the long hours of hard grind.

The importance of bowling partnerships is another facet of the game which is often overlooked. To have two bowlers supporting and complementing each other, building up pressure on the batsman and striving together to probe his weakness, is crucial to a team's success. Neil Adcock and Peter Heine, and Peter Pollock in tandem with Procter, were two such partnerships which gave South Africa great

Fast bowlers hunt in pairs. The Western Province and Springbok openers Stephen Jefferies and Garth le Roux swop ideas.

service. Unfortunately, test cricket saw only glimpses of the Pollock and Procter partnership when between them they took 41 of the 70 wickets to fall in the 1969–70 season.

It was Pat Trimborn who first showed me the value of a bowling combination, and the partnership we developed was not only mutually beneficial, but also a great aid to Pelham Henwood, who was consistently bowled first change by Richards in the early seventies. Henwood would regularly take a wicket in his first over as the opposing batsmen, tied down by the tight opening attack, tried to hit the spinner.

I was fortunate throughout my career to have superb new ball partners. Trimborn, Mike Procter, Ken Cooper (Natal), Wayne Daniel (Middlesex) and Rupert Hanley (Transvaal) helped enormously to keep the early pressure on opposing batsmen. This would be maintained by such excellent spinners as Henwood (Natal), John Emburey (Middlesex) and Alan Kourie (Transvaal), and these support bowlers were crucial to my success.

One of my disappointments was that Garth le Roux was never able to reproduce the excellent form he showed for Kerry Packer in Australia when he and I opened for the Springboks. A muscular, immensely strong man, Garth exerted great energy and force in his delivery stride. When he found his rhythm, as he did in World Series Cricket, he could be exceptionally quick but, sadly, injury has prevented him maintaining that pace in this country. Nevertheless, his effort has never slackened and he has always been an excellent competitor. This showed in his batting against the West Indians during the 1982–83 series and his aggressive approach at the crease provided the only spark in our lower order. His axing from the Springbok side the following year was greeted with delight by the West Indians who regarded him as South Africa's most penetrative bowler. His omission was not as a result of his poor figures, but because the selectors apparently expected him to achieve even greater heights.

Two outstanding characters who have made significant contributions to South African cricket are Wilf Isaacs and Charles Fortune.

Isaacs has been South African cricket's most loyal benefactor, taking numerous invitation teams to schools where young players have had the opportunity to watch and play against their heroes. His two tours to Britain—in 1966 and 1969—provided a number of South Africa's

South African cricket benefactor Wilf Isaacs relaxes with Geoff Boycott.

Charles Fortune in his beloved Wanderers commentary box. Laura Knight is the scorer.

leading young players with invaluable experience. On both tours he took just the right mix of the young and the old with the latter able to help with advice and coaching.

In one of the games, a young Pelham Henwood was coming in for heavy punishment against an exceptionally strong Invitation side. Clive Radley, an England batsman, was in his eighties when Isaacs decided that he would come on and show the youngster how to bowl to his field. Isaacs laid great emphasis on flight — in fact, he bowled a series of donkey drops. Nevertheless, he had a plan. He placed eight men to the off-side and one on the leg at mid-wicket. His first delivery pitched two metres outside the off-stump and had stopped by the time the wicketkeeper picked it up. The second ball also landed on the adjacent pitch, but Radley, a batsman of foresight, was ready. Like a sprinter out of his blocks, Radley charged into position well to the off, pivoted and cracked a superb hook to leg. While his timing was excellent, his placement was not, and the ball crashed into his stumps. He departed, played on. A few balls later the new batsman, following Radley's example, also swung one of Isaacs' deliveries to leg, but Pat Flanagan, fielding at mid-wicket, made metres around the boundary and dived to take a splendid catch. At the end of his spell, Isaacs called Henwood across and said, 'See, my boy, that's how you bowl to your field.'

The man who has done more for South African cricket than any other over the last three decades is commentator Charles Fortune. He has been a permanent feature of our cricket for as long as I can remember, and is highly respected by the cricketers, particularly the Springboks of the middle and late sixties who were close to him. Significantly, it was his advice that was sought before the Newlands walk-off in 1971. He perhaps does not give the score every 45 seconds during his commentary, but he does convey the atmosphere of the game to his listeners, and he has been responsible for introducing thousands, including numerous housewives, to the intricacies of cricket. His ability to sense the feel of a match is remarkable. Charles has made an immense contribution and will long be remembered by the cricket fraternity.

A worrying feature of modern South African cricket has been the lack of specialist spin bowlers. Only three South African spinners of international standard — Pelham Henwood, Denys Hobson and Alan

Kourie — emerged during my 15 years of Currie Cup cricket. One who might have made it to the top, but arrived on the scene late, was Baboo Ebrahim, the Indian left-hander. He burst into prominence in 1976 when he took six wickets for 66 for the South African XI against the International Wanderers in Durban. Ebrahim was already 32 by the time he made his Natal Currie Cup debut and, as most of his cricket had been played on matting wickets, he naturally battled to adapt. One wonders just how far he would have progressed had doors been opened earlier. Baboo has a delightful sense of humour. When a Natal player, who was even older than him, asked what pills he was taking during a break in the game against Rhodesia in the 1978–79 season, he quickly replied, 'Samoosa 45.' And, on one gloomy afternoon at Kingsmead during the same season, the crowd was calling on me, as Natal skipper, to 'give Baboo a bowl'. We came off for bad light before I had a chance and, as we were leaving the field, he turned round and said, 'What was wrong, Vince. Couldn't you see me out there on the fence?'

After 15 years in the first-class game, and being an armchair selector for most of my life, I cannot resist the temptation to pick the best South African cricketers I have played with or against. Of course, my selection leaves me open to attack, but I believe the side very nearly picks itself, though there are a number of other gifted players who have been left out.

My side would be: Barry Richards, Eddie Barlow, Peter Kirsten, Graeme Pollock, Lee Irvine, Clive Rice, Mike Procter (captain), Trevor Goddard, Alan Kourie, Ray Jennings and Peter Pollock.

This side contains a ready-made captain in Mike Procter, otherwise I would have chosen Ali Bacher to lead the team, replacing Peter Kirsten at number three. Jimmy Cook might be considered a more logical choice than Kirsten, but first wicket down is a specialist position, and the Western Province batsman's form in the late seventies, when at one stage he made five centuries in successive innings, should not be forgotten.

It could also be argued that Le Roux should be preferred to Peter Pollock, but I would not like to disturb the successful partnership of the 1969–70 tour. Dennis Lindsay was in his twilight years when I came on the scene, so Ray Jennings is the obvious choice as a specialist wicketkeeper.

The strength of the side would lie in its five all-rounders with

Barlow, Rice, Procter, Goddard and Kourie providing extraordinary depth to both the batting and the bowling.

This spread of talent gives some indication of what a remarkable era in South African cricket it has been. My players will be remembered as prolific performers, but they also played their cricket with style and flair. That is what I will remember long after the figures and scorecards, successes and disappointments have been forgotten.

A picture for the International Cricket Conference. A mixed crowd support Natal in the braai smoke of the Datsun Shield final at the Wanderers.

Hassan Howa, a man of courage and conviction.

CHAPTER FOURTEEN

At the crossroads again

In 1968, the late Prime Minister B. J. Vorster successfully buried South Africa as an international cricketing nation by refusing to allow Basil D'Oliveira to tour with the England cricket team. Sixteen years later, in the spring of 1984, South Africa's cricketing future again finds itself firmly in the hand of the Chief Executive, Mr P. W. Botha.

During the seventies, the demands and promises made by the ICC, led this country into an atmosphere of false hope. Through consistent hard work and by constantly challenging government policy, the administrators and players had quickly and defiantly changed the face of cricket — producing a non-racial controlling body and ensuring selection on merit at club and provincial level.

The goal in those early years was readmittance to the international fold, and South Africa's cricket fraternity attempted to take the future of the game into their own hands, removing it from the politicians' control. Reform came rapidly. Behind every change was the knowledge that they were morally and ethically right and just, though the fruits of promised rewards made the efforts stronger and more robust.

Just as our politicians had poked their noses into cricketing matters a decade earlier, so governments of ICC member countries began to exert enormous pressure on their administrators. It was not just the feared disruption and turmoil of South Africa's re-entry into world cricket that was a stumbling block for ICC members, but also their governments' interference. In the seventies, the ICC changed from an apparently autonomous body, concerned only with the future of world cricket, to an organisation which took decisions based on politics. South Africa's entire political and social structure came under the spotlight.

As Charles Palmer, of the Test and County Cricket Board, told Dr Ali Bacher, 'The goal-posts keep moving.' The ICC have shifted South Africa's goal from a non-racial controlling body, and selection on merit, to total acceptance of her social and political standards. Demands are now being made which are outside the domain of the cricket community.

So South African cricket, her players, administrators and supporters, must now wait on the whims of the politicians, at home and abroad, in the years ahead.

Hassan Howa's consistent stand, and one followed by his SACBOC successor, Mr Krish Mackerdhuj, a hardliner, is that there should be equal opportunity from junior school to the highest level for all the peoples of South Africa. The gap that still exists between SACBOC and the SACU can be bridged only by our politicians — by providing equal opportunity at school level. This presumably would satisfy SACBOC, but the rub is that the world's cricketing nations, or at least their government bosses, would still demand more.

In the mid-eighties, therefore, the outlook for South African cricket is gloomier than ever. Our playing strength has suffered from the retirement of the experienced core of Springboks, the loss of players to other countries and the effects of isolation on our cricket youth.

The euphoria of the rebel tours is behind us. The cost of importing the world's leading players is now too high, and the ICC countries have closed loopholes which allowed their cricketers to benefit from tours to this country.

At the time of writing, Dr Bacher, who masterminded the previous rebel tours, told me that there was no prospect of an international team coming to South Africa in the foreseeable future, adding, 'We are in the hands of the politicians.'

The earlier encouragement from the ICC behind closed doors, has finally been recognised for what it was: no more than back-patting within the cricket family. It is the politicians who hold the key today.

And so South Africa, after the excitement of the West Indian tours, seems certain to re-enter the wilderness, one which has become even more barren with the passage of time. Domestic cricket itself must now ensure that the game not only survives, but flourishes. It was in the early seventies that I heard Charles Fortune, guest speaker at a university function in Pietermaritzburg, say that South African cricket could prosper, even in isolation. 'There are many sports throughout the world that survive only within the domestic market — American gridiron and Australian Rules are healthy,' he added.

South African cricket will now be played in similar circumstances. The four supports of the cricketing table — the administrators, sponsors, players and the media — will have to stand firm if the future of this game is to be assured.

The situation cries out for a dynamic and innovative approach. The involvement of professional administrators in the Players' Association and in the SACU, can play a decisive and influential role in shaping our future.

An enlightened approach by the Players' Association and the administrators, an intimate understanding of each other's motives and open and honest communication, are essential. A dictatorial approach from the administrators, or a militant attitude among the cricketers, will prove disastrous.

In president Mike Procter and vice-president Dave Dyer, the Players' Association has two loyal and understanding men. Their foresight, and a sensible approach from the administrators, could carry South African cricket through difficult times to a secure future.

Even with the plethora of one-day cricket, and the strong counter-attraction provided by the second West Indian tour, the 1983–84 season saw an encouraging 11,5 per cent increase in crowd attendance at Currie Cup matches. This improvement was not matched by any of the other one-day competitions, and one hopes that these figures herald the re-establishment of the Currie Cup as the pillar of the South African game. If this is the case, and the influences of the three-day game continue to mould cricket technique, tradition and attitude, then our future is healthier than we believe.

South African cricket received a jolt last season when Rowe's second West Indian tour exposed several weaknesses in the Springbok side. They were not a full West Indian side, but they were most certainly stronger than most international teams. They also fielded a four-pronged pace attack, a modern phenomenon foreign to South Africans, and our batsmen struggled. The problems, however, are not insurmountable, though obviously our cricketers will have to work hard at perfecting their techniques and remaining conversant with developments in world cricket.

I remember an incident concerning Ian Chappell at Newlands in 1976 when the International Wanderers were in South Africa. Chappell had come to South Africa with the Australians in 1969–70 and skipper Bill Lawry, at the outset, had stated that his countryman was the best batsman in the world on all wickets. But Chappell had a disastrous trip, demonstrating a poor technique against the pace of Peter Pollock and Mike Procter. When he returned, in 1976, I decided to test him with a bouncer which he hit through mid-wicket for four. It was a perfectly-executed stroke and later I asked him what had changed since the 1969–70 tour. He told me that there had been no fast bowlers in Australian domestic cricket during that period and he had never had to develop the technique of playing the hook against real pace. As a result of his experience on the South African tour, he set out to correct this fault. Donning a motor bike helmet, he went into the nets and had his brother, Greg, hurl the ball at him from 15 paces. Eventually he became one of the best hookers in world cricket, but he had taught himself the stroke outside Australian first-class cricket. It is a lesson our cricketers will have to learn in the years ahead.

Isolation has also prompted several of our leading or most promising players — Kepler Wessels, Allan Lamb and the Smith brothers, Robin and Kippy — to look elsewhere for their international cricket. Their loss, at a time when Eddie Barlow, Mike Procter, Barry Richards and Graeme Pollock are leaving the game, has left the national side vulnerable.

There are gifted young batsmen, Adrian Kuiper, Roy Pienaar, Mandy Yachad and Mark Logan emerging, but the dearth of fast bowlers and specialist spinners is disturbing. One of the flaws in our system is the lack of a national coaching organisation, a central body to cater for the instruction of cricket at all levels. In a situation where our cricket could stagnate, it is essential to introduce a national scheme to facilitate the spread of new ideas and coaching methods throughout the country.

It also seems certain that the number of overseas professionals playing for each province will be reduced from two to one. The argument is that because overseas professionals in England have filled key positions — as number four batsmen and opening bowlers — in county sides, the strength of the test team has suffered. But it is wrong to compare our isolation to county cricket. In South Africa, there is no realistic chance of a tour in the near future, and we desperately need outside influence in our cricket. Overseas players will not only bolster the relative strengths of the Currie Cup and Castle Bowl teams, but will also keep South African cricket in touch with international trends.

The West Indians were ample proof of the need to maintain overseas ties in some form. The West Indians showed us a different approach to the game and I believe that for the next five years our coaching will show signs of the Caribbean influence.

If South African cricket is to be isolated, it is vital that we build up our internal competition and maintain it at a high level. With many alternatives on offer, the sporting public cannot be expected to support cricket willy-nilly. They will come only to watch the best players and entertaining contests. We must ensure that even if the Springbok becomes extinct, the standard and interest remains as high. I believe that the Graham Gooches, Sylvester Clarkes and Collis Kings are vital to maintain that enthusiasm. We must take a fresh look at this problem and not simply discard overseas players because they harmed English test cricket. If, by some miracle, regular tours were to become a feature of our game again, then obviously two professionals per province would be unnecessary, but at present we need all the outside influences we can get.

Residential qualifications have now been abolished in an effort to correct the imblance of strengths in our provincial cricket. This will allow provinces to sign players living in other centres and, at least initially, will be welcomed by the smaller and weaker provinces. But again, I believe, this is unlikely to solve the problem and it will not be long before the richer unions, such as Transvaal and, to a lesser extent, Western Province, again snap up the pick of the players and the polarisation of our cricket will continue.

The new qualifications will also swell the ranks of professional cricketers, who benefit in the short-term as salaries are increased. But I have a deep concern for the young cricketer who becomes a professional. So many of their English counterparts simply cannot answer the question: 'What are you going to do when you stop playing cricket?' I believe that administrators, both in the unions and the Players' Association, should help young professionals in planning for a secure future. Paddy Clift works for Barclays Bank in the mornings and coaches, on their behalf, at schools in the afternoons. When his playing career is over, the transition from a sporting life to one in banking will be easy. Unfortunately, Clift is an exception and most current professional cricketers' futures are much less secure.

My career, though played in the wings of the international stage, without a Springbok tour or a genuine test cap, spanned a remarkable period in the history of the game. It was exciting and invigorating to be part of this era and I was luckier than many other 'shadow' cricketers who were never given the opportunity to wear a Springbok cap.

My jaunts overseas, the opportunity to play against the SAB English and the West Indians, the fact that I had a relatively long, injury free career, the latter half during South Africa's first television age, gave me enjoyment, recognition and fulfilment.

The dream of a Springbok cap had been there from the start and, if my ambition was not entirely fulfilled, I did achieve far more than I ever thought possible. I savoured the full flavour of cricket — the fickleness, the delights and disappointments, the humour and tragedy. Cricket shaped my thinking and my life. Finally, when I transgressed late in my career, it taught the ultimate lesson — that the game is greater than the man.

Once again South African cricket is at the crossroads. The goal of international cricket is more distant than it was on that far-off day at Newlands in 1971. So it is up to the South African cricket community to ensure that the young player has every chance to flourish in the domestic arena. And, ironically, it is now up to the politicians to ensure that cricket's aspirations can be fulfilled. Politics and sport have become one, and a new era is upon us.

Vintcent Adriaan Pieter van der Bijl

Born in Cape Town 19 March 1948. One of only five SA families from which three generations have played first-class cricket.

WP Nuffield XI in 1967. Toured England with Wilf Isaacs in 1969.

First class debut for SA Universities in 1967–68. Natal debut in 1968–69.

South African Cricketer of the Year 1971. Selected for cancelled Springbok tour to Australia in 1971–72.

In 1979–80 Natal granted him the first-ever benefit season in the province.

New South African record of 75 wickets (average 14,92) in one domestic season (1981–82). Highest wicket-taker for Natal and any Province 587 first-class and 532 Currie Cup (South African record).

10 wickets in a match 12 times; 5 wickets in an innings 46 times.

Captain Natal from 1976 to 1980 winning Currie Cup and Datsun Shield in first season.

33 captaincies and 109 appearances for Natal. 101 Currie Cup appearances for Natal, a record; the last 93 in succession.

Eight Currie Cup appearances for Transvaal in the 1982–83 season. Took 40 Currie Cup wickets.

One season for Middlesex in 1980, awarded cap. Headed England first-class averages with 85 wickets at 14,72 apiece. Wisden Cricketer of the Year.

Hat-trick v Eastern Province in Durban 1978–79.

Holds the South African record for the most wickets in the Datsun Shield competition.

His highest first-class score is 87 for Natal v Zimbabwe in 1979–80.

Best Currie Cup bowling was eight for 35 v Western Province (match analysis of 13 for 53) in Pietermaritzburg in 1971–72 season.

Best match analysis 14 for 93 v Northern Transvaal (1981–82)

Best Datsun Shield bowling five for 25 Natal v Western Province in Cape Town in 1975–76.

Announced retirement before 1983–84 season.

Married in 1973 to Beverly and has three daughters Sarah, Chloe and Louise.

Named one of Wisden's Five Cricketers of the Year in 1981, Citation: 'Few Cricketers have made a bigger impact in a single season of English county cricket than Vintcent van der Bijl made in 1980. He took 85 wickets at 14,72 apiece, finishing *virtually* top of the first-class bowling averages. He made a massive contribution to Middlesex's victories in the Schweppes County Championship and the Gillette Cup, not only with wickets but with controlled hitting when runs were needed. When he arrived in April, he had a long tally of broken records in South Africa and, on a variety of pitches in an uneven English summer, he more than justified the reputation which had preceded him of being one of the best fast-medium bowlers in the world. Most of all he brought, as is generally agreed, "a breath of fresh air" with his immense enthusiasm, his love of playing cricket, and his bubbling friendship for other cricketers.'

V. A. P. van der Bijl — Career record

First-Class Cricket

	M	I	N.O	Runs	H.S.	Average	100	50	Cts	Runs	Wickets	Average	10 in Match	5 in Ings	Best
1967/68 SAU	1	2	0	11	6	5,50	—	—	1	82	1	82,00	—	—	1/52
1968/69 Natal/SAU	7	9	4	53	16	10,60	—	—	2	493	24	20,54	—	1	5/60
1969/70 Natal/SAU	6	8	3	71	23*	15,20	—	—	—	437	28	15,61	—	1	6/60
1970/81 Natal/The Rest XI	6	9	2	65	27	9,28	—	—	5	508	26	19,53	—	2	4/35
1971/72 Natal/SAU	9	13	2	68	35	6,18	—	—	2	725	48	15,10	1	4	8/35
1972/73 Natal	9	15	3	83	22*	6,91	—	—	4	832	39	21,33	—	2	5/44
1973/74 Natal/Invitation XI	12	11	6	139	50*	27,80	—	1	1	1 037	64	16,20	1	3	7/45
1974/75 Natal/Presidents XI	10	9	3	58	30	9,66	—	—	7	960	49	19,59	1	2	6/46
1975/76 Natal/Invitation XI	13	17	7	173	31	17,30	—	—	6	1 084	65	16,67	1	3	7/24
1976/77 Natal	8	8	1	56	19	8,00	—	—	3	734	36	20,38	—	1	6/58
1977/78 Natal	8	14	0	233	49	16,64	—	—	6	715	37	19,32	—	2	8/56
1978/79 Natal	8	14	1	330	61	25,38	—	3	1	684	46	14,86	—	6	5/32
1979/80 Natal	8	13	2	249	87	22,63	—	3	5	503	37	13,59	—	2	5/37
1980 Middlesex	20	16	3	331	76	25,46	—	1	5	1 252	85	14,72	1	5	6/47
1980/81 Natal	8	7	3	93	37*	23,25	—	—	1	513	54	9,50	—	3	6/30
1981 Middlesex	1	—	—	—	—	—	—	—	—	38	1	38,00	—	—	1/32
1981/82 Natal/South Africa XI	11	13	5	178	53*	22,25	—	1	2	1 119	75	14,92	4	10	8/47
1982/83 Tvl/South African XI	11	10	3	80	30	11,42	—	—	—	976	52	18,76	—	1	7/42
	156	185	48	2 269	87	16,56	—	9	51	12 692	767	16,54	12	46	8/35

Limited Overs Cricket

			BATTING							BOWLING				
	M	I	N.O	Runs	H.S.	Average	Cts	Overs	Maidens	Runs	Wickets	Average	5 in Ings	Best
Gillette/Datsun	41	21	5	200	45	12,50	11	434,5	108	1 074	62	17,32	2	5/25
One day Internationals	9	4	2	11	7*	5,50	2	67,2	4	230	12	19,16	—	3/19
Benson & Hedges	6	1	0	2	2	2,00	1	56	14	206	14	14,71	1	5/30
Protea Challenge	1	—	—	—	—	—	1	11	0	30	2	15,00	—	2/30
Connoisseur Brandy	1	—	—	—	—	—	—	5	1	10	0	—	—	—
Computer Sciences	6	2	0	13	13	6,50	—	53	10	142	11	12,90	—	3/17
	64	28	7	226	45	10,76	15	627,1	137	1 692	101	16,75	3	5/25

Currie Cup Bowling (101 matches for Natal, 8 for Transvaal)

Matches	Runs	Wickets	Average	Best	10 in Match	5 in Match
109	9 395	572	16,42	8/35	9	36

*Not Out

Postscript and gallery

Vince van der Bijl was simply one of the world's greatest fast-medium bowlers

He is recognised as such by South African cricketers but it is depressing to think that he has not gained the reputation he deserves at international level.

Australian Max Walker is a household name in world cricket but you could never convince me that Vince was not a far better bowler than he. He deserves, I believe, to be ranked with West Indian Joel Garner as the finest fast-medium bowler of the seventies.

He suffered more than most from South Africa's cricket isolation. He was the finest bowler I have seen who has not played genuine test cricket.

Vince was one of the best exponents of swing and cut of the wicket and we had many exciting duels in the nets. In the Natal side he was once our destroyer, workhorse and non-stop trier throughout a succession of summers.

His only fault, perhaps, was that he was occasionally a little too 'nice' out in the middle. 'But I might kill him, Boer', he once replied when I asked him to bowl a bouncer at a lower-order batsman who had overstayed his welcome. But, then, that is a refreshing trait in what has become a harsh and unkind sporting arena.

His charitable attitude to various tail-enders did not prevent him becoming enormously successful. His outstanding record speaks for itself. But, of course, he was much more than just a record-breaking South African bowler. He was an ideal team-man, refreshing, helpful and intelligent.

If Vince brings those same attributes to his chosen business career, he will prove immensely successful and popular. It was a pleasure to be associated with him.

BARRY RICHARDS

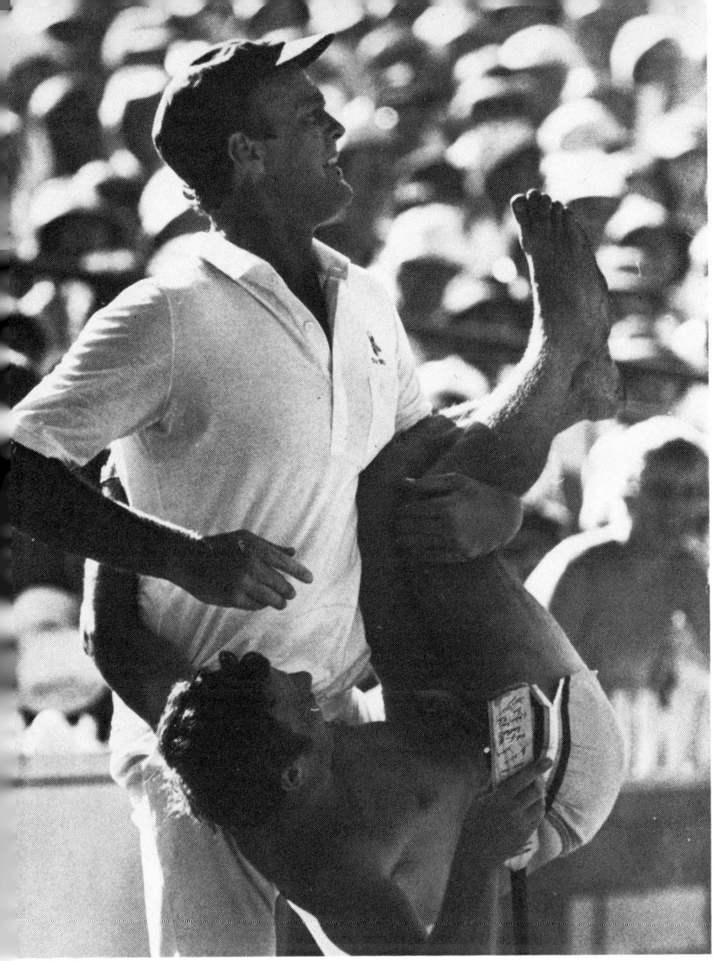

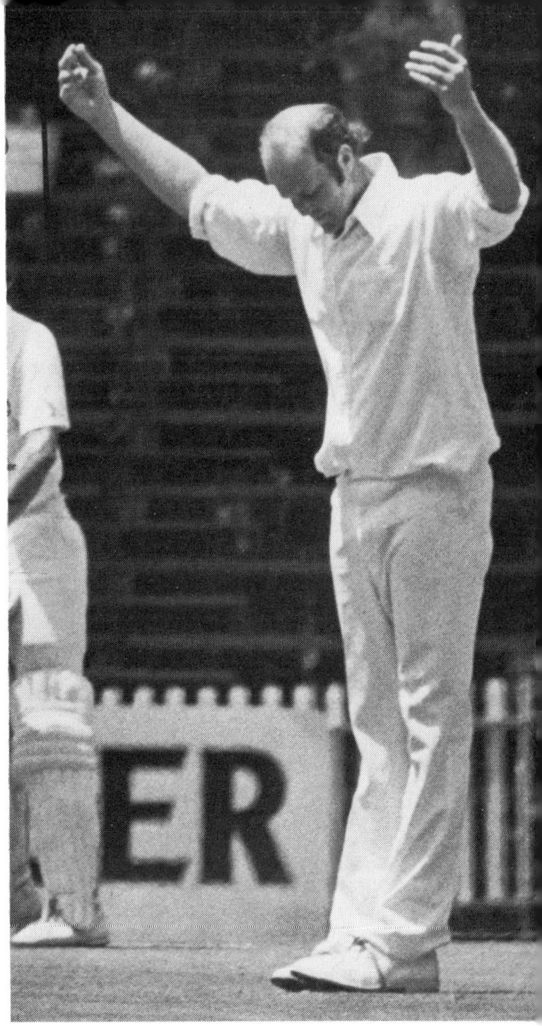
ER

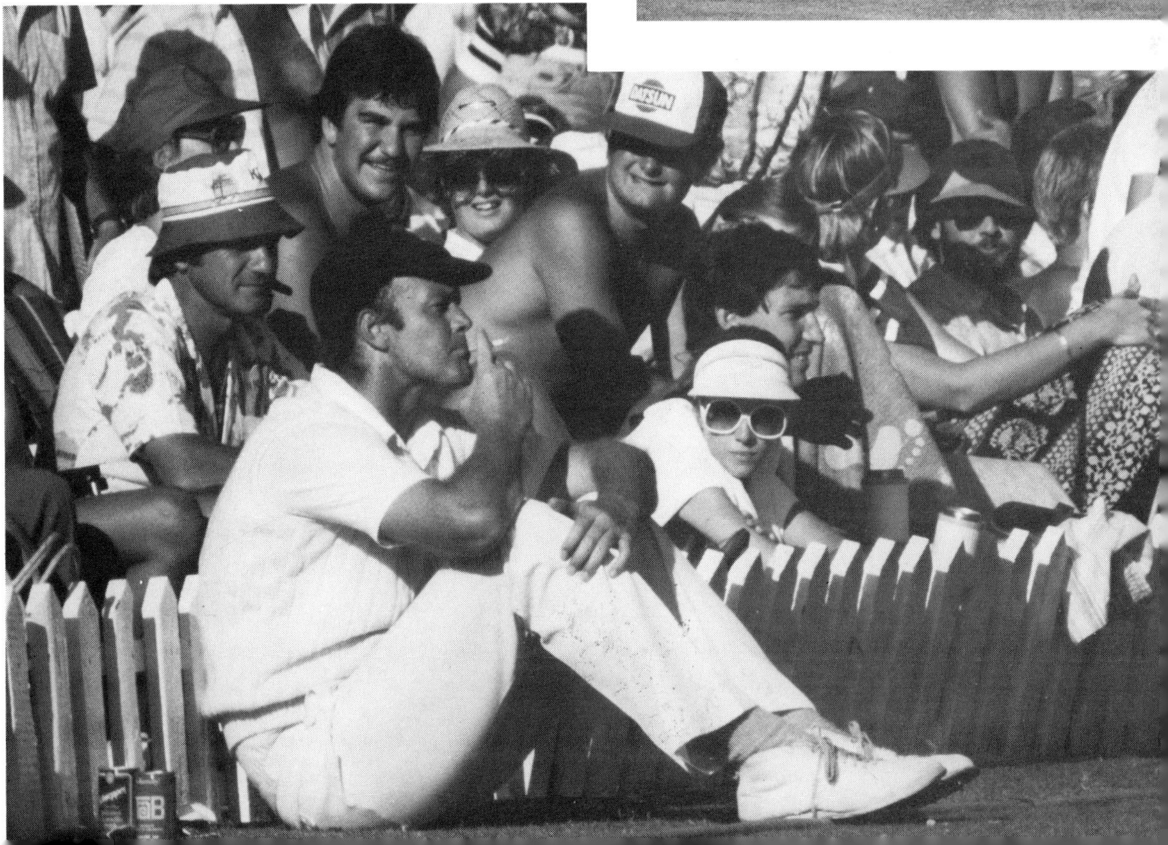

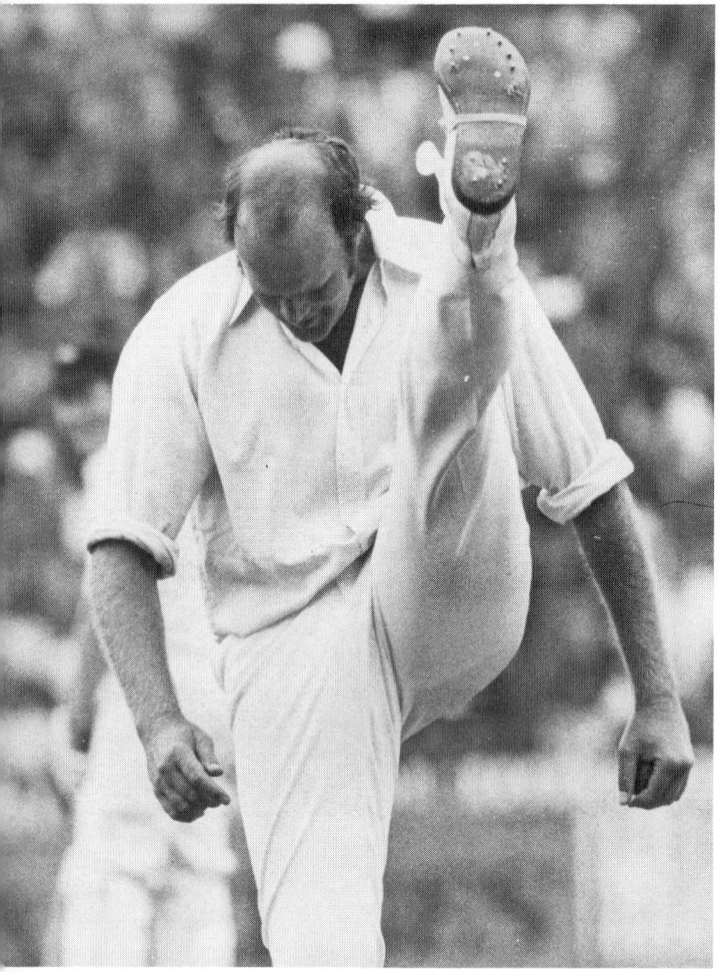

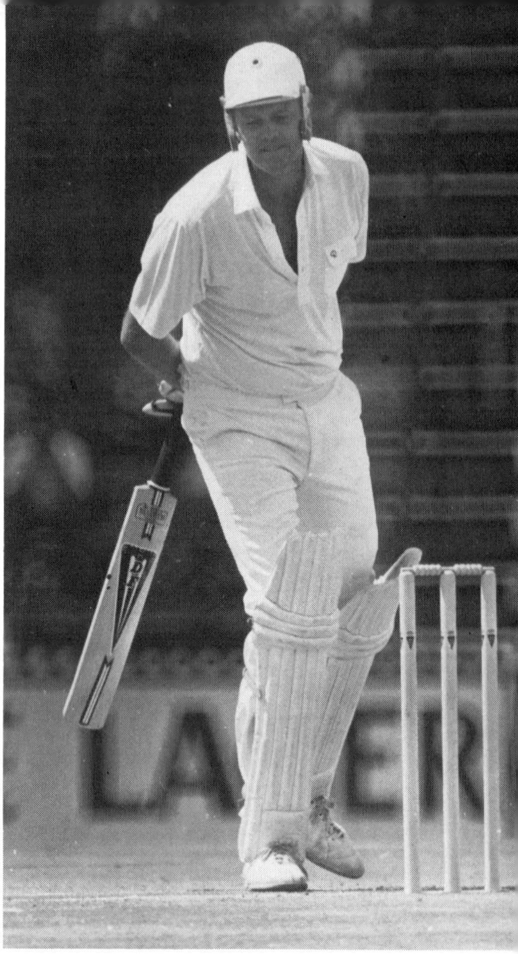

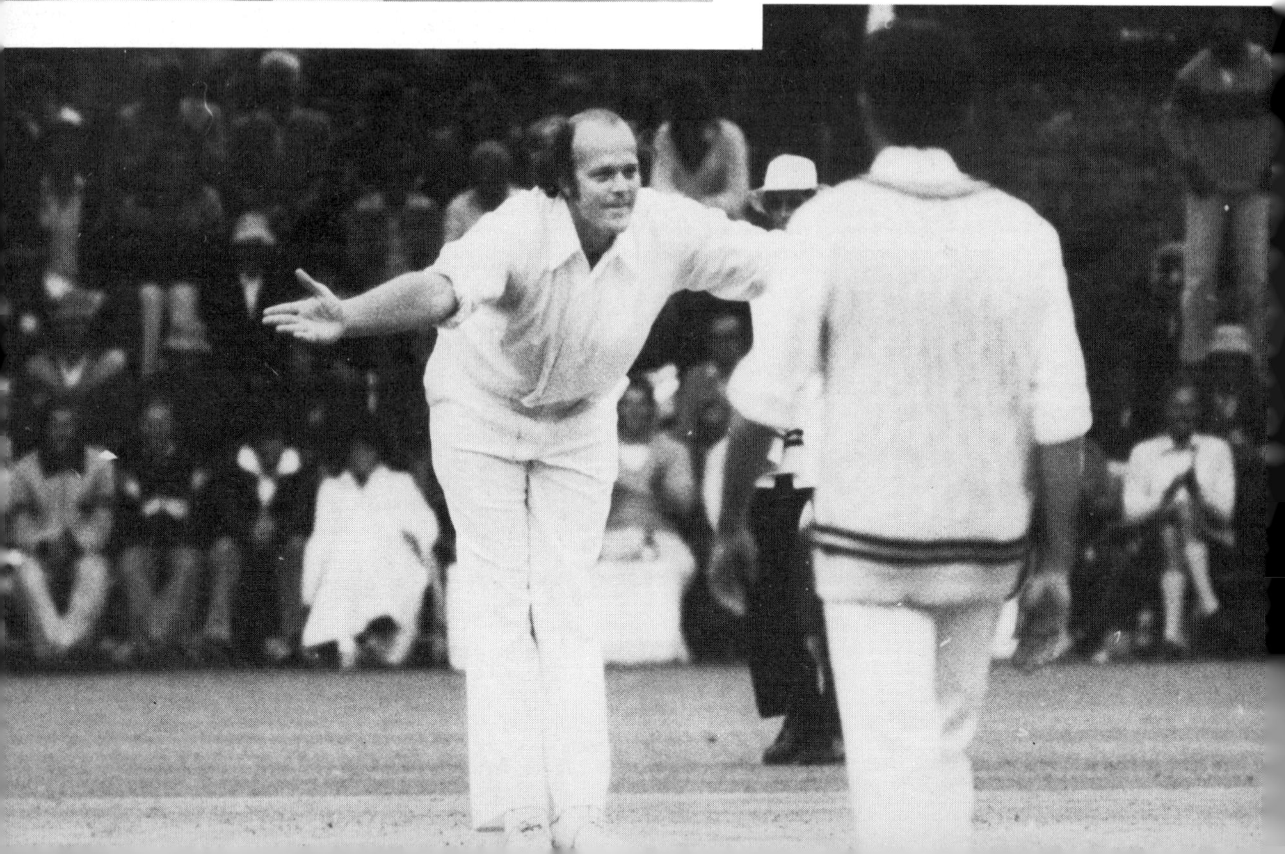

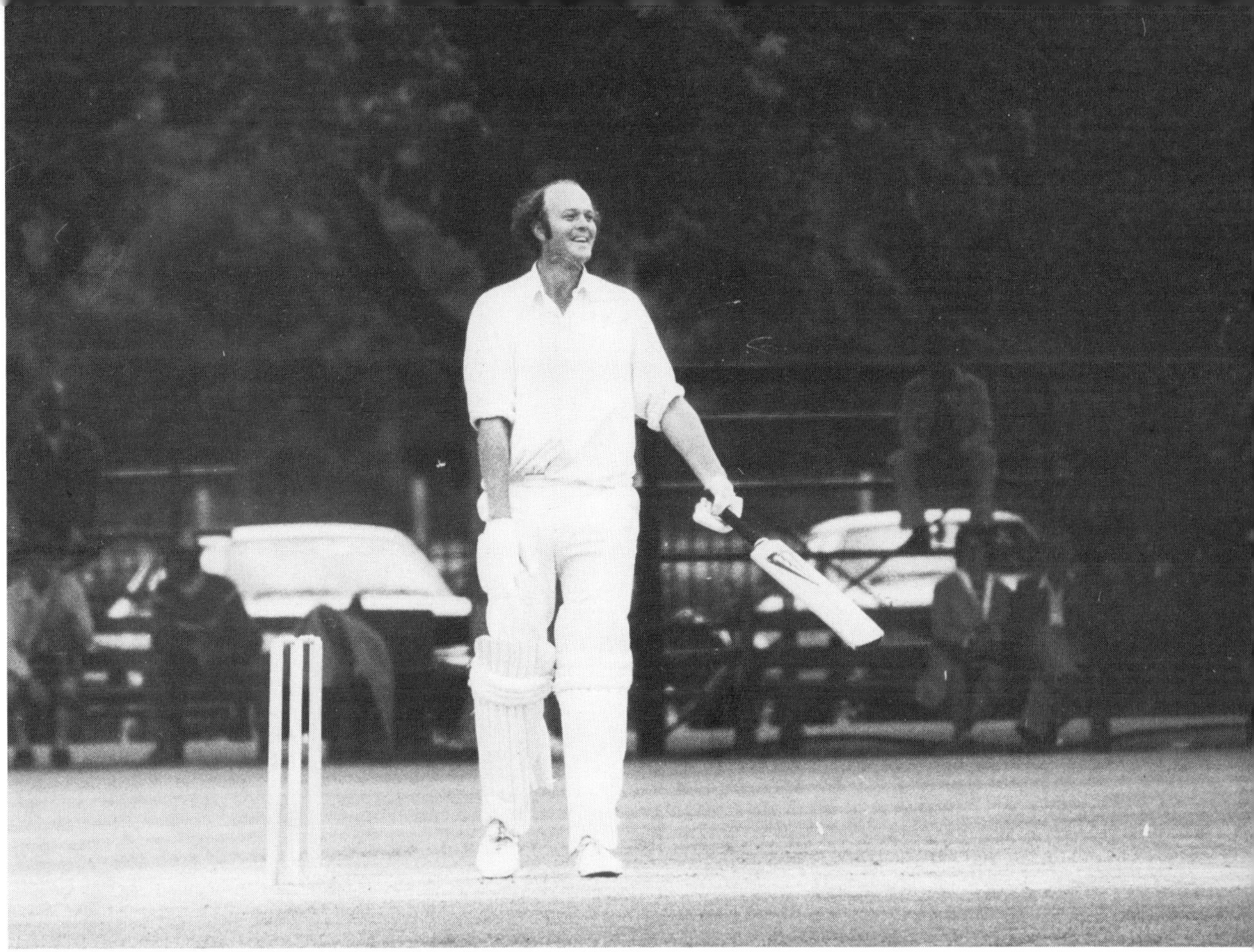

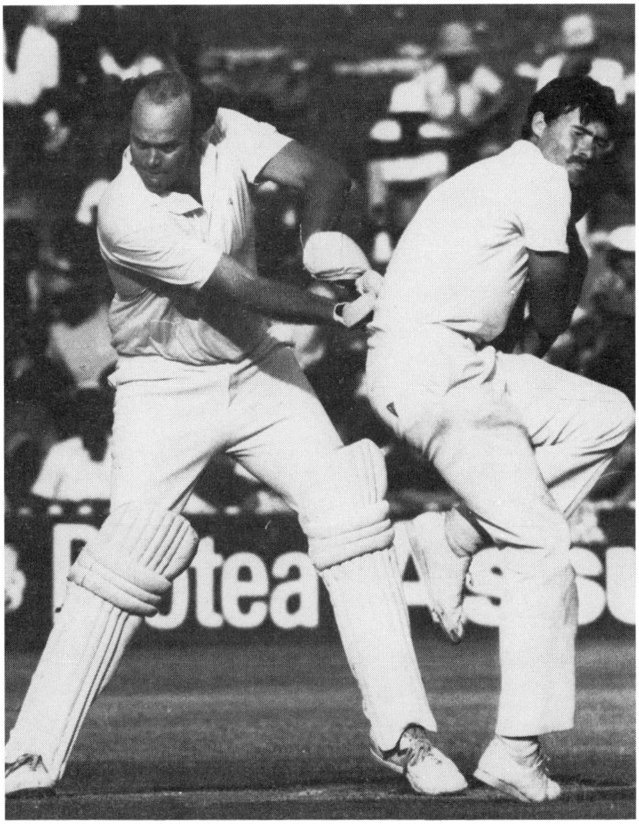

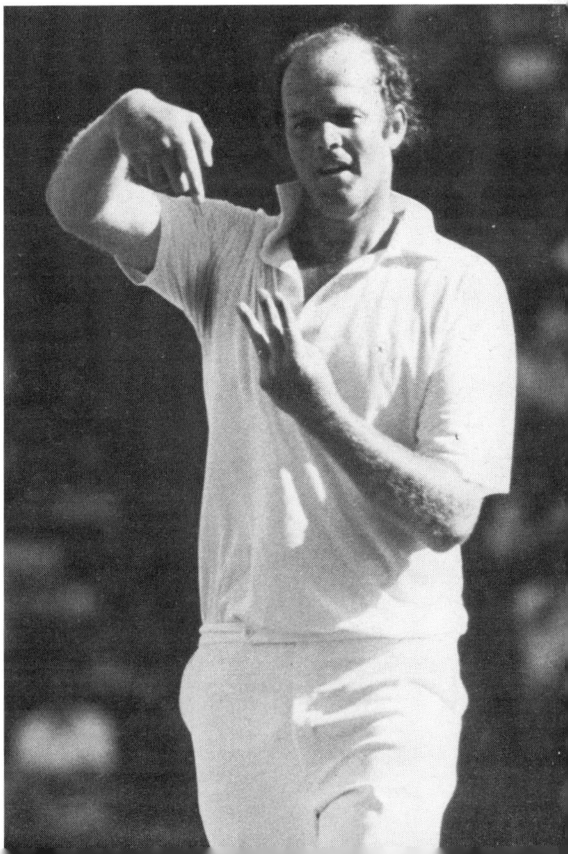

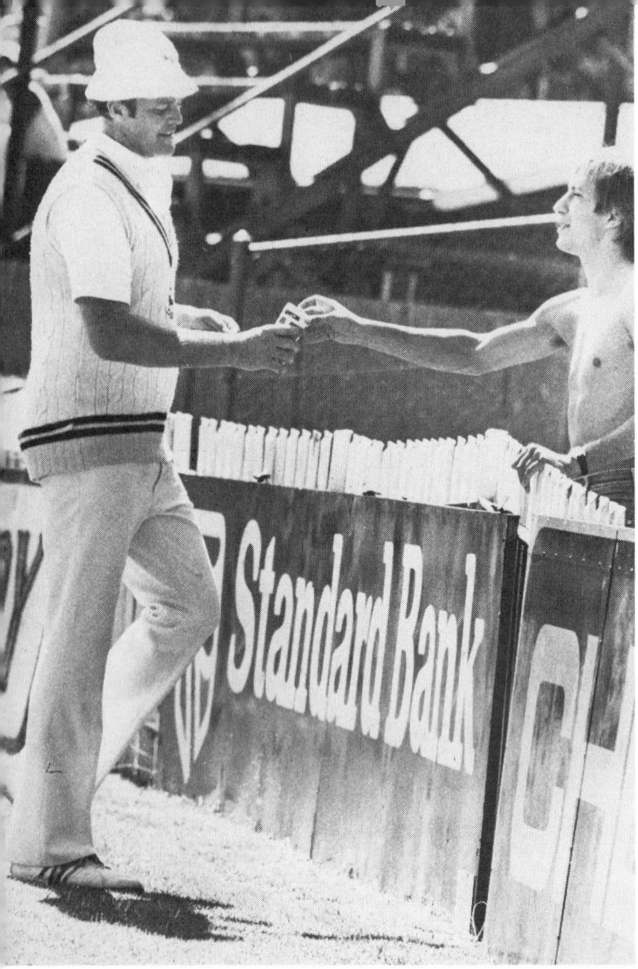
Standard Bank

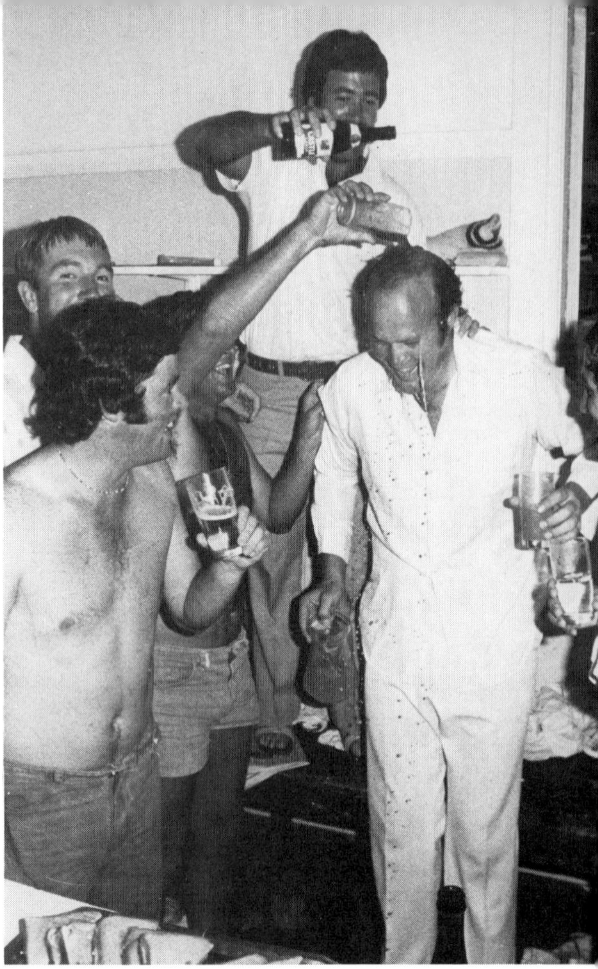

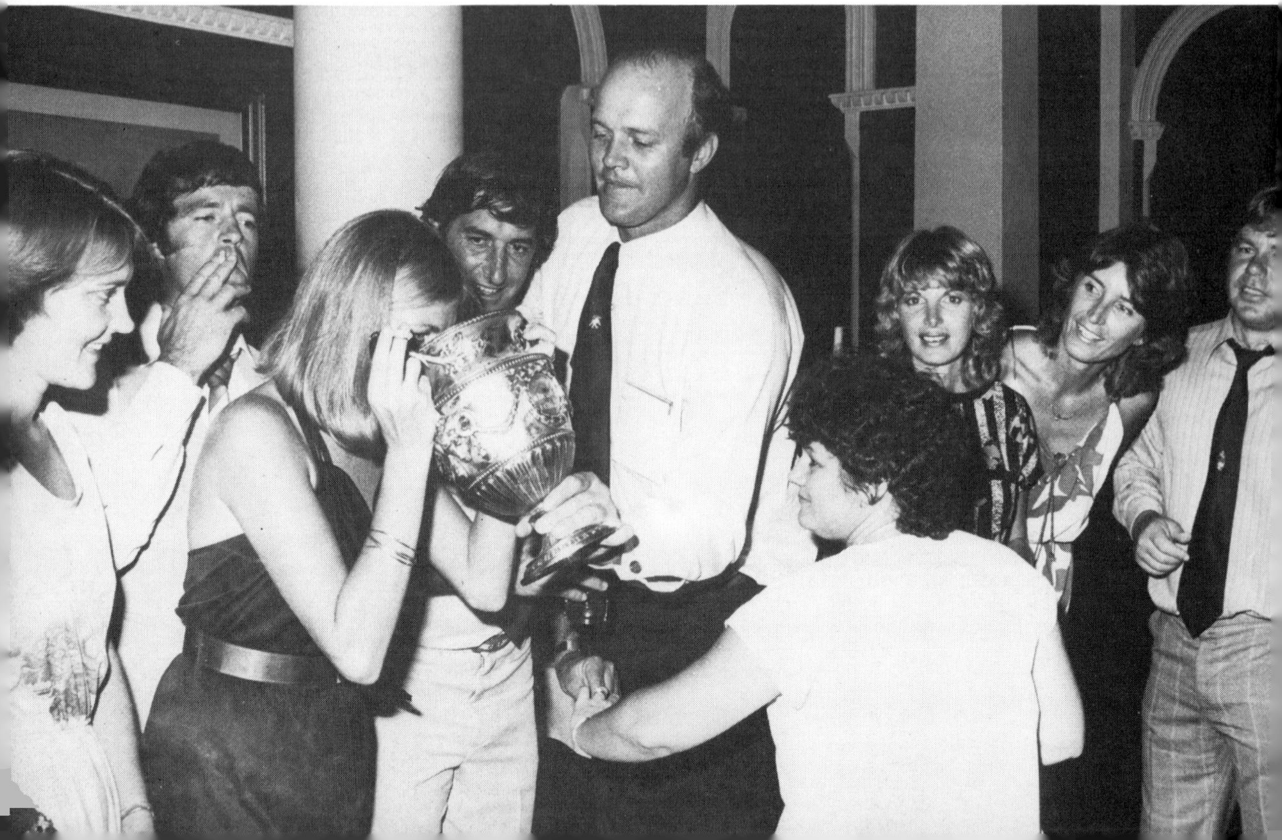

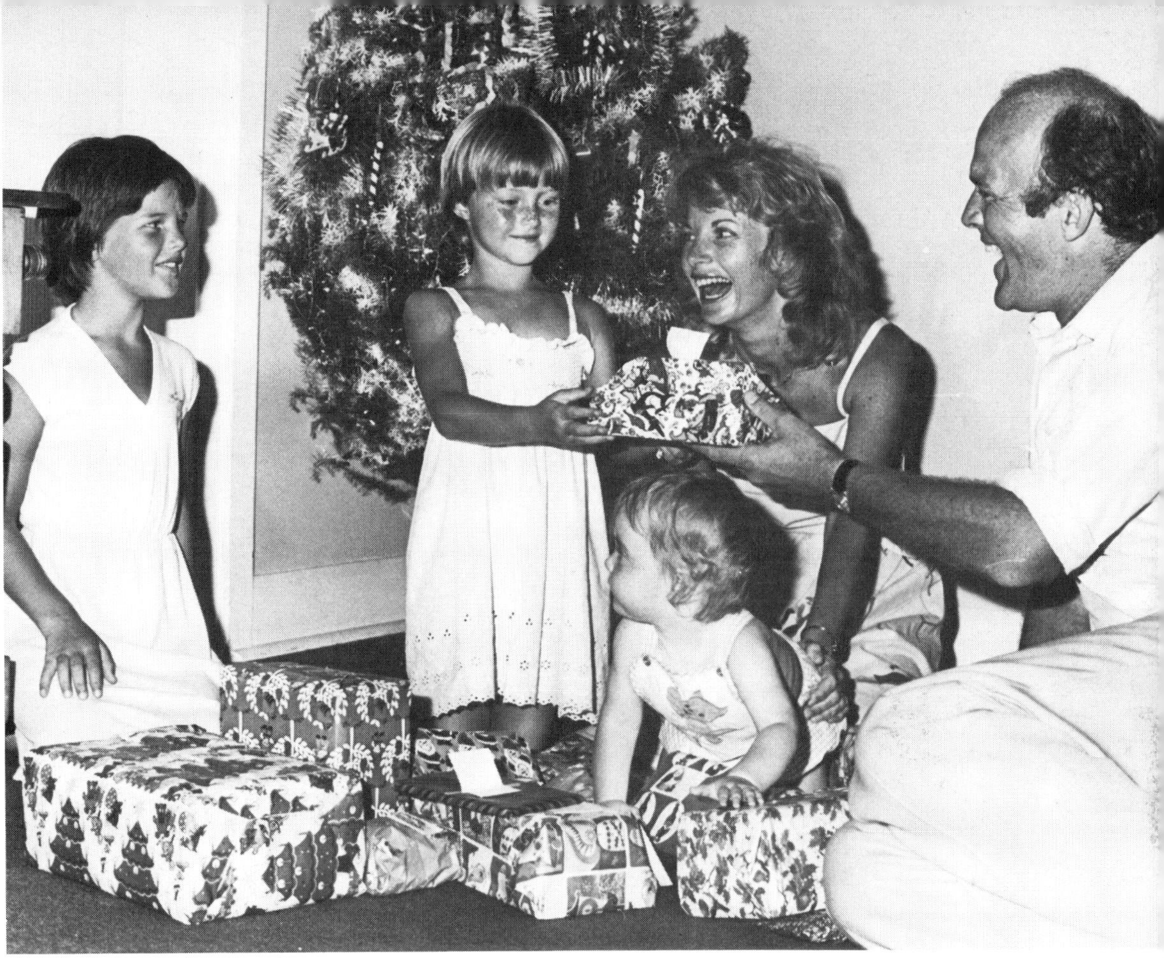

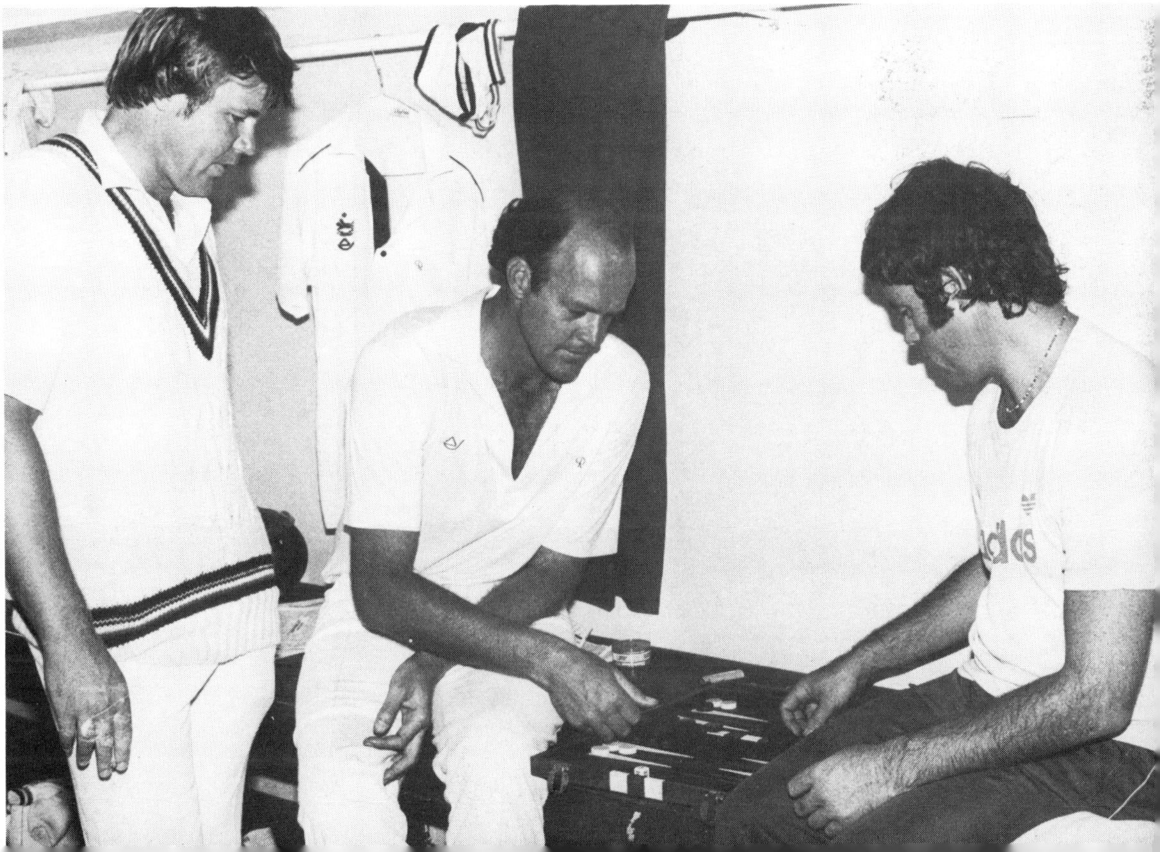

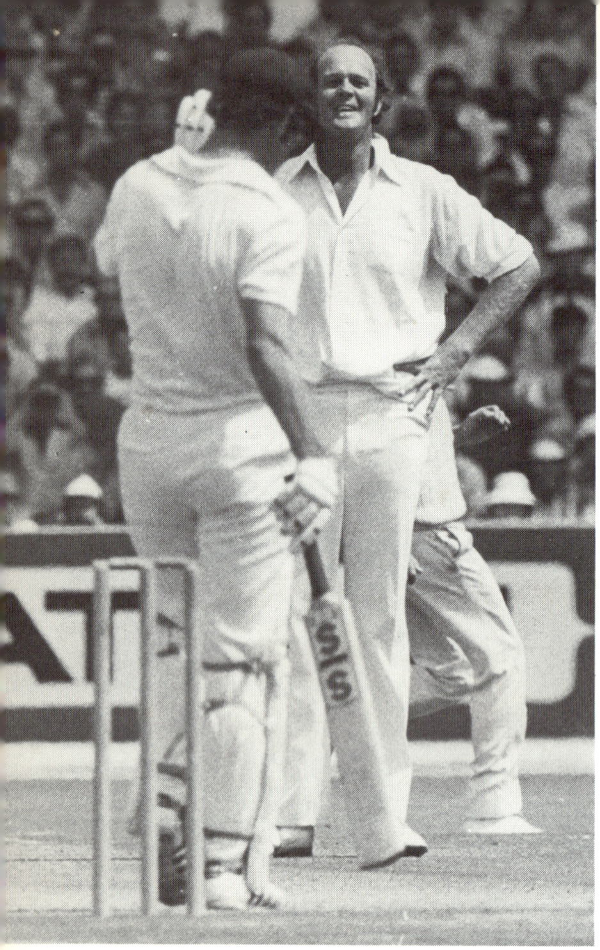

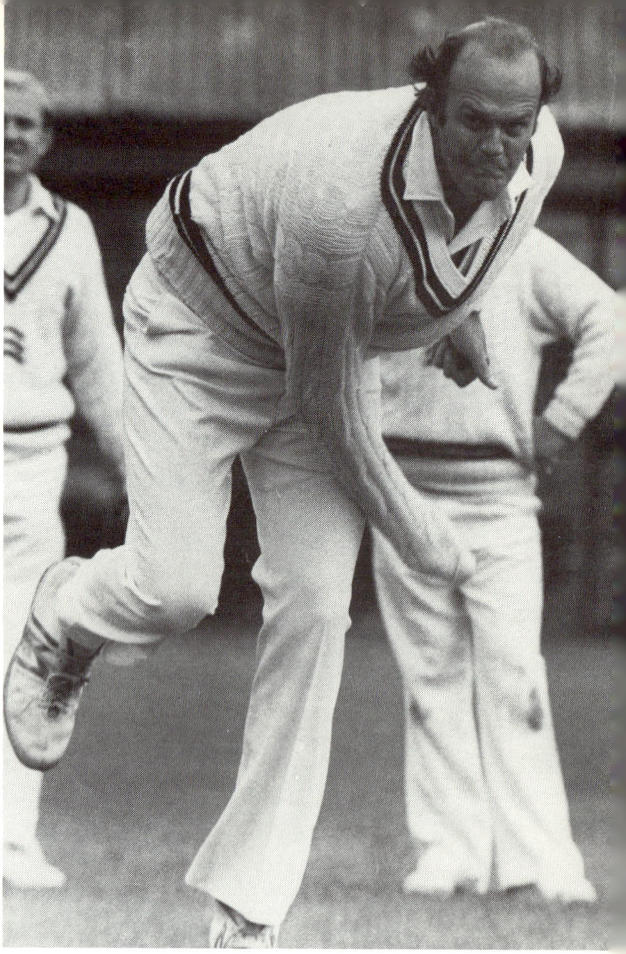

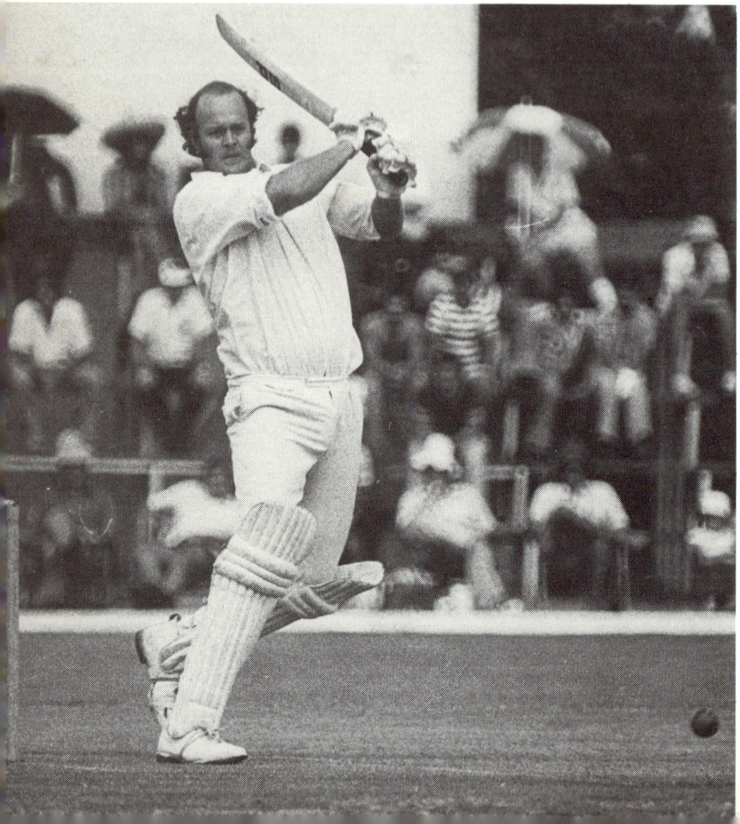

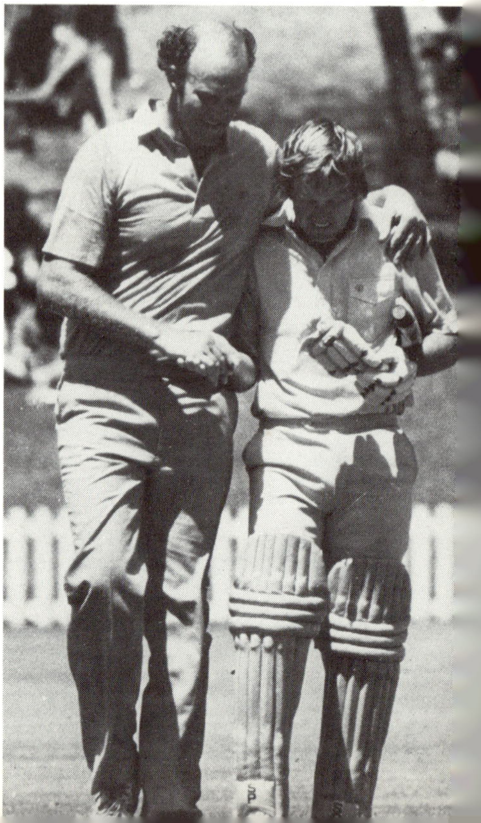

"BIG VIN"

BIG VINCE

Unification of

Mirror CRICKETER OF THE MONTH

VINTCENT VAN DER BIJL
Middlesex

THE cricket season is over. And so is the English career of Vintcent van der Bijl, the massive man with the balding head who became the most popular new player on the circuit, if not with batsmen and quite a few bowlers.

Vince—not Wayne Daniel, Mike Brearley, Mike Gatting, John Emburey or any others you care to name—took Middlesex to a marvellous Schweppes Championship title. He could also win them the Gillette Cup, too, tomorrow.

But the big man, having topped our bowling averages and smashed some of our bowlers, is going back to his native South Africa, he says, not to return here as a player.

Not for him the naturalisation that Mike Procter has achieved.

He said: "My company let me off for six months to play for Middlesex. I've got to go back. But it has been wonderful playing for Middlesex who are a marvellous side."

As the Mirror Cricketer of the Month, he will be presented at Lord's tomorrow, with a cheque for £250 and a framed portrait.

Vince's fondest memory of his great season was his 76 against Nottinghamshire at Lord's. Middlesex went on to win that match by an innings and virtually extinguished Surrey's attempts to catch them.

Brearley, the former England captain, says: "Vince has been an inspiration to the side this season. We will miss him badly."

The great South African has been a marvellous bowler and an excitingly aggressive batsman who never sacrificed style for sheer brute force. He'll be a great loss to the English cricket scene.